ALSO BY CHARLES GRODIN

It Would Be So Nice If You Weren't Here

How I Get Through Life

WE'RE READY FOR YOU,
MR. GRODIN

Behind the Scenes at Talk Shows,
Movies, and Elsewhere

CHARLES GRODIN

A LISA DREW BOOK

CHARLES SCRIBNER'S SONS
New York   London   Toronto   Sydney   Tokyo   Singapore

CHARLES SCRIBNER'S SONS
Rockefeller Center
1230 Avenue of the Americas
New York, NY 10020

SCRIBNERS and colophon are registered trademarks of Macmillan, Inc.

Manufactured in the United States of America

1 3 5 7 9 10 8 6 4 2

Book design by PIXEL PRESS

Library of Congress Cataloging-in-Publication Data
Grodin, Charles
We're ready for you, Mr. Grodin: behind the scenes at talk shows, movies,
and elsewhere/Charles Grodin
p.   cm.
"A Lisa Drew Book."
1. Grodin, Charles—Anecdotes. 2. Motion Picture actors and actresses—
United States—Biography. I. Title.
PN2287.G74A3   1994
791.43'028'092—dc20   93–43696
[B]   CIP

ISBN 0-02-545795-0

Contents

Contents

Contents

PREFACE

PREFACE

The 100 Most Powerful People in Hollywood

Each year I see the *Premiere* magazine list of The 100 Most Powerful People in Hollywood, and I always feel bad I'm not on it —I mean not close to on it. I'm so lacking in power I hardly even *know* anyone on it. Oh, there are a few people I know, but mostly it's a passing acquaintance type of thing. Here are some names from last year's list and my relationship to them.

Bob Daly/Terry Semel—Chairman and President of Warner Bros. I've never met Bob Daly. I met Terry Semel in 1978 at the house Warner Bros. keeps in Acapulco. A mutual friend told me he doesn't like me.

Michael Ovitz—Top man at CAA, considered the industry's most powerful agency. I was represented by CAA for a short time, but left because they wouldn't let me meet Mike.

Peter Guber—Chairman and CEO Sony Pictures Entertainment.
Met him on a plane once—said he was a big fan. He felt I
should always be starring in a movie with "someone else." I
guess because he's never offered me a job, he hasn't figured
out who someone else is.

Stanley Jaffe—President of Paramount Communications.
Never met him.

Jeffrey Katzenberg—Chairman, Walt Disney Studios.
Had a mini run-in with him when I did the movie *Taking Care
of Business* for Disney. The picture starred Jim Belushi and
me, and Jeffrey chose an ad that had a full figure of Jim with
my face the size of Jim's foot.

Tom Pollock—Chairman, MCA Motion Picture Group.
I've had my biggest successes in recent years for him. There's
a statue of him in my foyer.

Steven Spielberg—Producer, Director.
He actually wanted me for *Jaws*, but I couldn't meet him
because I was busy trying to help a friend's play that was in
trouble out of town. It's been nineteen years and I just
stopped thinking about it last Tuesday.

Joe Roth—Producer.
Never met him.

Mike Medavoy—Chairman, TriStar.
Once read a script of mine to him. It's about a guy who sees a
woman and falls for her on sight. Halfway through we took a
break and I said, "I think this has happened to every guy at
least once." He said, "Not me." The second half of the script
was a tough read.

Larry Gordon—Producer.
I once had a chat with him on a plane shortly after he became head of 20th Century Fox. He told me the only thing he liked about the job was reading the announcement he had it.

Robin Williams—Actor.
I met him once at a party. He kept referring to me as Mr. Grodin, so I asked him to get me a Coke. When I spotted him later I chastised him for not getting it, so he did.

Michael Douglas—Actor, Producer.
I did a picture with him, but we never met until much later at a party at his house where I observed Sylvester Stallone pick up a beautiful blonde.

Jake Bloom—Attorney.
Never met him.

Ivan Reitman—Producer, Director.
Asked me to play the dad in *Beethoven*. Asked me to write a movie for him that I will also be in. Two statues of him in foyer.

Eddie Murphy—Actor, Writer.
Never met him.

Sylvester Stallone—Actor, Writer.
Watched him pick up gorgeous blonde at Michael Douglas's house.

Robert Shaye—CEO, New Line Cinema.
Once had lunch with him and discussed possibility of my doing a role where Whoopi Goldberg was their first choice.

Kathleen Kennedy/Frank Marshall—Producers, Directors.
Never met them.

Bert Fields—Attorney.
> His firm represents me. I once called him, but he didn't return my call.

Marty Bauer—Agent.
> One of the co-heads of the agency that represents me. Never met him, but have spoken to him once on phone. Hope to meet him.

Adrian Lyne—Director.
> Never met him.

Bruce Berman—President of Warner Bros.
> He likes to tell how when he was a young executive at Universal years ago, he sat in a room and listened to me read a whole script of mine aloud. I don't think he liked it, because he tells the story as though he can't believe it happened to him. I like him though.

Ismail Merchant/James Ivory—Producer, Director.
> Never met them.

Whitney Houston—Singer.
> Never met her, but she stole my sound.

Clearly my connection to The 100 Most Powerful list is relatively minimal with a couple of notable exceptions. However, it should be said that there are hundreds of people having extremely successful careers who are *not* on the list, which begs the question—Is this the most important list? Perhaps, and this is just a suggestion, the list should be The 100 *Happiest* Successful People in Show Business or maybe The 50 Happiest Successful or if it really puts the list makers' backs to the wall The 25 Happiest Successful. There's no question that's a more exclusive list, but the one most worth aspiring toward. Obviously if you want to make the Happiest Successful list, rather than the Powerful one, your choices might be different. I recommend it. You look better. You feel better. You live longer, and so does everyone else in your life.

It's my personal judgment that overwhelmingly the people on The 100 Most Powerful list wouldn't make The 25 Happiest Successful list—not to say there aren't any really happy people on that powerful list—just not a whole bunch of them.

So on second thought maybe I shouldn't feel *bad* I'm not on The 100 Most Powerful list—but *good*.

Yeah, that's it. Shoot for happy successful and watch out for powerful.

TALK
SHOWS

Banned by
Johnny Carson

I Am Not a Jerk

When I got into the movies it never entered my mind that people would think I was like the parts I played. Unfortunately I played a lot of jerks.

I realize now that I, too, believed movie people are like they are on screen. I've always assumed Robert Mitchum really was a tough guy or more recently Kevin Costner's a great guy. Maybe they are—maybe Henry Fonda was really a nice guy, or Spencer Tracy—maybe, but maybe not. Would anyone ever doubt that Clint Eastwood or Charles Bronson really are tough guys? I wouldn't, but who knows? It's not like there's all these real life stories of these guys rushing into burning buildings rescuing people in their free time.

So given my roles, I shouldn't have been so surprised that the moviegoing public assumed I was a jerk. In my first big movie, *Rosemary's Baby*, I played Mia Farrow's good-guy obstetrician. That's how I saw it anyway. I was the good-guy obstetrician and Ralph Bellamy was the bad-guy obstetrician. Ralph is secretly involved with a lot of witchcraft stuff with Mia's husband and neighbors. When she gets on to them she comes back to me, her original man, for help. The audience is thrilled, but after hearing her story, I assume she's hysterical, give her a sedative and call her husband and bad-guy witch obstetrician. The audience was outraged. More than one person confronted me with, "How could you do that?! She came to you for help and you betrayed her!" "Hold on a minute," I'd say, in defense of my behavior, "her obstetrician is one of the top men in the field. I, as Dr. Hill, couldn't know this witch stuff was real. It's not like Dr. Hill was watching the movie with the audience until his scene came up—then went in and betrayed her! Give me a break," but basically people remained outraged.

In my second big movie, *Catch 22*, a black comedy about World War II, I played the part of Aardvark, who sleeps with a girl, throws her out the window, and then defends himself by saying, "A lot of people get killed during war. What's everyone so excited about?"

Aardvark was a good part. I got nice reviews and was feeling fine about it, until at a dinner party a woman seated next to me asked what movies I'd been in. It turned out she'd seen both of them, and I swear to you she quickly got up and changed her seat in a snit.

My next movie was my first starring part, *The Heartbreak Kid*. I played a young man who, on his honeymoon, tells his wife he wants a divorce after he falls for Cybill Shepherd. This time I was a little wary. I asked the director if it was really necessary to show my wife crying alone in her hotel room while I was out carrying on with Cybill. It was. At the first screening of the movie, the audience hissed me. The picture was a success, but I had pretty much indelibly stamped myself into the moviegoing public's consciousness as a jerk—at best.

In a later picture I was responsible for the death of one of the screen's most beloved and touching creatures, King Kong, and a few years after that I played Lily Tomlin's husband in *The*

Incredible Shrinking Woman. There's a scene in that one where tiny Lily drops a stack of dishes, and instead of helping her pick them up I just remain seated at the breakfast nook and shake my head. My mother's friends (I'm not making this up) were offended by my poor behavior. My mother felt compelled to ask me about it. I said, "Look, Mother, tell your friends the way they make Lily tiny is to make the dishes huge. If I had rushed in to help I would have been tiny too, and that's not the story. Besides my reaction was filmed on a whole separate day. I wasn't even *there* when Lily dropped the dishes!" My mother felt my explanation was too complicated and I should just forget it.

The Tonight Show

Sometime after *The Heartbreak Kid*, I thought it might be a good idea to get on the Johnny Carson show, so people could see I really wasn't such a bad guy. A publicist for the movie made some phone calls, and about a week later I was in my apartment in New York, and I got a call from a man named Bob Dolce from "The Tonight Show." Bob and I chatted about this and that for about twenty minutes at the end of which he said, "You're a very interesting person, but I see you more as a Cavett guest than for us. We're more interested in instant entertainment." I said, "Uh huh, well, thanks," and hung up the phone. I sat there for a long moment surprised—mostly that the call was actually an audition. I thought I was just having a chat—albeit a chat that would eventually lead to what I might do with Johnny Carson. Bob's conclusion on what I might do with Johnny Carson was not appear.

I called him back. I said, "Bob, I didn't quite get what we were doing in our chat; what *specifically* are you looking for, with someone like me on 'The Tonight Show'—theoretically?"

He quickly said, "Funny stories. Have you got any?"

Now this seemed like a question that might have come up in our first chat, but I think Bob and I actually got interested in whatever we were talking about, and the funny stories concept

just didn't emerge. Now that it did, I said, "Bob, I have some
funny stories."

He said, "Let's hear them."

I told him a few stories. He laughed and arranged to have me
flown to L.A. the following week to be on the show.

Once booked, however, and confronted with a TV audience of
millions, a huge studio audience, a large band and Johnny himself—I completely let go of the establishing my niceness idea
and was basically trying to survive.

My first appearance on "The Tonight Show" was in January
1973. At that time the show ran from 11:30 to 1 A.M. Johnny
brought me out at 12:53 A.M. I had seven minutes. Even though
I had been in show business for almost twenty years, I had never
experienced anything like that. For something remotely compa-
rable, I have to go back to the first time I got up in acting class
to do a monologue at the University of Miami in the fifties when
I wished the ground would open up and swallow me and my
nerves. Now in spite of years of theatre, television and even
movies, I was overwhelmed with the feeling of "How in hell did
I get into this?"

I was immediately helped by Johnny commenting on how
much he enjoyed *The Heartbreak Kid.* I hadn't even assumed
he'd seen it. He asked me if my family enjoyed it, and I said
they were waiting till it got to their neighborhood theatre. That
broke the ice. The audience and Johnny laughed, and somehow
I got through the seven minutes without forcing the network to
go to black. Three weeks later I was on again, this time at
12:50. I had ten minutes. The next day I got a call from Bob
Dolce telling me Johnny wanted to put me under exclusive contract as a talk show guest. I had never heard of that. Bob told me
he had only done it twice before with Joan Rivers and David
Steinberg. I asked, "Why me?" Bob said Johnny's explanation
was, "That kid really knows how to tell a story." Of course, I was
enormously flattered and accepted. It meant I'd be on every
three weeks between 12 and 12:30.

6

I had an odd evolution with Johnny Carson. I appeared with him over a twenty-year period interrupted by long stretches where I was banned from appearing with him. Here's what happened.

In watching these TV talk shows over the years I have never assumed that the hosts are particularly interested in what anyone else has to say. They are putting on a *show*, and, of course, they want it to be good—but actually *interested* in what the guests have been up to?—highly unlikely.

This belief has kept me away from the standard chat—"I'm very excited about my new . . . He was wonderful to work with . . . I'm really looking forward to . . ." etc. I once expressed this opinion on "The Tonight Show" after Loretta Lynn had said how excited she was about her new album. She was understandably offended, and so were her many fans who wrote in attacking me. I hadn't meant my comment specifically about what Ms. Lynn had just said she was excited about, but it no doubt came out that way. Actually maybe I did mean it about her, as she had just read Johnny Carson's palm and predicted some really bad news. I said on the air, "I don't know that it's O.K. to say that to Johnny on national television." She said, "I just report what I see." It was shortly thereafter I said, "No one is that interested in our new anything." I figure if your new thing is really good there will be plenty of time for the audience to get excited on their own.

I've always thought of a talk show appearance as a performance. Most talk show guests fall into the trap of believing a tale of "what they've been up to lately" will make compelling television.

Of course my point of view definitely has its drawbacks. In an effort to look for something different, I did the following to reactions of either bafflement or silence:

Walked off "The Tonight Show."

This was on a night when there were what felt like no laughs on the show. At one point when I was about third down the couch, Johnny looked at all four of his guests, and in an effort to be amusing, tried to determine the degree of blame for each of us for the failure of the evening. When he fixed his gaze on me—I said, "You looking at me?" He just shrugged and I got up, *pretended* to be annoyed and walked off. Even though I came back on, I don't think my walk-off was appreciated. Personally I felt it was a good move given the situation.

One night when there was virtually no response to the guests that preceded me, I told Johnny, "It would be pointless for me to attempt to be entertaining in this atmosphere, so why not run a clip from an earlier show where I got a nice response?" Johnny stared at me. It would be a good year before I was invited back again.

As time went by, Johnny continued on occasion to be uncomfortable with me, but sometimes I didn't really know why. I would come on with stories and basically tell them to the audience. While the audience was laughing I was turning "The Tonight Show" into an evening with Charles Grodin. Not that Johnny was competitive, that's just not what the show was. Even when guests like Don Rickles *did* take over the show, they did it *including* Johnny (in Don Rickles's case by insulting him). Johnny was probably as supportive and noncompetitive a host as there ever was—one of the many reasons for his longevity. In any case after several appearances, "The Tonight Show" was no longer an evening with me, *or* an evening with me and Johnny. I was gone.

Guest Hosts

Johnny no longer wanted me, but the guest hosts did. So I appeared with Joan Rivers, David Steinberg, Bill Cosby, Rich Little and several others.

I remember an appearance with David Steinberg that was to portend the different type of "tense" appearances I would later have with Johnny Carson. I had appeared on Broadway with Ellen Burstyn in the two-character play *Same Time Next Year*. It was a huge success, standing room only. We both won best actor awards, and it was sold to the movies for one million dollars. When they made the movie, however, they did it with Ellen Burstyn and Alan Alda. The reason for that would have to be explained by someone else, but, of course, it's not uncommon. I gave all this information to Bob Dolce and told him to have David Steinberg recount all my success with the play on Broadway and then ask me how I felt about Alan Alda doing the movie. When David asked the question, I just stared at him for a long time and then it went like this:

ME
(disbelief)
They're making a movie out of *Same Time Next Year*?!

DAVID
You didn't know that?

ME
No.
(a pause)
And who's playing my part?

DAVID
Alan Alda.
(a pause)
How do you feel about that?
(a long, long silence as I stare at the floor)

ME
(disdain)
I don't care *what* they do!
*(I continue to stare at the floor in silent anger,
as they go to a commercial)*

9

When I got back to New York, one of my closest friends said, "I can't believe he asked you that insensitive question."

Back with Johnny

Johnny evidently watched some of these appearances, was amused, and eventually had me back. However, my problems continued. Once for some infraction I can't remember, Freddie DeCordova, the producer, turned off camera and said, "The door just closed again on Mr. Grodin." Bob Dolce, in the spirit of the Freedom of Information Act, passed this on to me. So once more I'd not see Johnny, but be back with guest host Joan, or whomever.

Throughout all this, Bob Dolce would advise me on how not to offend Johnny when I would eventually be let back in for another try. "Wear a suit and tie. That will help legitimize you. Don't speak first. Let Johnny speak first." I went with the suit, but when I got out there I couldn't help myself—my instincts for entertainment took over. I still spoke first, because not doing that put me in a passive position that made me uncomfortable, and believe me, you really want to reach a certain level of comfort—before *anything* happens. Diane Keaton had several appearances where all she talked about was her nervousness. I feel anyone that nervous (and I really believe she was) would be better off not going on. Obviously, experiencing that much nervousness is not good for your health in the long run.

During these years of the in favor/out of favor business, I would get back on with Johnny and make reference to my most recent ban. First Johnny denied it with a smile, and then when I said, "Oh yeah? I was only getting booked on Armed Forces Radio," he started to laugh. I said, "I didn't realize you had that kind of power," and he laughed again—partially, I think, because he saw I took the whole banned thing as funny, not hurtful. I will admit that when Bob Dolce told me once after a short appearance, Johnny exasperatedly said, "Those ten minutes felt like an hour," that stung a little, but more because that's how *he* felt. I wasn't uncomfortable at all with the ten.

On that occasion I told a true story about going for a meeting to see about playing the pope in a movie. I didn't think the script worked, but the producer said I was their number-one choice, so the agent, a warm guy named Jack Gelardi who's married to Annette Funicello, urged me to go. The comic point of the story is that I went from no interest to, by the day of the meeting, wearing a very long white outer shirt that really hung low—not to the knees, but *low*. When I left the house, I asked my girlfriend, "How do I look?" She said, "Great!" (In show business, everything is a little exaggerated.) I then said angrily (as a joke to my girlfriend), "Yeah, but *do I look like the pope*?!" The audience didn't know I was joking when I said that line to my girlfriend, and they hissed me. *That* didn't even make me uncomfortable. I figured anyone who thought I would seriously shout at my girlfriend and then talk about it on the air—well, I can't worry too much that they don't get what I'm doing.

Anyway, after about ten years of banned—guest hosts—not banned—banned—guest hosts—not banned—I stopped being banned. I stopped directing my remarks to the audience, and now spoke only to Johnny. Things were going well. In fact, things were going *so* well that once during a commercial Johnny leaned over to me and said, "Y'know, I never really knew what to do with you, but now I can see I can do *anything* with you." I said, "Right," and we nodded. What I think he understood is that no matter what I'm doing I'm goofing and there's no way you're going to bother me in this entertainment venue, and, more importantly, don't take too seriously what I say either. In a living room—maybe, but on TV I'm playing. After we reached that understanding, I decided that I was no longer really interested in doing stories based on the preappearance notes—but more interested in a free-form thing that might lead anywhere: where that was going to lead I could never have imagined.

"Tension" with Johnny

Bob Dolce and I had a tug of war on these notes for twenty years. Bob always wanted to get as much information out of me as possible on what I thought I could talk about, and I wanted to give him as little information as I could get away with. Bob wanted to know the punch lines to the stories. He swore he wouldn't tell Johnny. He just first wanted to judge whether they were funny enough. I wasn't comfortable with that. I felt I had proven after many years that I didn't tell unfunny stories, and also, while I believed he wouldn't tell Johnny the punch line, it wasn't even O.K. with me that *Bob*, who was sitting about ten feet away by the camera, knew the punch line—or for that matter the story itself. I just don't like telling a story if someone sitting ten feet away has heard it. I've been approached about appearing in clubs, but I could never get past the two-show-a-night concept. People argued it would be a different audience at the second show—they wouldn't know the stories, but I always said, "The waiters would." So Bob and I went back and forth on this for years. Once he invited me and my wife over to his house to have dinner with Bette Midler and her boyfriend. I think he was trying to soften me up. I knew and liked Bette from New York. She once came to see me in a Broadway show I was doing. My back was hurting and Bette worked on it for a solid ten minutes even though she admitted she didn't know what the hell she was doing.

Anyway, back to the notes. Finally Bob swore to me he would only tell Johnny as little as he would need to know about what the subject was, so Johnny might have some pithy comments. I got tired of arguing and eventually decided to tell Bob all the stories—punch lines—the whole enchilada. Then I would go on and not do the stories. I didn't plan this. I probably had a subconscious resentment of still auditioning material after ten years, and even though Bob meant well, he probably had something to do with me entering a decade-long phase of on the air "tension" between me and Johnny Carson that no one enjoyed more than me and Johnny.

Once Johnny had in effect said, "Anything goes," I decided to go with anything I felt. It went something like this:

JOHNNY

So, how are you?
I just stare at him.

JOHNNY

That one too tough for you?

ME

It's hard for me to answer a question from someone who doesn't really care about the answer.

JOHNNY

I care.

ME

Do you really?

JOHNNY
(thinks a moment)

Not really.

ME

You don't really care about *anything*, do you?

JOHNNY

No. I'm just here to scoop up the money and take it home.

13

Or, it might be something like this:

ME

Who are you anyway?

JOHNNY

What do you mean?

ME

Do you know who you are?

JOHNNY

I'm Johnny.

Sometimes Johnny would be genuinely taken aback by my grilling but *never* really uncomfortable. He would be comedically uncomfortable, even if he really didn't know how to respond. Another time he asked me one of those stock talk show questions. The exchange went like this:

JOHNNY

What's the funniest thing that ever . . .

ME

(interrupting, mockingly)

What's the funniest thing that ever happened to *you*? What's the weirdest thing? What's the hardest thing you ever did?

JOHNNY

Talking to you.

The audience would roar with laughter but a certain percentage of the millions of viewers, unaware of how many times I had appeared really thought that this was televised animosity. I

14

mean, plenty of people thought so. Johnny and I would discuss this during the commercial breaks. He would even say in his introductions that I was a little weird. He was trying to convey to the viewers who were upset that this was all in fun. Still the "tension" we created overrode everything, and to this day I'm certain a significant percentage of the viewers believe they were watching a feud, and that I was about the most unpleasant guest who had ever been on "The Tonight Show." So much for going on to show what a nice guy I was!

When it finally became clear that Johnny was going to leave the show I was reluctant to make my final appearance. I wasn't all that comfortable going out in a blaze of insults, but we had been insulting each other for so many years that I wasn't confident we had another way to go. I went on and immediately said it was difficult for me to think of this last appearance as special, because for years all my appearances had felt like they might be the last. We needled each other some more for quite a long time. During the first commercial Johnny leaned over to me and said, "I hope you know that your appearances have always been special to me." I nodded, and said they were to me too, and was surprised how moved I was by his remark. This had been my longest relationship in show business—a profession not particularly known for longevity in relationships. As he said good-bye on the air to everyone on the panel at the end, I said, "I will miss you as much as anyone. I'm not kidding." He looked at me quite seriously and said, "I know you're not." Afterward he said off the air with a smile, "You had to blow it at the end, didn't you?"—meaning let people know we really did like each other.

Once about ten years ago on the air he looked at me and said quite sincerely, "Why don't we have dinner some night?"

I said, "I'm out here with my wife."

He said, "Yeah?"

I said, "You want to have dinner with me and my wife?"

He said, "Yeah, I'm alone."

I asked, "Alone?"

He said, "Well, not *alone* alone."

It never happened though. Neither of us pursued it. We both probably thought it might spoil our on the air "tension." The truth is the only real tension I ever felt with John was backstage. I told him it was so tense running into him backstage that while I never memorized anything I'd say *on* camera—off camera I memorized everything I'd say if I ran into him. There was truth to that. It's kind of like with girls when I was young. If I really liked someone I could really play and tease with her better if there were people around. Alone it was tense. The electricity with Johnny brought out the long-gone teenager in me. That's why I miss him.

Suing
David Letterman

A different version of the Johnny Carson experience developed with David Letterman.

I have been appearing with David for about ten years. They are kind of acerbic appearances (no Mr. Nice-Guy here either), but the audience seems to enjoy the exchanges, although again a significant percentage of people think we really dislike each other. David, for those of you who don't stay up that late (I don't either), is not really a host, but a wonderfully sardonic humorist who happens to be called the host. He heard me say this once on the Tom Snyder radio show, and during a commercial at one of my appearances with him, whispered in my ear that he had heard me attacking him on the host thing on Tom Snyder.

I said, "Was I saying it jokingly?"

He said, "No." When we came back on the air I told the audience what had just transpired off the air. David countered with, "Well, you're not exactly what I'd call a *guest!*"

I said, "I've never *claimed* to be a guest!" In the strictest use of the words you have a nonhost talking to a nonguest.

Anything is fair game for David. One night I happened to catch the show when he was interviewing Marilu Henner. We had worked together on something, and he asked her what I was like. She said nice things, but he responded with, "I think he's a whiner." I know that's one of David's favorite funny words. He might use it on anyone. He likes to say it. It never means he thinks you're a whiner. In fact, the less of a whiner you are the better for his joke. The problem is people don't know he's joking. So the audience didn't laugh and Marilu just muttered something about her not finding me a whiner. On my next appearance, I brought it up as though I was really offended. "You called me a whiner the other week!"

"No, I didn't," he said.

"Yes, you did, I heard you."

"Well, you *are* kind of a whiner, don't you think?"

"Yes," I joked, "but still . . . " So much for *our* animosity.

Another time, Bob Morton, David's producer, called me and said they had a bit they'd like to do with me. I would come out, but David wouldn't be there. He supposedly couldn't get to the show, because he had to stay home to wait for the cable people. Actually he was in his office at NBC, so I just talked to him on a TV monitor. I was supposed to be annoyed over his not showing up. I went on, took my seat, saw on the monitor his explanation for why he wasn't there and then I began to attack him. "Hey, I could have last minute things come up too, but I had a commitment to be here, and I really resent you're not!" Well, they actually got plenty of mail ripping me for not being more gracious about David's last minute cancellation.

I had been made aware, mostly by friends who keep later hours than I do, that David would *regularly* attack me on the show when I wasn't there. I always knew he was kidding, even if the audience didn't. Of course, with many people he's not kidding, like celebrities who use their names to promote endless hair sprays or perfumes or exercise videos, diets, etc., etc., etc. I knew his needling of me when I wasn't there would be to inject some juice into the segment while he was interviewing a friend or colleague of mine. One week on consecutive nights during interviews with Carol Burnett and Dabney Coleman, two good friends of mine, David called me psychotic and let Dabney call me "a pain in the ass" without disputing it.

I probably see Dabney as much as any friend when I'm in L.A. Dabney really enjoys blistering people, but he is so witty at it, I don't mind when he does it to me.

Anyway the week I was called "psychotic" and "a pain in the ass" on David's show, I called Bob Morton and told him I wanted to come on and do a bit with an attorney about suing David. Bob agreed. I called the wonderful burlesque comedian, Joey Faye, with whom I had worked years earlier on "Candid Camera." Here's how the show went:

DAVID
(to audience)
An old friend of the show, Charles Grodin, seems to be annoyed about something that happened here last week. Since we have a warm relationship with Mr. Grodin, we've invited him on in the hopes that we can straighten out whatever this situation is.

I then came out. It was actually my third appearance in a month (a record). I walked out pretending to be really fuming and refused to shake David's hand. At this point, the audience wasn't sure if this was a joke or not.

19

DAVID

Boy, you're really upset about something.
What's the problem? I'm not really aware of
it.

ME
(annoyed)

What do you mean, you're not aware of it!?
You were right here when it happened! I'm
so upset that I've brought my attorney, Neil
Fraymens, who's the senior partner of . . .
(and then I made up some firm)

David then brought out Neil Fraymens (A.K.A. Joey Faye, who
carried a small leather notebook and looked pretty distinguished). Joey shook David's hand a little too warmly for my
taste, and I shot him a look.

ME

Why don't we run the two clips where I was
attacked on your show last week?

DAVID

O.K. Fine, but I don't think we have anything actionable here.

ME
(grimly)

We'll see about that.

The director ran the clips where I'm called "psychotic" and "a
pain in the ass." The lights came up and I was steaming. Joey
Faye was just sitting there shaking his head very soberly, as
though we're talking major lawsuit here. I then began to turn on
David when Joey tapped me on the shoulder and whispered in

my ear like counsel at a Senate hearing. I listened to what Joey whispered, and looked exasperated.

DAVID

What? What is it?

ME

My attorney would like a glass of water.

David produced a pitcher from behind his desk and poured Joey a glass of water. Joey took one tiny sip—then told David how much he enjoyed his show while I fumed some more. I then began to go at David again when Joey once more tapped me on the shoulder. I leaned over to hear his latest whispered counsel and he did this enormous (fake) sneeze all over my blue blazer. By now, of course, the audience had no doubt it was a joke. As David handed Joey some tissues to wipe me off, Joey "sneezed" all over me again. I stormed off the show in disgust as Joey and David watched. After I left Joey turned to David and said, "You're right, he *is* psychotic." That was one of the only cases where I was confident that the audience knew we had just done an elaborate joke, but for the most part, this walking-the-edge thing that I can't seem to resist just further supports the audience's opinion that I am just as much a jerk as any jerk role they've seen me play in the movies.

Maybe the most interesting aspect of appearing with David Letterman is how many people have actually come up to me on the street to shake my hand for "telling David off." I think when we go after each other (in our minds totally for entertainment) a substantial number of people think I'm a jerk and just as large a group thinks he is. Hopefully the largest number finds it entertaining. I'm not sure though.

One of the Funniest People in the World— Albert Brooks

Once I did a wonderful bit thought up by the brilliant comic filmmaker Albert Brooks. Albert, for reasons I don't know, was taking over a radio talk show out of Texas for a week. He arranged to phone me in New York and we did something like the following on the phone that went out on the air live.

> ALBERT
> I'm on with the actor Charles Grodin, from
> his apartment in New York. Charles, are you
> there?

> ME
> Yes, I am.

> ALBERT
> Now, Charles, the reason for the call is I
> read in a local paper here that you went on

location with the movie *Scarface* even though you weren't in the picture. Can you tell us what happened there?

ME

Well, Albert, last year Al Pacino was cast in a romantic comedy film, *Author, Author*. That was a role I felt I should have played, so when Al was cast as Scarface I decided to go to where they were filming to play the role of Scarface—off camera.

ALBERT

This was your way of getting even?

ME

That's right. Al was very nice about it. He understood. The producers weren't happy. They thought it was a distraction. They refused to tell me where they were going to film each day, but I just waited in the lobby where the crew stayed and followed them out to location.

ALBERT

This was in Florida?

ME

Yeah, right. It was very pleasant—a little muggy sometimes, but all in all pleasant, and a lot of the crew felt I was doing as good or better a Scarface than Al.

After the broadcast Albert and I spoke. I said, "The problem is 90 percent of the audience will think this really happened and that I'm nuts." Albert said, "More like 99 percent." Albert, however, is irresistible to play with. Years ago when I first met him, a group of us were just sitting around the living room of Penny Marshall and Rob Reiner's house. (They were married at the time.) There was a lull in the conversation, and I looked across the room at Albert and said, "You're very close friends with David Nelson, aren't you?" I picked David Nelson, whom I didn't know, and who I assumed correctly Albert didn't know because, at least, what he portrayed on "Ozzie and Harriet" was the opposite end of the spectrum from Albert—middle of the road as against hip/oblique. Without missing a beat Albert said, "The thing about David is no matter how many times I go over to his house, he insists on showing me around—I mean, every room. I say, 'David, I've seen all this many times,' but he does it anyway." I doubt there were many there who guessed he had never met David Nelson.

Another time I called Albert on the evening of the day of the Kentucky Derby and said, "Albert, why would you have entered the Kentucky Derby? Everyone knows a human can't run anywhere near as fast as a horse, and falling down right out of the gate like that . . . "

There was only the slightest pause before he said, "You've never met my manager."

From Merv to Arsenio

John McLaughlin

The people who saw me with John McLaughlin consider it the roughest appearance I've ever had on a TV talk show. John McLaughlin is, of course, the growling host of "The McLaughlin Group." He also had a full hour show on cable, CNBC, and wanted me for his sole guest.

I had always been intrigued by his Sunday morning show out of Washington. He has four or five veteran news correspondents with him—each of whom seems at least as knowledgeable as he is, but nevertheless he snarls at them, patronizes them and other things of that nature. They all seem to take it in good spirits, and it makes for a lively show.

I was sure he'd do this with me, because that's his thing, and I was really looking forward to dealing with him a little differently from what he was accustomed to—all for the purpose of entertainment.

I showed up for the taping at Secaucus, New Jersey, and eventually was ushered out to a chair on a platform in front of an audience of about sixty people sitting in bleachers. John was not quite ready, so someone weirdly figured why not have me wait out there onstage in front of the audience who, by the way, didn't seem to have the least idea who I was. I looked at the audience. They looked at me, and we all just sat there. I thought it was an extremely strange place to have a guest wait, but "strange" for me often leads to what I consider some fun ideas— so after a minute or so of me looking at the audience and them looking back at me, I said to them, "I just want to say, I didn't do it! I wasn't even there, and I think when the evidence comes out I'll be vindicated." Nobody laughed. For all they knew, I *was* accused of a felony and I was coming on McLaughlin prior to trial.

Soon John appeared and launched into quite an extensive and flattering introduction of me. Then he started in on me in his accusatory style of a prosecuting attorney. The funny thing about it, his snarling questions were innocuous items like, "Why do you live in New York?!" but asked as though it was "Why did you kill so and so?!" I chose to answer everything he asked in the same manner he was asking. In other words, I snarled back. He looked startled. I don't believe anyone had ever spoken to him like that. After a few minutes of this back and forth snarling, I felt he was secretly enjoying the confrontation. Sometimes when he'd come after me in that "closing in for the kill" style with a painless question about working in the theatre versus movies, I would act as if he really had me cornered and any second I would break down and confess to *something*.

An hour is a long time in an interview, so eventually I decided to really go after *him*. I should say before I recount this that I would never have done it if I hadn't spotted the little twinkle in his eye telling me he was enjoying it. He had been reading aloud every project I ever did off cue cards and asked me to just jump in if I had anything to say about whatever project. Eventually, I stopped him.

ME
(snarling)
What are you doing?!

McLAUGHLIN
(taken aback)
What?

ME
You're just reading all these cue cards. How did you get this show anyway?

McLAUGHLIN
I have a lot of shows!

ME
(stunned)
You do?!

McLAUGHLIN
Yes, I have four shows.

ME
I'm shocked! You don't seem to have any ability for this at all.

McLAUGHLIN
No?

ME
I mean, I've seen your Washington show, and that's O.K., but you're *sitting* there, aren't you?

McLAUGHLIN
Yes.

ME

Personally, I don't feel you can stand this long and ask coherent questions. I offer that to be helpful.

McLAUGHLIN

You do?

ME

Yes.

The snarling went back and forth for the whole show and John and I both had a wonderful time. The producer told me the show was rebroadcast more than any show they had ever done. The reactions I experienced ranged from Mel Tormé telling me it was the single best appearance he'd ever seen on a talk show, because I said what a lot of guests might think and never say— to, on the opposite end of the spectrum—my wife, who had to stop watching it after about sixty seconds, and my aunt Ethel, who asked my mother, "How could Chuck talk to John McLaughlin that way?" She evidently saw John as quite a distinguished figure.

I saw John shortly after the show at a screening, and we continued to needle each other off-screen. He even invited me to come as his guest to some press corps dinner in Washington for the Clinton inauguration—probably to convince his colleagues that the whole thing was in fun. I considered going, but it was black-tie and I'd have had to stay overnight in a hotel there, so I chose to stay home.

A few months later the producer of the show asked me to come back on again. I really didn't want to, as I didn't figure I could top it. They persisted, and after several more calls I said, "O.K." Then I didn't hear anything. Eventually I got a call from the producer, explaining that due to a strike and a changing of facilities or something, they wanted to delay my return engagement. I couldn't really follow what they were saying but said, "Sure, fine." They never called again. I think after they got me—someone must have asked, "Do we really want Charles Grodin to come back on and question John's ability to do a show?"

Andy Kaufman and Hutch Saxony

Shortly after that some people at the Fox network got the idea to do a special around me as an interviewer attacking my guests. I thought about it, but figured since a lot of people think this is for real, I don't need a special to have more people get nervous when I show up.

The late brilliant comedian, Andy Kaufman, used to do stuff like this except more so. He would appear in concert first as Tony Clifton, a hostile, mediocre lounge singer, as the opening act for himself. A lot of the audience didn't realize Tony Clifton was Andy Kaufman and when Tony started to attack the audience—they would hiss and boo and call for Andy. I once suggested to Andy he bring Tony on later to let the audience in on the gag, and he simply said, "But, Chuck, Tony's my opening act." If I had known he also insisted on a separate contract and dressing room for Tony, I probably wouldn't have broached the subject.

I had a character I used to do called Hutch Saxony, who was an equally hostile predecessor to Andy's Tony Clifton. In 1969 I was directing a television special for Simon and Garfunkel. I came into the recording studio one day and Roy Halee, their producer, called out to me, "Hey, Hutch, feel like recording?" Hutch Saxony along with Rommie Genta and Christopher Fargo was one of the three names I considered changing mine to when I was starting out in show business. Roy and Paul and Art often called me Hutch.

Anyway, Roy had the tracks of a big ballad that Frank Sinatra was going to do and never did. He wanted to play the track for me, but I said that wasn't necessary, just put it on and I'll record a song. I explained I didn't have that much time. Simon and Garfunkel positioned themselves beside me. They were going to be my backup, the Saxonaires. It would be Hutch Saxony and the Saxonaires. It turned out the music had a lot of unexpected modulations. It would suddenly soar up, then quiet down, then soar up again. About thirty seconds in, Paul and Art started laughing and just fell away from the microphone, so there went the Saxonaires. It was just Hutch Saxony singing a big ballad. Since I had never heard the music before, and, of course, was making up a lyric as I went along, it ended up with some strange phrases like, "I'll meet you tonight by the synagogue." It was called "Please Don't Go," and if you play it at a really noisy party you really can't tell I'm no good—which is what Paul did at a big party he threw about six years later. I was talking to Faye Dunaway when Paul walked over and said to her, "That's Chuck singing." Faye listened for a moment and said, "You have a love-ly voice." Like I said, it was very noisy. Anyway, somewhere along the line I struck up a communication, I think through Paul, with a Warner Brothers record producer named Russ Titelman about Warner's recording an album with Hutch, who was always referred to as a friend of Charles Grodin, although everyone was in on the gag.

We conducted a rather ugly comic negotiation through the mail. Russ, who recently has won a lot of awards for producing Eric Clapton, tried to present his qualifications to produce Hutch, and Hutch wrote back that he had no interest in Russ or his qualifications—that both were irrelevant—that the way Hutch worked, all someone had to do was press a button to start a track and he would record. The whole session would take as long as it took to play the music once. We actually made a date for me to record three songs.

On the day of the recording session in Los Angeles I got my pal, Richard Martini, to drive me and my girlfriend (now wife) to the recording session. We all wore Panama hats and dark glasses. My girlfriend was referred to as Mrs. Hutch and never spoke. It was understood there would be no conversation with Hutch. I would come in, record—and leave, period. They put on three instrumental tracks I had never heard before. I sang three songs—one I called "My Dog" is rather touching, if I do say so myself. My friend Luana Anders came in in the middle of that one and told me she instantly got tears in her eyes. She wasn't kidding either. Hutch isn't good, but he's sincere. At the beginning of the track you can hear me put down the facility by instructing Richard not to let them put much of a rental charge on for the studio. When it was over Russ came out from behind the glass and asked Richard if he could at least shake Hutch's hand. I glared at him from behind my dark glasses and left. I've always felt they could release Hutch's first endeavor, "Please Don't Go" and it would be a hit. Just a personal opinion.

Merv Griffin, John Davidson, Joan Rivers

Back to the talk show hosts. In truth I liked all of them. I mean, I didn't know any of them, but as far as I knew them—I liked them. I appeared a lot with Merv Griffin. Once before an appearance someone from his staff called and asked if I would like to win the Meridian Award on my next appearance. I said, "What's that?" Evidently it was some kind of a tie-in with a new magazine or something, and everyone on the panel that night who was already booked would win one for their field. Abigail Van Buren (Dear Abby), won hers for communication, Swifty Lazar, the legendary literary agent, for business. I won for entertainer of the year. I was really surprised that the other recipients seemed to actually take the award seriously. I took mine, looked right into the camera, and said, "I'd like to thank the members of the Academy."

Merv interrupted with, "It's not the Academy Award, it's the Meridian Award."

I said, "What's the Meridian Award?"

Merv said, "Never mind," and we went to a commercial. Merv loved to kid as much as I did and it's never more fun to fool around than when the other guests are being serious. You may be accused of "inappropriate humor," which I have been, but it's worth it.

I once persuaded the producers of "The Merv Griffin Show" to let me bring my pal, the aforementioned Richard Martini, on with me. Richard is a young writer/director and a real favorite of mine. He's one of those people who by his presence makes any group better. I told Merv's producer that he was an "aura guy," that his aura would enhance my appearance and therefore the show itself. They reluctantly agreed. Richard took a small ad in *Variety* announcing his appearance with a photo of himself under which it said, "May accept employment." Richard and I rehearsed what we would do, but neither Merv nor his staff had any idea. First I went on for a while, then I said, "Let's bring out Richard Martini." Here's how I recall a piece of what happened next. Richard entered to welcoming applause, looked around, then spotted Merv, who went to him and shook hands.

                    RICHARD
          You're Merv?

                    MERV
          (shocked, to audience)
          He didn't know who I was.

Richard took a seat to my right, not the main seat.

                    MERV
          So, Richard, what do you do?

                    RICHARD
          Chicago.

32

ME

Hold it. Hold it, Merv. This is his first
appearance. Go easy.

MERV

He's memorized his answers!

ME

Bear with him. Bring him along slowly.

Eventually Richard moved into the main chair and told a story
about watching a celebrity being very gracious, signing auto-
graphs in a restaurant. Merv looked uninterested until Richard
revealed the celebrity was Merv. At which point Merv said,
"You're right. He does have a nice aura." He meant it, too.

Once when I taped an appearance with John Davidson on his
show, he tripped and fell flat on his face on his entrance. He
had them stop tape and start again. I told him seeing a celebrity
fall flat on his face is exactly what the audience wants to see.
I'm sure I'm right.

Joan Rivers once invited me to dinner at her house with a few
other people. She told me on the phone that she really couldn't
vouch for the food, so I decided as a joke to take a tuna sandwich and keep it in my pocket—just in case. I drove by her
house three times before I realized the sprawling estate with
huge fences and attack dog signs was Joan's. She was really
sweet and funny. There were a lot of servants around, and, as I
recall, in tuxedos yet. When they served dinner, I put my hand
on my tuna sandwich in my lapel pocket as the food got closer. I
clearly was craning my neck to see what was coming. People,
including Joan, started to stare at me. As the food got close
enough for me to see, I took my tuna out, as though I had made
my decision. Joan and the others got a good laugh out of that.
What happened later, though, wasn't too funny. There were some

kind of small porcelain horses or something floating in, I think, the finger bowl. I didn't realize they were valuable and thought they were party favors. I said, "Oh, Joan, these are nice; can I keep them?" honestly thinking I was supposed to, but just checking. Joan hesitated for a moment, then said, "Sure." So I did. Later one of the butlers said there were two missing horses. Joan looked over at me uncomfortably and said, "I told him he could keep them." I realized I had made a faux pas, and forked the horses over. By the way, Joan's two books, *Enter Talking* and *Still Talking*, are two of the best books on show business I have ever read.

Regis and Kathie Lee

Regis and Kathie Lee are favorites of mine. I have been appearing with Regis for decades, first when he had a show in L.A. I remember him interviewing me on a lawn outside the studio and asking if I was going to be doing any campaigning for an Academy Award I was being mentioned for. I said, "I'm just going with the blimp and let it go at that." I'm sure a large portion of his audience believed I'd hired a blimp with my name and reviews on it cruising above L.A.

Regis and Kathie Lee have a silly show much of the time, and I really enjoy that. To me "silly" has gotten a bad rap in recent years. Regis puts a feeling of fun in the air better than any man I've ever met. He creates an atmosphere for laughter. To me he is much more than a talk show host. He is very much underrated as a comedian. People think of comedians as "stand up," but they can be sitting down and conducting a show. Regis throws himself into the center of every situation and becomes the besieged everyman. Through it all he displays an underlying "fun" disposition. Recently I was at a party talking to Robert De Niro. Regis came over and immediately urged us to do a sequel to *Midnight Run*—with *him*! For the rest of the evening he was telling everyone that very serious talk was going on for *Midnight Run 2* with Bob, me and himself. He was putting a feeling of fun in the air. He's a pleasure on and off camera.

I'm really fond of Kathie Lee. I saw her appear for half an hour on Larry King. You could really see why she is so enormously successful. She tells the truth. Whatever she's discussing she talks as though to a trusted confidant. That's unusual, because she seems willing to touch any subject. She's also genuinely kind and it comes through. Recently I saw her as the honoree on the television show "This Is Your Life." She was genuinely moved, sometimes to tears, by everyone who showed up for her. I found that impressive, but I was really knocked out by her ability to end the show with a rousing rendition of "If They Could See Me Now."

Dr. Ruth, Arsenio, Tom Snyder

My reputation certainly preceded me when I appeared as a guest on a program Dr. Ruth was doing on cable, of course, dealing with sex. Dr. Ruth, whom I really enjoy, came into the makeup room to meet me before the show. She marched over and looked up at my eyes. I think she came to just above my belly button. After gazing at me a few moments she said, "My producer told me you attack talk show hosts. I just watched you on Letterman, and you gave it to him pretty good." I was just smiling, listening to all of this. Then after looking at me intently, she said, "But I don't think I have to worry about you. I think you're a nice guy." I said, "You don't have to worry about me attacking you." With Dr. Ruth, attacking wouldn't be funny, because it only works if someone takes a shot at me first, which is not her style. On the air, she, of course, opened with some question about sex. I don't think it had the word penis or vagina in it, but I looked at her, shocked. I said, "Are we on the air?!" She said, "Yes," and asked me another question about sex. I acted like I thought I was on a cooking show, and said, "What are you *doing*?!" as though I had wandered onto a totally dirty show which clearly it wasn't. I got a lot of mileage out of continually being startled by her questions as though I was a priest or something.

With Arsenio I opened with, "I have a cousin, Fred Rudin, who was a communications major at Kent State with you in the early seventies, and he told me at the time you were 'a white Jewish man.'" The line got no response whatsoever from the audience and kind of a blank look from Arsenio, who only said, "What's your cousin's name again?" I quickly changed the subject into a serious interview about dealing with rejection in show business. It turned out to be one of the few substantive interviews I've ever given in the short talk show format. It sure made a number of my friends happy who always fear the audience will believe the rough guy act. Some of the people I know actually leave the room when I'm on Letterman or Carson, and at least one, a sophisticated woman, watches while peeking through her hands. I got a sweet note from Arsenio saying something to the effect that I turned out to be a dream rather than a nightmare. He had admitted to me on the air that he'd had a nightmare the night before my appearance about what I might do. Personally if I ever had my own show, I'd never book someone like me. Who needs all that nervousness?

Once, in fact, I did take over as host of the old "Tomorrow" show, which used to be on NBC at 12:30 A.M. following "The Tonight Show." Tom Snyder was the host, and I had been a guest of his quite a few times. An opportunity presented itself for Tom to go to Egypt to interview then-president Anwar Sadat, and they asked me to take over for him for about four days. As it turned out, Sadat canceled and Tom stayed home, but the decision was made by Tom and his producers to let me host anyway. The most uncomfortable guest I had was Tom. He was only sitting a few feet from where he usually sat, but he was in the interviewee's chair and he admitted it really threw him. The show was ninety minutes long, as I recall, and I spent an enormous amount of time preparing for it. My guests ranged from the journalist I. F. Stone to the economist George Gilder to a very funny friend of mine named Nick Arnold, who has cerebral palsy. Nick was the booking who made the producers nervous. You do have to concentrate to understand what he's saying, but he is hilarious—even more so, because most people don't expect him to be. He also in his premarital days was quite a ladies' man—kind of a stage door Johnny around Broadway, sending flowers and a limo to various lovelies. It worked, too.

Larry King

On my book tour for *How I Get Through Life* I appeared with Larry King, and we took some calls. They all seemed to be from people I knew as a little boy growing up in Pittsburgh. I know Larry sees me as kind of a "put-on" comic, so he seemed amazed to hear what a nice little kid they all claimed I was. I get a big kick out of Larry King. I love Albert Brooks's line that if Larry was interviewing God his first question would be, "Why *seven* days?" I believe Larry is so popular because he has the attention span of America. He asks the questions the country wants to ask and stays interested about as long as your average American, which isn't that long. It makes for a good show. I also probably like him because just about anything I say or do that's intended to be funny makes him laugh. Recently I saw him at Phil Donahue's twenty-fifth-year anniversary show where we appeared together. Afterward I shouted across to him, "Hey, Larry, there's a rumor Liza may show up later." He laughed. I'll bet very few people would find that amusing—understandably. Here's why it's funny to me. Years ago I read an item in a gossip column that went something like this: "It was rumored that Liza Minnelli would be showing up at Studio 54 last night. Her representatives denied it, then confirmed it might be true, but she didn't show." That's why "Hey, Larry, there's a rumor Liza may show up later" is funny to me. Larry will have to explain why it was funny to him.

New York at Night

I'm allergic to cats. The booker of a television talk show called "New York at Night" was aware of that from reading something I had written. I was to appear on one of their shows where a later guest would be an animal trainer with a leopard cub. She sensitively asked me if that would be a problem. I said if I wasn't that close or holding the cub, it would be fine. Besides, I didn't want to inhibit their entertainment potential. The animal trainer came out last. Initially he made me a little wary when the host asked if the snake with him had a poisonous bite. The guy said, "No," then looked at his notes and said, "Oh, yeah, it does." Later he came out with the leopard "cub." It was a full-grown black leopard he held tight on a chain. It had those green slits in his eyes and gave me a look I could have done without. I watched the show later, and I wasn't on camera when the leopard appeared, but you can hear me on the sound track in a startled voice saying, "Oh no! This isn't for me." Actually when the leopard came out I seriously considered leaping over the back of the couch and off the set, but I saw the women guests just sit there, and since I sometimes play romantic roles, I thought it wasn't in the interest of my image to jump set.

Good Morning, America

Years ago I got a request from "Good Morning, America," where I had appeared several times, to come on and talk about an upcoming production of *Charley's Aunt* I had done for cable. The producers had sent them clips they thought were funny, and "Good Morning, America" invited me. I was living in Connecticut at the time and really didn't want to go into New

York. You have to get up very, very early, because it's broadcast live. They said they'd send a car and the *Charley's Aunt* producers really were looking for some promotion, so I agreed. A booker for GMA called for a preinterview. We chatted for about five minutes outlining areas of questions. I then decided to go into my New York apartment the day before the show, so I could sleep later the next morning rather than being picked up at 5 A.M. in Connecticut. I hadn't heard what time I was on the next day, so I called the P.R. people for *Charley's Aunt* to get the information. A woman uncomfortably asked me, "Didn't anyone tell you they canceled your appearance?" I said, "No, why?" It seems the booker for GMA decided I wouldn't be that funny talking about *Charley's Aunt*. In other words, some fifteen years after my first phone call "audition" for "The Tonight Show," I had another one—unbeknownst to me. I had successfully appeared on television talk shows for years. I say "successfully" by the only real barometer—they kept asking me back. As I've said, I had even been under contract to Johnny Carson, and someone from "Good Morning, America" decided I couldn't hold up five minutes on what I didn't even see as a comedy appearance. That may have been the problem. To me "The Tonight Show" and David Letterman, for example, are comedy shows, and the morning shows like the "Today" show," "CBS This Morning," and "Good Morning, America" are news and information, where you might be amusing, but it's not the same thing. These morning show appearances are usually less than five minutes long, don't have audiences, and can be sandwiched between disaster stories. None of this stuff is comedy's playground. So when I was having this telephone "audition" with the "Good Morning, America" person, I didn't know I was supposed to be funny. I simply thought, as I've said, we were outlining areas for questions—a procedure I had done with the morning shows, *including theirs*, dozens of times. Someone speculated that the reason for the cancellation wasn't any of this at all, but really because I was going to be on network television promoting something on cable. That may have been the real reason, but that's not what they said, and I was mad. I made some phone calls. By that time my reputation as a talk show guest had grown to the point where *Rolling Stone* actually did a huge spread on me as the best talk show guest in the country. (Forgive me for this self-aggrandizement; I'm trying to make a point about stupidity.) *Rolling Stone* actually constructed a replica of "The Tonight Show" set for a photographic session, and then never ran the piece. Maybe they decided I *wasn't* the best talk show guest in the country. I have no idea, but my point is it was odd, to put it gently, to be canceled from a five-minute appearance on "Good Morning, America," a portion of which would have been taken up with funny clips from *Charley's Aunt* with me dressed like a woman. David Hartman, who at the time was their main interviewer, was away on vacation during all of this, but called me as soon as he got back and heard about it, and apologized, saying, "You're welcome here anytime you want to come on for anything." Shows want to be careful about this stuff. If there's too much insensitivity or power play nonsense, people don't want to get near them. That's what happened to Jay Leno's female producer who was fired by NBC when he took over from Johnny Carson. At this writing I've never appeared with Jay Leno, but even I was aware of complicated considerations about when you could be on David Letterman or other shows if you were on "The Tonight Show" under her reign. I had heard she'd had some personal tragedies in her life, and I assumed that was what was causing this aggressive behavior, but then I heard she had been acting that way for years. It was her position of prominence as producer of "The Tonight Show" that put a spotlight on her and caused her trouble. Later, after she was fired, there were the usual claims that if a man had acted that way it would be considered, by many, acceptable. Years ago there was truth to this. But now, happily, society's standards have changed so that aggressive bullying men are just as disliked as aggressive bullying women. It always surprises me that otherwise intelligent people don't realize that if you treat people badly, it will eventually come back to you. It's fascinating that the offenders seldom seem to know how much they are offending until they're fired or told to screw off. Then they seem to be the most shocked people on earth. Sad.

A note on television ratings. It seems for years now that I've been reading in the papers who's on top, "Good Morning, America" or the "Today" show or "CBS This Morning" or whatever they call it. There are weekly reports on this just as there are on who's ahead, Peter Jennings, Tom Brokaw or Dan Rather—just as there is constant reportage on who's leading, CBS, NBC or ABC and where is Fox? *Who cares*?! I mean, with all due respect, aside from their employees and people who buy air time to sell products, who really is concerned with all of this?

I realize the papers also publish the ten leading movies. I guess that's to help people choose from what's popular, but do fans of "Good Morning, America" or Tom Brokaw, for example, really switch because a competitor got rated a touch higher one week? I doubt it. No, I think the papers sometimes publish what primarily interests *them*.

I suggest they give this stuff a rest and find some good news to publish in its place. Contrary to the widely held belief, people *are* interested in hearing some good stuff from time to time. It might help us all breathe a little easier.

MAKING A
CAREER

Making a Career?

How Do You Know If You Should Get Out of Show Business?

One of the things I wish I could do over again has to do with my first book, *It Would Be So Nice If You Weren't Here*, which is all about dealing with rejection in show business. I get the impression that most of the people in show business who read it take it as an inspiration to continue. The rationale is, "Look how much rejection Charles Grodin dealt with." While I'm pleased the book inspires people, I meant it just as much as a warning. I do say in there that you don't want to spend ten years in this profession and end up nowhere but ten years older. I say that *even if you're not publicly recognized, there must be plenty of signs along the way that you're really good to encourage you to keep going.* I did have a lot of praise in my unrecognized years, but I found it awkward putting all my compliments down on paper. As a result, I feel a lot of actors gloss over that consideration, which is a crucial one. It's a terrible truth that people going into show business generally have no idea how stacked the numbers deck is against them. There's no question you have a far better chance in Las

Vegas. The other harsh reality is you could actually be very gifted and still not have a career—a fact of life generally not true in other professions. I urged my daughter who, in my opinion, is an extraordinarily gifted actress and writer to pursue writing. Happily, she hasn't been out of work in years. That would be highly unlikely for an actress—even an outstanding one. Of course, all of this advice means nothing to those who are determined to try it. You must have talent, unending perseverance, thick skin and, as Walter Matthau once said, "All you need are fifty good breaks." I feel duty-bound to say one more time:

1. This is a dangerous profession, because you can be seduced into thinking you have a career when you really don't. It is so difficult to get anywhere that if you get any job—any job at all—it's easy to believe it counts—it matters, when it usually doesn't.

2. Of those who attempt it, there is just the tiniest percentage of people who make a living as actors. Please try to understand this and be realistic—not an actor's strong suit, because we are dreamers. You must have some real evidence you should be doing this. It can either come from people employing you or extraordinary praise from several sources seriously leading you to believe employment is just around the corner.

3. It's true I was doing this for twenty years before I was widely recognized, but I had received extravagant praise from estimable people while in my early twenties. I played a large role on a live network television show when I was twenty-three. Do not think of me as one who was so completely rejected for twenty years before I made it, because it's not true.

4. Please don't let years of inactivity dominate your life. Study, work hard, and if real signs of success aren't there after *five* years (an amendment to my first book where I said ten)—

don't spend a lifetime of knocking on doors and waiting for the phone to ring.

5. Reach for it, but don't fall off the end of the world. I wish you could all get what you want, but there's nothing as valuable as a useful happy life, and rumor has it there are some people who have achieved that who aren't actors.

My wife cautioned me that the above could sound like the Sermon on the Mount. My assistant, Clay, said about it, "It would have saved me ten years I put in pursuing acting." Most actors probably won't pay attention to what I've just said, but a few might, so that was for those few.

My Friend John's Show

Movie money is weird. I had no money at all when I got my first starring role in a movie in the sixties called *The Fun Lovers*. I thought, "My God, the starring role, I'll probably make a hundred thousand dollars." Then I learned that was the budget for the whole movie. I would get three hundred and fifty dollars a week for five weeks. Half kidding, I asked the agent to make sure I had my own room. He checked, and I didn't. When I mentioned to the director that I realized we were on a low budget, but was it really necessary for everyone's body and face to be made up with the same sponge, he apologized, saying, "Sorry, I haven't had time to dive for sponges today."

The whole thing turned out to be really fortunate though, because I shared a beautiful suite with the other leading guy in the movie, a talented actor/singer named John Gabriel, who to this day is one of my closest friends. John's stories of dealing with rejection in show business are so funny that I encouraged him to do a cabaret act using them. The act was very well received. The only problem was people kept coming up to him after the show expressing their sympathy over all his rejection, so he had to figure out a way to let the audience know they shouldn't feel sorry for him—that he actually was very successful, which isn't that easy a thing to get said gracefully in a show about rejection. I suggested he put his bio on the tables in the night club. His bio is longer than both my arms, but he said no one read it, and they still came up after loving the show to express their condolences. At this writing we're still trying to figure a way to let the audience know that someone doing a show about dealing with rejection actually has a job—*this show.*

You Need the Breaks

The good breaks are always a necessity. I'm certain I was about the fifth choice for *Beethoven,* but the people ahead of me were either unavailable or not interested, and its success has put me into a position I've never been in. A position where I still need good breaks, I should add.

My first really big break would have been impossible to know at the time. I was directing a short piece written by and starring Renée Taylor and Joe Bologna for public television. Halfway through the first day of rehearsal I looked at Joe, who was lying in bed with his wife Renée, and said, "Y'know, you should be directing this, and I should be playing your part." He said, "Well, we really based the role on you."

I said, "I knew there was something about it."

Joe climbed out of bed. I climbed in. A few months later Elaine May saw it. She was a friend of Renée and Joe, and shortly after we met she said, "I'm being offered movies to direct and I want to find one for you to star in." That's how I ended up in *The Heartbreak Kid.* Another big break was when Marty Brest, the director of *Midnight Run,* decided he wanted me instead of the biggest star who was interested—Robin Williams. That was highly unusual. I also considered it a break that Tom Pollack, the head of Universal Pictures, would star me in a big-budget movie when others wouldn't. I, of course, had information I threatened to use on Ms. May and Messrs. Brest and Pollack. That last line is the kind of thing I might say on a talk show or for that matter write here, and some people might take me seriously. Like the time Marlon Brando didn't accept his Oscar for *The Godfather*, and I said on "The Tonight Show" I'd take it. I'm sure some people thought that I was serious. (I was—a little.)

Avoiding Helpful Relationships

The business of Hollywood has always been something from which I tried to keep my distance. That's one of the reasons I always lived in New York even when it would clearly have been in my interest to live in Los Angeles. I formed no friendships over the years with Hollywood people who could have helped my career. It was almost as though I would question my own reason for cultivating the relationship so I didn't do it, even though there were several people I met who probably were potentially just nice enjoyable friends. One of my closest friends today is Phil Donahue, and I have told him if someone representing something I'm involved with suggests me to be on his show—reject it. I have been on his show twice in the past, once with Carol Burnett and once alone, but I've said, "No more," unless I turn up on the cover of *Time* and it's good for his ratings, but I don't think we have to worry about that. Not only have I not sought out potentially helpful friendships—I have actively avoided them. I was once at a party where the powerful Hollywood producer Ray Stark was present. I had met him once. Some people with me said, "Go over and say hello to him." I didn't.

Later Ray came over to me and said, "Someone told me you're a hell of a director, but I can't remember who it was."

I said, "It was probably me." I'm not real proud of this flippancy. In fact, I think it can get neurotic, and I'm working to get over it. Years ago I was at a large gathering at the home of

Frank Price, who was then head of Columbia Pictures. I had just done a couple of pictures with them. As I was leaving, Frank came over and said, "Why don't you and your girlfriend join my wife and me for dinner some time?" Now the truth was I really liked Frank a lot and would have loved to have had dinner with him, but I responded, "Send me a memo. I always obey your memos." I could see the hurt cross Frank's face at my stupid joke. We, of course, never had the dinner and he didn't speak to me again for ten years. I saw him recently. He's not running a studio now, and in a short conversation I was reminded of why I liked him so much in the first place. I've known Barry Diller for years. Barry, for about as long as I've known him, has been one of the most powerful people in show business—running various studios, etc. Mostly all I've ever found myself saying to him is, "What exactly do you do, anyway?" I honestly didn't mean to suggest he wasn't doing anything. I really was curious to know exactly what a studio head did, but I can see more clearly now how it could be taken as a dig.

The reality is that somewhere in there I probably have been defensive and resentful toward people with power. Today when I meet one I make a real effort to control myself, as I have no idea what might slip out.

My Friend Detachment

I used to be very active as a director, but my experience there, even though successful, was so filled with dealing with one problem after another—I'm thrilled when someone else takes on that job. I just don't enjoy coping with various people's temperaments as a way of life. My own is enough for me. As I once explained to the aforementioned Clay Alexander Dettmer, my right arm, assistant, associate, who really helps me get through life, "I'm low-key, but I'm high-strung. Don't mistake my easy-going manner. I'm a person who can comfortably stand in front of a thousand people and perform, but it really bothers me if my bed blanket falls on the floor." Actually, in a lot of hotels they throw them on the floor when they make up the bed. Clay and I put a stop to that, at least when we're watching.

I probably have always been low-key and high-strung, but for most of my career I think I benefited enormously from being detached. This detached thing took care of the high-strung thing, as the blows never really got through to me the way they seemed to others. Somehow even early on I found excessive abuse kind of funny—maybe knowing it would make a good story someday.

The head of the acting school who, by way of audition, gave me a kind of Rorschach test—"What does this shape remind you of?"—was trying to see if I was nuts, and I ended up thinking *he* was. The speech teacher who exploded at me, "Why should anyone pay money to hear you, the way you speak?" and I applied the question to people who spoke the way she wanted—"affected" (at least for an American character). The great teacher, Uta Hagen, who got angry at me for not rushing up onstage to practice opening an imaginary window just made me quizzical. Detachment has been my friend, in dealing with theatrical blows anyway.

Three Nice Show Business Calls

An actress/writer friend of mine said she'd gotten three nice show business calls in one day. We were all impressed and asked what they were. She said, "This producer liked a script I'd written. Somebody else called and wants to meet me about a writing job, and my acting agent phoned to say she didn't want to represent me anymore." I said, "Geez, that third call, uh . . ." She responded, "She didn't *have* to call." So even a call of rejection was a *call*, instead of the silence that surrounds most careers. Show business can play funny games with your mind. Beware.

Critics and Other Problems

Critics

I used to be friends with the *Los Angeles Times* critic Charles Champlin, who is now their critic emeritus or whatever they call it. In his review of *Sunburn*, a picture I did with Farrah Fawcett and Art Carney, he said something like, "It looked like everyone was down there to collect a paycheck." I was turning down opportunities to do commercials when I was a cabdriver, so I really don't qualify as a guy who will do something for the check without concerning myself with its quality. I've never explained to Mr. Champlin, who is actually a very nice man, why I haven't embraced him when our paths have infrequently crossed over the years. I'm not that easy to insult, believe me, but cracks about people on movies who are there to pick up paychecks or actors who looked like they phoned it in get me. People who write this stuff obviously have never been on the set of a movie from beginning to end. Just showing up somewhere every day for twelve to sixteen hours for three or four months should be enough to disqualify movie people from those cracks. The only thing about a movie that can be phoned in is a review.

Critics, of course, have a job to do, and personally if I had to see hundreds of movies a year—I'd probably have a breakdown, and end up saying weirder things than the guy who interviewed me during a press junket for *Midnight Run* and asked if I was concerned about losing my faculties as I got older. I said I hadn't actually been thinking about it and made a mental note of the questioner's name. I think he'd probably been to so many screenings he was worried about losing *his* faculties. Another question I got a lot during that time was, "Were you intimidated working with Robert De Niro?" I tried not to sound arrogant when I said, "I've never been intimidated working with anyone, including Anthony Quinn, who was a superstar when I was in my twenties working on Broadway with him." I can't really afford to be intimidated. I'm not quite where Ethel Merman was on the subject: "If somebody from the audience could do it better than me, then they'd be up here." Merman was tough. After she retired she went to see a show where the leading lady didn't quite hit a note to Ms. Merman's satisfaction. People in several seats nearby were able to hear her say, "Oh, *please*." Confidence is hard fought for and gained after many years of effort, and feelings of intimidation are to be avoided if at all possible.

It's Worse Than You Think

A few years ago I was in New York and phoned an actor friend of mine, Joe Sicari, in Los Angeles. When I asked him what was going on, he told me about a problem he was wrestling with. He had an offer to go into the long-running stage hit *Tamara*. The show had been on for years and Joe would be about the sixth replacement in the role, so it wasn't a showcase for him, but it was a paycheck.

Tamara, for those of you not familiar with it, is a unique theatrical event. It's a romantic historical saga set in a mansion and as a member of the audience you choose to follow whichever part you want, as the actors split off into different directions. Joe went to see the play to check out the role they wanted him for. He followed the actor who was leaving the production, as he went down a flight of stairs into a basement. Basically Joe was trying to see if the guy's costume could be altered to fit him. The rest of the audience had gone elsewhere, so it was just Joe and the actor down in the basement. The actor, grateful that at least one member of the audience had followed *him*, really was putting a lot of passion into his monologue as Joe looked on. Joe considered quietly interrupting to tell the guy to take it easy, since he was only there to check out wardrobe but thought better of it and remained a polite audience.

I'm sure the actor thought it a bit pathetic that he had an audience of one. Of course, the unimaginable truth was worse, which reminds me of the time a former partner of mine was made the head of a studio. We had been producing partners on a script I'd written. When I called him in his new position to present our script, he said, "Come out to the house over the weekend. It's too crazy around the office." Naturally I took that as a good sign. I played out every scenario in my mind on how it all might go, except the one that actually happened. When I called him over the weekend, he didn't return the call.

Troublemakers

When I did my play *One of the All Time Greats* in New York, the director Tony Roberts told me some of the actors would come to him and ask if they could change the lines this way or that—not for comedy—just for basic language. I write the way I feel the characters talk—not always according to proper rules of grammar, and some of the actors wanted to clean up my syntax, which Tony flatteringly referred to as Grodinesque. I don't know about Grodinesque, but I was as startled as Tony was by the request. For whatever reason, playwrights are accorded rights by their union that very few screen writers can get. You simply can't change anything in a play script without the playwright's approval. Tony was fond of saying, "This isn't a democracy!" I was happy to have Tony in charge. I had long since lost interest in directing, which I had done off-Broadway, on Broadway and on television specials. I eventually found it a tedious job in the theatre, a grueling one in television, and observed it was an unending one in the movies. You have to give at least a year of your life to prepare, film and take care of postproduction on a movie, and I'd much rather write or act. The tedium in the theatre comes from the necessity of watching the same thing over and over, which I found even more trying than acting the same thing over and over. Mostly though I tired of dealing with all the various personalities. Tony told me in his twenty-five-year acting career he had never raised his voice. In directing my play he more than once had to raise it—really raise it, threaten to leave and worse—and the play wasn't in trouble, it was a success. I saw my role as supportive of Tony. I would really get involved only for something of a trouble-shooting nature, which unfortunately was needed from time to time. Early on though I felt somewhat alienated from the production. I came to the first run-through I believe at the end of the second week of rehearsal. Prior to this I had disagreed with Tony and the producer, an unusually talented man named Doug Aibel. I belong to the school that believes in the theatre the actors must spend considerable time learning their lines *before* rehearsal begins. I don't go as far as Noel Coward, who insisted that everyone show up on day one fully knowing their lines, although I'd like to. I think you have to be Noel Coward to get the actors to go along with that. I certainly agree with Jerry Zaks, the very successful director of *Guys and Dolls* among many other shows, who expects a full-out, word-perfect run-through two weeks in. Tony and Doug didn't agree with me. They felt everyone works differently and the actors would be resentful and feel pushed if we insisted on what I wanted.

55

Years ago I had read an interview with Paul Muni where he dealt with the subject. He definitely believed in learning his lines ahead of rehearsal. One of the arguments used against this is you get into patterns of line readings and you can't "find" your performance in rehearsal. I don't acknowledge this as a problem at all. I believe the opposite is true. When Muni talked about learning his lines ahead of time he definitely did not mean *how* to say them, just what they were. You could learn them the way you'd learn the alphabet—by rote. Then when you got into rehearsal you wouldn't have to spend so much time trying to figure out what the words were and could use that focus to get more deeply involved in the situation of the play.

Anyway, Tony and Doug weren't buying it, so when I saw the run-through midway into rehearsal—it was shaky. I wasn't at all surprised that a number of the actors didn't know their lines. I had the opportunity to speak to the company afterward, and after saying some supportive things I made my speech about the importance of learning the lines. This was supposed to be a fast-paced ensemble comedy. I had directed an early version of the play twenty years ago in stock, and then, too, most of the actors didn't know their lines well enough on opening night. I said you didn't want to be giving a significantly more solid performance a month after the critics had been there. I spoke of two outstanding acting experiences I'd had, one with Ellen Burstyn on Broadway in *Same Time Next Year* and another in movies with Robert De Niro in *Midnight Run*. I said what they had in common was the extraordinary amount of time we had drilled the lines. In Ellen's and my case, after a full day's rehearsal we'd go to my apartment and run lines for three more hours. We found there was no other way to master this two-character play in the amount of time we had. By the way, Ellen ended up winning the Tony, and we both won the Outer Critics Circle Award as best actors.

In the middle of this pep talk, one of the actors angrily rose and said, "I'm not interested in hearing about Robert De Niro and Ellen Burstyn! What you're really saying is if you were in the play you'd know your lines by now. I take that as a criticism."

I said, "That's exactly how I mean it." In fact, I really wasn't singling this actor out. He was more prepared than most. I meant it as a general note, and he really got his nose out of joint over it. Another actor quickly rose and said he personally appreciated the reminder and acknowledged he probably hadn't worked hard enough. This didn't mollify the first fellow, who was still steaming about it weeks later. Of course, he also found other things to steam about that had nothing to do with my speech. When you want to steam—you steam. I couldn't bring myself to point out if it wasn't obvious to everyone that Robert De Niro and Ellen Burstyn and I, for that matter, had reaped a lot more rewards from show business than anyone in that company, and I believe that principle of learning lines had something to do with it. Ironically, the guy who was offended is unusually gifted and really should be a star actor. He's that good. By the way, after the speech he was seen putting in extra time on the lines—I'm sure out of spite. I'll take it any way I can get it. Anyway, for me and eventually for Tony it wasn't that thrilling a place to hang around. What I've described is just a tiny part of it. There was a lot of backbiting within the company, threats of union charges being brought—it was a mess. To paraphrase the title of my first book, I'm so glad I was hardly there.

It's amazing to me how actors don't seem to realize that being troublesome will impact their careers. Working on the other side of it as a producer, director or writer, I can say that the first question that comes up when people are interested in hiring someone is, "What's he like to work with?" And word gets around quickly. Employers call each other, and you definitely can get hurt if you cause people grief.

I personally would not be in a hurry to work again with the actor who chose to debate every one of the director's directions or the more than one actor who denigrated a script on a consistent basis after agreeing to play the part for what I'm sure was a considerable amount of money. Then there was the young actor in something I'd written who refused to stop doing something the director asked, even though he knew that both the director and I felt it was sending a truly inappropriate message. The actor persisted and absolutely cost himself future employment. That's the way it works. We all want to work with not only talented but cooperative people. I once directed an actor I was trying to get more out of. He said at one point, "If I feel like someone's really pushing me, I want to kick them in the face." You know I'll be running to work with him again! I'm also not in a hurry to work again with anyone who yells at people, and I've seen actors and directors and producers do that.

I have no interest in working again with a star actress whom I found to be a snob. She spoke only to the makeup and hair people when she felt like it, and wasn't much better with me. I've since learned that was a phase and generally not what she's like today. My purpose in talking about all this is to call attention to the negative behavior. I've learned from experience that many of these people, amazingly, aren't even aware there's anything wrong with what they're doing, but chalk it up to "I was in a bad mood" or say chucklingly, "I have a terrible temper."

Once on a book promotion tour for my last book, *How I Get Through Life*, I found myself in the, for me, highly enviable position of sitting in the broadcast booth between the New York Mets baseball announcers, Tim McCarver and Ralph Kiner, a boyhood hero of mine as a home-run hitter for the Pittsburgh Pirates. Ralph had picked one line out of the book that particularly appealed to him: "People who yell at people are hated— usually forever." So, of course, all this bad behavior isn't appreciated any more out of show business than in it.

Press Agents

I place myself somewhere between my friend, the playwright Herb Gardner, and a "show business person." On the Herb Gardner side I have not moved to Hollywood, done commercials, or, for that matter, anything else just for money. Although, there is certainly nothing wrong with working *just* for money, as long as it's legal, doesn't embarrass you too much, and doesn't affect possible future employment, which show business missteps often do.

I have had a public relations person on occasion—but mostly not. I never was able to figure out if it was necessary to have one. They are expensive and generally can promote you only if you're doing something, which the movie company or Broadway show or publisher's P.R. people are hired to do.

The first time I got one was about twenty years ago when a big ad for *The Heartbreak Kid* appeared, understandably dominated by the writer Neil Simon and the director Elaine May. Even though I played the title role, my name was listed with the same prominence as the production assistants (tiny), as was everyone else. I hired a guy who I learned later was primarily known for keeping people's names *out* of the paper.

I once hired a press agent with misgivings, because her office was in an open area surrounded by other people. She assured me I needn't worry about private communication. I find any conversation about public relations embarrassing even if it's only with a press agent. Anyway, one day someone came to the press agent's "office" to do a story on her. The reporter listened as the press agent was on the phone with me. I was asking what time a car was going to pick me up in Connecticut to take me to a press junket. I also asked if a story had appeared in some magazine. I promise you, innocuous stuff, innocuously asked. I don't give "attitude," as hundreds of people who have worked with me can attest. The reporter, hearing only the press agent's side of the call, wrote a story for *Spy* magazine characterizing me as demanding or words to that effect. It was all totally bull. The reporter assumed my attitude from hearing one end, and got it all wrong, but totally. That, and once reading in the paper that I personally demanded the film company of *Midnight Run* go to do a rapids sequence in New Zealand rather than Arizona, which was also totally made up, makes me look warily at a lot of reported outrageous show business behavior. If I had enough power to tell a movie company where to film—I probably wouldn't even bother going to work.

At some point I got tired of people pursuing things on my behalf, so now I don't have a public relations person, although there are some I think are good, and like personally. If anyone wants to do a story on me or have me appear, they find a way of getting the request to me. It's nice to not "want" it and a lot cheaper, too.

Richard Martini Improvises

My pal Richard Martini told me a funny show business story the other day. As I've said, Richard is a writer/director. He's also a sometimes actor. He got a call from an agent in Pasadena—one of many to whom he'd sent his resumé. He drove out to meet the guy, who was a tall black man with dark glasses. The agent sat behind his desk and put Richard through a series of improvisations. "You're in Vietnam. You're the only one left in your platoon. The Vietcong are closing in. You grab an M-16 rifle. Go!" Richard picked up an imaginary gun and dashed around the office, ducking and firing off rounds. After a few minutes of this, the guy said, "O.K. It's 1929, the Wall Street crash, you go into your accountant's office and he's lost all your money and shot himself. Go!" Richard started screaming, then dragged the imaginary dead accountant's body to the window and threw it out. The guy said, "Great! I really think I could do something with you. I'm blind, but from what I've heard, you've really got it." Another time Richard got an assignment to rewrite a script and set it in Poland, as Polish money was financing it. When he completed it, the producer told him the financing had fallen through, but now German money was available, and they wanted the story to take place in Germany. Richard rewrote it with German characters and locations. This time when he handed it in the producer told him the whole thing was off because "I've almost gone bankrupt doing movies like this."

The People I
Started Out With

One of the odd, troubling things I've experienced in my career
has to do with what happened to some of the people I began
with. As I've written elsewhere, when I started at the Pittsburgh
Playhouse school, I was what felt like lower than the low man on
the totem pole. There were two young actors highly touted by the
head of the school, Bill Putch. In thirty years I've seen one of
their names once and the other never. Bill gave me a scholar-
ship but soon appeared to have little or no faith in me. He tragi-
cally died in his early fifties. Of course I appreciate the success
I've had, but when I think of Bill and the others at the playhouse whom I've never seen, there is only a kind of rueful feeling. I feel even stranger about all the outstanding people who
were my classmates in New York who probably, for lack of real
opportunity, just dropped out of the profession. The strangest,
saddest experience of all relating to this has to do with my first
agent, Bruce Savan. Bruce had an up-and-coming young client
who was the favorite of the agency. His name was Bobby Drivas.

Bruce used to tell me, "Someday Bobby will be unavailable and you'll get your chance." Both Bruce and Bobby died of AIDS.

It was not the warmest of beginnings. I'll never forget Bruce's partner, Barry Levinson, not the great director, answering my question of whether I should have pictures made. He said, "Of course, get pictures. Then the people who don't want to see you will at least know who it is they don't want to see."

I once was friends with an actor who was older and more well known than I was. We used to watch basketball games together. As time went by, I became more well known than he, but I never mentioned anything about what I was doing, sensing he wouldn't particularly enjoy hearing it. I would go over to his place and he'd be holding a newspaper. He'd look at me and say, "You never told me you were starring in a movie." I'd try to shrug it off, but as it continued over the years, he got increasingly uncomfortable. I was having the career he'd imagined for himself. Eventually we drifted apart. So I never tell other performers I'm doing anything, and if they ask, I try to low key it as much as I can.

I wasn't so aware of this on the opening night of my first Broadway show, *Tchin-Tchin*. It was a real breakthrough for me. I had gone from being totally unknown to playing an important role in essentially what was a three-character play with the other two characters being played by the stars Anthony Quinn and Margaret Leighton. Not only that, but I got great reviews, and the show became standing room only. I was in my apartment, after the opening-night performance, talking about it with two close friends, a couple, when the woman said, "You've been talking about this for twenty minutes already!" Naturally that stopped me, and just as inevitably my friendship with this couple eventually went away. We were all young actors together, and the woman, at least, couldn't handle my success. Often it's not the person who becomes successful who changes.

Acting Classes and Other Weird Things

I got a letter recently from the famed actress and acting teacher, Uta Hagen, with whom I studied for three years early in my career. She expressed regret that she had read in my first book that I never understood the reason for the years of opening imaginary windows or carrying imaginary suitcases in her classes. I also said wonderful things, but you always remember the dig.

This imaginary stuff still goes on today. Uta Hagen excepted, most acting teachers never made a living as actors. That's how they have time to teach all this imaginary stuff—imagining showers—pretending you're an animal—feeling heat—feeling cold. I'm not saying there aren't some, but I have never personally met a working actor who uses any of this stuff.

Then there are the speech teachers who try to get all of us Americans to sound English—and do. So you have a lot of unemployed American actors who sound English. I always felt the main value of acting classes was they were the only place you could get up and act. Then someone could tell you how you did, and next week you could try again. Certainly there was no place else a beginner could get to do that.

The main thing, as I see it, for actors to do is try to get experienced enough to get over their nerves. The only way to do this is to do so many scenes it becomes if not second nature, then close. Also, as I've said, learn your lines as well as you know the alphabet (no less!) so you can "listen" the way you listen in life to know how to answer the other person. The functioning of an actor is much like life and when you feel less real than life—you'll know you're "off."

I was at a dinner party recently. The subject of acting came up. I was the only actor there, so I could claim the authority position. After hearing a few of my observations, a woman in a clearly hostile way offered, "But acting's fake, isn't it?!" I said, "No, this [dinner party chat] is fake. Acting is real." I believe acting is more real than most life behavior, which is superficial and fake. Try dinner party reality on the screen, and we won't get to see you again, unless it's in a dinner party scene.

When I first came to New York the two gods of reality in acting were Lee Strasberg, who was running the Actors Studio where virtually no one could get in, and Elia Kazan, the most celebrated director of his time. Both were distant, removed, almost mythic figures to a young actor. I auditioned for the Actors Studio a few times, and while encouraged to try again, I was worn down by the process and happily settled for being in Lee Strasberg's private classes for three years. The circumstances of auditioning for the studio made it almost impossible to get in. You were ushered up a narrow stairwell into a large room where two spotlights hit you. You could vaguely see three figures sitting on some kind of elevation. You were asked to state your name and the name of your scene. If you could do anything but shake after that—you were a pretty good actor. I always advised people to audition playing characters who were supposed to be nervous.

It was after I appeared in *Same Time Next Year* on Broadway that I was invited, at the instigation of Ellen Burstyn, to become a member of the Actors Studio. It is a cherished moment for me that after my first session at the studio when I thanked Lee Strasberg for inviting me to join, he said, "You belong here."

It was about thirty years after I first came to New York that I finally met Elia Kazan at a party at Robert De Niro's apartment. I had appeared with Bob in *Midnight Run* about a year earlier and when Kazan came in I was introduced to him along with about three other people by Bob. I got the impression Kazan thought I was a business associate of Bob's. Because of a lifetime of admiration for his work, I considered approaching him later, but realized I had nothing to say that I was sure he hadn't heard thousands of times. Later I was sitting in a corner talking to some people when I heard Kazan call out, "I found him, I found him, here he is!" I turned to see who Kazan had found and was startled to realize it was me! He was genuinely excited to meet and talk with me and planted himself beside me for a long time. How strange it all can be. The unimaginable was happening, and it was difficult to grasp.

What is exceptional about my career is not that it took so long for all this to happen but given the odds, that it *ever* happened.

Early Strange Behavior

I sometimes shudder when I think of my naïveté at the beginning of my career. I was going out with a girl whose manager was planning a musical he was going to call *Tennessee*—I guess because of the success of *Oklahoma*. One night the three of us were at dinner and he casually mentioned there might be a walk-on for me in it. I imagined I could do something in that imagined walk across the stage in that imagined musical that would launch me. Imagine!

It astonishes me that someone who would later write a book about surviving in show business once believed if I could get my hair to fall *way* down over my forehead—that would be a ticket to stardom, as a lot of the young successful actors in the fifties had that look.

Also early on I was an extra, one of Robin Hood's men, in a sketch with the comedy team Wayne and Shuster on "The Ed Sullivan Show." I actually averted my face from camera thinking to be seen in this context would hurt my career—which at the time was non-existent.

I'm embarrassed to admit I was doing silly things later as well. I was the Broadway director Gene Saks's assistant in a Theatre Guild production of *The Millionairess*, starring Carol Channing. Even though I was in my late twenties, Gene had to gently remind me it probably wasn't a good idea for me to sit in the second row at rehearsals smoking a cigar—with my feet up yet. Carol was a pistol in that one. She had a big scene with Gene Wilder, who hadn't figured out what to do in it yet, so he just sat there softly saying his lines. Carol, who was really carrying on in the scene, turned to Gene when it was over and said, "I just love what you're doing!"

Before I was really in a big movie, I had an interview for a studio picture called *1000 Plane Raid*. Again, as with Wayne and Shuster, I didn't want to be in it, even though I didn't have all that much going for me. I met with the producers and fooling around said, "I understand you're painting a backdrop on the lot with a thousand planes on it." They vehemently denied it. I then referred to their star. I said, "Doesn't it make you nervous that the star of your picture has just completed his third movie in a row that the studio feels is unreleasable?" They looked at each other stunned by the information. Somewhere a little after that they realized I was kidding about everything, and offered me a role in the picture. To everyone's amazement I turned it down. In other words, what we had there was a cocky, hostile young actor—I'm sad to say. It was all a defense mechanism about being rejected. Luckily I didn't act that way often, but I sure do cringe when I remember when I foolishly did.

Authorities Who Don't Know What They're Talking About

Three examples leap to mind. About eight years ago I was show-ing a cut of a movie I'd produced to a man who was actually running United Artists. There was an audio cut in one of the scenes—meaning the sound of a scene continued over the pic-ture of the next scene. The dialogue was people describing a character and that continued as the picture went to the person being described. This is, of course, a quite common device used for years. The studio head didn't seem to know that and crankily called out, "The sound is still on from the last scene!" There was only silence when I called back, "It's supposed to be!"

More recently a man in quite a position of power in the Broadway theatre criticized a play I'd written, because it has a narrator who helps advance the action. He firmly told me, "You can't do that!" I had to gently remind him a narrator has been an acceptable device in the theatre since there's been theatre. Most recently on Broadway we had two award-winning plays use it—*Dancing at Lughnasa* and *Conversations with My Father*—not to mention *Our Town* and untold others.

A friend of mine recently had her script rejected by a movie studio, because while they loved the writing, they didn't care for the concept. They had hired her to write it, and it was *their* concept! Many people in the business side of show business are too cavalier, spread thin and unfocused to even have the ability to communicate intelligently with the artists. The inherent problem is while the artist is usually involved with one thing, the business person inevitably is involved with several.

If I'm continually surprised to learn anything about show business, it's the *extent* the profession is filled with people who speak with great authority and don't know what they're talking about. I had lunch recently with a man who had produced about twenty-five movies—none of which I'd heard of—which should have warned me. I was there with some other associates because I was told this man had liked a script I'd written and wanted to arrange for some European financing. He opened the meeting by saying he'd like to see less dialogue and more visual ways to tell the story—something any screenwriter should agree to. I said, "Great! I'd love to hear any ideas you have on that." He quickly changed the subject. Later he actually said that any movie should be just as effective with the sound track turned off. After he said *that*, I decided to proceed with the lunch, if only for later anecdotal purposes. Imagine *When Harry Met Sally*, or a thousand other movies, without hearing what they're saying. When he sent a few pages of notes a couple of weeks later, they were so nuts that I thought he was joking. He even had me hearing a horse talk to me that no one else heard. To really understand how crazy that note is you'd have to know no horse appears in the picture. This guy was the epitome of the person who speaks with great authority who doesn't have a clue.

Because of lack of specific requirements for most jobs in show business, this profession has way more than its fair share of incompetents telling everyone what to do.

PERSONAL APPEARANCES

One Man Show

I first had the idea to do a one-man show in the early eighties. This was somewhat born out of writing comedy scripts and having business people tell me they weren't funny. I wanted an opportunity to write something—show it to no one and then go onstage and do it. The only judge would be the audience. I wrote the show over a period of about a year. It was actually the genesis of my first book. The first time I tried it out, it was about two hours long, and I had an audience of one, my wife. It's so hard to talk nonstop for two hours that the only way I could do it was lying on the sofa. After that I refined it to about an hour forty-five minutes, and did it again in my living room for a couple of patient friends. Next a group of about thirty-five of my mother's friends were assembled in a living room. They were an audience of older people and some were hard of hearing. At the end of one story the punch line is, "And that man was Noel Coward." I heard one woman in the last row ask another, "Who?" The other woman answered, "Noel Howard," as both women nodded. Eventually I called Shelly Schultz, who's an agent friend of mine at William Morris, and told him I had a one-man show that I wanted to do in my hometown, Pittsburgh. I said I had been president of my high school class four years in a row and really not since Gene Kelly had an actor come out of Pittsburgh and become known in the movies. I thought it was an ideal place for me to draw a crowd, and Shelly quickly agreed. He had represented some major attractions, most recently Eddie Murphy, and he had clout as an agent in the field. He called the local concert producers in Pittsburgh, Engler/Ross, and asked them to arrange what would be called "An Evening of Humor with Charles Grodin" at the Stanley Theatre in downtown Pittsburgh. They put a thousand seats on sale, and virtually no one bought a ticket! Well, a few people did. Let me put it this way: my brother, an attorney and CPA who lives there, was buying more tickets for his clients than the whole city of Pittsburgh bought. I got on the phone with the local producer, Rich Engler, and said, "Rich, maybe it would be a good idea to put flyers up at the universities there, Carnegie Mellon, the University of Pittsburgh, the Pittsburgh Playhouse, where I graduated.

He said, "We've done all that." Unconsciously at that moment I became more of a New Yorker and less of a Pittsburgher.

I said, "Given my background with Pittsburgh and movies and all that, how do you explain my brother out-buying the city?"

He said recognition in one area of show business clearly didn't transfer to another. In other words, if I was appearing in a play locally that might be one thing, but as a monologist doing an evening of humor, well, so far we had sold forty tickets. After a couple of weeks of my brother out-buying the city two to one, Rich called me and said, "How would you feel if we got the mayor to designate the day of the concert Charles Grodin Day? Would you be comfortable with that?"

I didn't quite get the question. I sure wasn't comfortable the way it was going. Charles Grodin Day sounded like a great idea to me. It had certainly never entered my mind, given the city's response to me so far. I said, "Could you do that?"

He said they had some connections in the mayor's office and thought they might be able to do it. After about a week I was talking to him about the poor ticket sales and I awkwardly asked, "By the way, any news on my day?"

"We're working on it," he said.

This went on every few days for the next couple of weeks: "Anything on my day?"

"We might hear something next week."

"What's up on my day?"

"We'll hear something real soon."

I could just imagine these conversations, Rich Engler saying, "C'mon, give the guy a day!" and the mayor's representative saying, "Who is he again?" And Rich hitting them with all my movies and Broadway shows. He probably threw the president of the class thing in there, too. Anyway, after about a month of this, the day of my concert *was* miraculously designated Charles Grodin Day. That afternoon there was an official proclamation in the mayor's office. My wife, my brother, my daughter Marion, and a couple of friends along with a little gray-haired lady everyone thought was my mother were there. My mother, in fact, was home in Los Angeles. I'd like to say she had mixed feelings about the whole thing, but her feelings definitely weren't mixed. I remember the first time I told her about my plan to do this. She said, "Alone?"

I said, "Well, yeah, it's a one-man show." She just shook her head in silence. I said, "What?"

She said, "I don't like this."

I said, "Look, Mother, you didn't think it was such a hot idea for me to be an actor, and that worked out."

She said, "Yeah, but as an actor you're up there with other

people. This is *alone*." I said I felt I could do it. She said, "Neil Diamond, I could understand."

So my mother chose to stay in L.A. for this one, nervously waiting by the phone to learn if her son had made a fool of himself on the stage of the Stanley Theatre in his hometown. The little gray-haired lady at the Charles Grodin Day ceremony was actually Mrs. Snyder, who was one of our neighbors when I was growing up on North St. Claire Street in Pittsburgh. Unfortunately I couldn't resist pulling a gag on poor Mrs. Snyder when people referred to her as my mother. I said, "My *mother*?! I've never seen this woman before in my *life*!" Mrs. Snyder looked shocked and cried out, "I'm Mrs. Snyder! I was your neighbor when you were growing up!" I quickly put my arm around her and assured her I was joking, but I'm sorry to say it took a long moment for Mrs. Snyder to recover.

Later in the day I was alone in my hotel room wondering what I had gotten myself into. The combined total of sold tickets ended up being about a hundred and fifty, and about eighty had been bought by my brother. The Charles Grodin Day announcement certainly hadn't created a stampede on the box office. The producers in order to avoid an 85 percent empty house filled the place with complimentary tickets, so that meant 85 percent of the audience had not paid to see me. I had no idea who they were, and they probably didn't know who I was either. To make it even more frightening, when we put out complimentary tickets in the theatre quite often English is not the first language of the complimentary ticket holders. While I was pacing, rolling all of this around in my head, the phone rang. I answered and there was a young man on the other end of the phone calling from the lobby of the hotel. The conversation went something like this:

YOUNG MAN
Is Charles Grodin there?

ME

Speaking.

YOUNG MAN
(startled)
This is Charles Grodin?

ME

Yes. Can I help you?

YOUNG MAN
(flustered)
Mr. Grodin, I had no idea you'd answer the
phone!

ME

Well, what can I do for you?

YOUNG MAN
I can't believe I'm talking to Charles
Grodin!

He turns and shouts out to people in the lobby of the hotel:

YOUNG MAN
I'm talking to Charles Grodin! *I'm actually
talking to Charles Grodin on the phone*!

At that point I hear a woman's voice call out, "Who's Charles
Grodin?"

YOUNG MAN
(to woman and others in lobby)
Charles Grodin! He was in *The Heartbreak*

We're Ready for You, Mr. Grodin

Kid, Heaven Can Wait, Seems Like Old Times!

The woman calls out, "Ask him what Goldie Hawn is like."

YOUNG MAN
(to me)
What's Goldie Hawn like?

ME
She's very sweet.

YOUNG MAN
(to woman)
She's very sweet.
(to me)
Mr. Grodin, I'm so embarrassed. I'm the
only one down here who knows who you are!

With that call ringing in my ears, I headed for the theatre.

Oddly enough, in spite of everything, I had one reassuring thought in my mind. A few years earlier, in casual conversation, my friend Paul Simon had referred to me as a world-class anec- dotist. Paul is one of the most critical people I know, mostly of his own work. He is sure not a guy who passes out easy compli- ments. So I figured if I could get that kind of assessment from Paul Simon—I should be O.K. in front of this crowd, even if they were strangers. I'm sure Paul had no idea how much that casual comment of his meant to my confidence. There was a local singer the producers had gotten for an opening act. I asked Rich Engler to take me from my dressing room to the back of the theatre while the singer was on. No one had told me he was going to be lip-synching his act to a prerecording. The audience seemed indifferent—at best. I thought to myself, I've got to be able to do better than this.

About a half hour later I stepped out on the stage as a monologist for the first time in my life. A thousand people stared at me. I looked back at them a moment, and then told the story of the phone call from the young man in the lobby. The story, the point of which was that no one had heard of me, seemed to relax everyone, including me. It got a big laugh. In fact, for an hour and twenty minutes the laughs were there. It went absolutely great. It was all true stuff, and started with growing up in Pittsburgh, which certainly didn't hurt. I felt vindicated that all the comedy I had written which had been rejected by business people was probably a lot funnier than they could tell. Of course, scripts are meant to be performed, not just read, and that's always been the problem. The ability of the reader—his sense of humor, etc., clearly has a lot to do with the reaction.

As soon as the concert was over my mother got a call from a friend of hers who was there reporting the reaction, and she told me later she'd never been so relieved in her life. Actually, after years of cautioning, "Do you think you can do this?" from my mother about performing, directing, etc., she is now prepared to believe I can do anything. Of course, if I told her I was next going to sing—the red light would go on again.

The reviews for the show were wonderful, and Shelly Schultz, who had booked it in the first place, was now ready to book me around the country. I was surprised I had no interest in doing that. I just wanted to prove to myself I could do it. So I did no more of it for about eight years.

Bankers Trust

Last year I got a call asking if I would be interested in hosting a mock Academy Awards ceremony for a group of international traders for Bankers Trust. I didn't really understand what it was they wanted me to do, and I didn't particularly want to fly to Florida where they were awarding themselves, until I heard how much they were willing to pay me. I knew nothing about

Bankers Trust or international traders, but I figured I'd bone up on it and somehow figure something funny to do. I asked that they send me some literature. I read it, but unfortunately had no idea what most of their terms meant—futures, swaps and about twenty others, some of which even friends of mine in financial fields had never heard of. I had lunch with the two people responsible for putting the thing together, a Japanese woman and an American man based in Japan. They laughingly said even people who worked at Bankers Trust had a hard time figuring out what most of this was about. Worse yet it wasn't even clear if the awards were really given for achievement or a joke or what. "Kind of a joke," is what they said. I again called everyone I knew who might enlighten me—my business manager, my brother, my friend Gideon Rothschild (no relation), my cousin Joey in Chicago, who actually did something like this for another company. After all these conversations and further study of the literature—I was really nowhere. Not only couldn't I fathom what they did—as hard as I tried I couldn't figure out what award was a joke or serious or what. It was a mess. Right in the middle of all of this, Hurricane Andrew hit Florida. I was secretly hoping they'd cancel the event, which was set for Key Largo, but all they did was move it north to Boca Raton.

I flew in on the afternoon of the event and was met by the guy I'd earlier had lunch with who was based in Tokyo. He started to further explain what was going on, but I stopped him. Here's what a conversation with my Bankers Trust contact sounded like to me.

ME

So these awards, they're a joke, right?

B.T. GUY

Well, in a way.

ME

In a way?

78

B.T. GUY

Some are—partially.
A pause.

ME

Give me an example of one.

B.T. GUY

Most borders crossed to close a deal.

ME

Is that a joke?

B.T. GUY

No. It is given to the person who crossed the
most borders.

ME

So, it's *not* a joke.

B.T. GUY

Well, it is in a way.

ME

Because it's the most borders?

B.T. GUY

Right.

ME
(lost)
Uh huh. Give me another award.

B.T. GUY

Best-dressed broker.

ME

That's a joke, right?

B.T. GUY

Well . . .

ME

Is the winner well dressed?

B.T. GUY

Some people think so.

A pause.

ME

I'm not really getting a clear shot of the humor here.

B.T. GUY

Want to see some literature?

ME

I've got literature. I can't understand it.

B.T. GUY
(laughing)

Most people can't.

ME

What's an L-Tranche?

B.T. GUY
(laughing)

Nobody understands that one.

ME
(increasingly lost)
Uh huh.

(a pause)
Give me another award.

A pause.

B.T. GUY
Hardest sale to complete.

ME
Did the winner complete a hard sale?

B.T. GUY
We're not sure who the winner is yet.

ME
Did the nominees complete hard sales?

B.T. GUY
(laughing)
That's a matter of opinion.

A pause.

ME
Do other people have difficulty following
what you're talking about?

B.T. GUY
(laughing)
All the time.

The whole thing reminded me of the story of the famous double-talker Al Kelly, who sat down next to General Mark Clark on a train after World War II. Al Kelly said, "General, it's a tremendous honor to serve in the situation of your bravery, and our organization, the People's American Unified Forever, has asked me to approach you to be given the estovel pranken appreciation service, because in the history of America, no one indigenous battle or peacetime in the sense of your county. Would you accept it, sir?" The general paused for a moment, then nodded. At least he didn't have to speak about Al's organization.

In the car on the way to the hotel, I said, "John, I just can't follow what you're talking about. What I want you to do is get me a chair on the side of the lectern and my own microphone. Let someone else pass out the awards. I'll make comments, and we'll just see where we go." I figured my ignorance was all I had going for me, so I'd try to use that.

They took me to the presidential suite. When they opened the door to the living room, it looked like the lobby of a pretty good-sized hotel. There were about nine rooms off the living room—conference rooms, banquet rooms, etc. I mean, I was alone and this was accommodations for a dozen people. This place was so big there could have been ten people in there you might never discover. I said, "Have you just got a bedroom, somewhere I can go and lock the door?" There was an elevator that took me to one of the upstairs bedroom suites with two large bedrooms. One of them had a bed you had to climb a ladder to get to. I guess that's where whatever president slept. I climbed up there and lay on it. It put you close enough to the ceiling that you could see imperfections in the paint. Since I would be staying over after the show, I wanted to sleep up there for the fun of it, but I was concerned if I fell out of bed I could break my leg. Normally, of course, I don't think about falling out of bed, but on the other hand I don't sleep six feet off the ground. I phoned my wife and asked her what she thought. She felt, at this stage of the game, to worry about falling out of bed was a touch irra-

tional. I figured this concern about falling out of bed might have
something to do with my deciding to "wing" my whole performance there in a few hours.

When the time came to go on, I went out in front of about five
hundred or so of these international wheeler-dealers and before
taking my position beside the lectern talked to them about
money. I was certain that was one subject they'd be interested
in. I said, "I have for this event the equivalent of what in the
movies is a pay or play contract. That means if I show up, even
if the event was canceled [because of the hurricane] I'd be
paid." I said, "I formed a plan to drive south toward Florida
knowing the roads would be clear going in that direction
because of the northerly evacuation from the hurricane, and
when I got to a point where there were roadblocks going deeper
into Florida, I planned to get out of my car and go on foot
through swamps in the storm if necessary to show up to qualify
to be paid." They loved that. I think they were comforted, even
though they knew I was joking, to be in the company of someone
who would go to extremes for money the way they did. In fact, as
I've said, I've never done anything in show business for money
alone. The reason I've never done a commercial, for example,
even though I've been offered a lot of money to do them, is I
couldn't bring myself to use whatever ability I had to sell people
something they probably don't need and lie about what the prod-
uct could do for them—to boot. I don't judge anyone who does
it. In fact, maybe someday I'd even do one, if it were for a lot of
money and shown only in a foreign country where I wouldn't
ever see it. Whatever that makes me, that's what I am. Recently
I was persuaded to consider doing voice-overs, but I found when
the possibilities presented themselves, I couldn't do that either.
I, of course, didn't want to say this to these international traders,
because they'd probably stone me for saying something as anti-
capitalist as that. Instead I told them, "Frankly, I'm only here for
the money." They loved that, and it certainly was true in the
sense I wouldn't have been there as a goodwill gesture toward

Bankers Trust, but the difference was I was there to entertain, not endorse. I then told them, "I have no idea what you do," and that was the biggest laugh, because I was told they hear that all the time from family and friends. Then I took my position beside the lectern and basically needled presenters and award winners. I still couldn't tell if the awards were a joke. One Indian guy came up dressed only in a tee-shirt and slacks. I asked him why he was wearing a tee-shirt. He said, "This tee-shirt costs three hundred dollars. How much does your suit cost?" The audience loved him giving it to me. All in all what started out as a nerve-wracking engagement ended up being a good time. Oh yeah, I didn't fall out of bed.

Watch Out for Me

Professor Brown and the United Jewish Appeal

Sometimes I feel like I've gone over the line—not too far over—
but over.

Sometimes I will walk a fine line in life as well as in appearances, if I feel something really funny can come out of it.
Recently on *Heart and Souls*, the movie I'm doing now, the costume designer, a thoughtful, unusually creative man named
Jean-Pierre Dorleac, came to me and said, "Charles, you are the
consummate professional. You are always courteous, on time,
you know your lines. There are only two actors I've ever worked
with who can compare to you and they were Fred Astaire and
Henry Fonda." Well, of course it was pleasant to hear, but the
praise was so fulsome I just knew it was time for a joke, so I
looked at him for a long moment and said, "I wish I could say
the same about you." He stared at me, stunned for a moment—
then thankfully, laughed.

On another occasion there may have been a more lasting
sting. I had been scheduled to appear at a benefit for the United

Jewish Appeal at Town Hall in New York. A fellow I've known for years, Professor Richard Brown, was putting the whole thing together, and I happily agreed when he asked me to participate. Richard Brown is a brilliant interviewer. He has been conducting seminars at the New School in Manhattan for a long time, and he attracts your top talent in movies mostly for his classes of five hundred people. He also interviews screen legends like James Stewart and Katharine Hepburn on the American Movie Classics channel. He has always been effusive in his praise of me and regularly invites me and mine on these cruises where he provides the entertainment, even though I've always told him I'm not cruising anywhere, unless it's on the way to work. I have to travel so much, I'm really not inclined to go anywhere I don't have to. Richard is a supporter and a booster, and I genuinely like him. Along the way, however, there have been a couple of bumps in my relationship with him. Around 1985 when my picture *Movers and Shakers* was having its media screenings, Richard volunteered to supply me enthusiastic audiences from his classes. By the way, I have learned that the response of an audience at a screening has very little or no bearing on a critic's review. To digress a moment, even knowing this, I was nonetheless taken aback by Frank Rich's *New York Times* review of my play *Price of Fame*, in which I appeared. Unbeknownst to me at the time, he saw it on a preview night where the response of the sold-out audience was extraordinary. We never got such a reception before or after, although the audience always liked it. Frank didn't particularly care for it which, of course, is his right, but he actually noted something like, "Even fans of Charles Grodin will be hard pressed to like this one." When I realized he'd seen it with an incredibly responsive audience I was sorely tempted to write him a letter, but I figured he probably already got enough mail.

Back to Richard Brown. I was organizing screening dates and times with him so he could provide good audiences for *Movers and Shakers*. I wanted to make sure we didn't overbook, because as much as I wanted these small screening rooms to be full, I sure didn't want a lot of angry people to be turned away. That can definitely affect lobby ambiance. Anyway, it's not a one-call thing. Somewhere in getting this all worked out, Richard got on the phone with me and snapped, "Yeah! What is it?!" I completed the arrangements with him, and then didn't take his calls for a couple of years. I know that sounds harsh, but I'm not too big on snapping. Believe it or not, I've never done it to anyone (in a work situation). Loved ones, I believe, are allowed to snap every few years. The screenings arranged by Richard, by the way, were a mess—overbooked and of course a lot of angry people were turned away.

However, that screening mess doesn't take a thing away from Richard's wonderful interviewing skills, his insights and vast knowledge. He is absolutely tops in his field, and is always genuinely interested in his subjects, which is unique. To this day, I am always inclined to show up when Richard asks me.

So he called for the UJA. and I said, "Yes," in no small part, of course, because it's the United Jewish Appeal, and in case I haven't mentioned it—I'm Jewish.

I told Richard I would write something about emigrating from Pittsburgh to New York as a young man and having nothing, and now wondering if I had been eligible for aid from the UJA. I ultimately decided my idea was too trivial for the occasion. When I arrived at Town Hall for the event, I was ushered backstage where other performers were milling around. I spotted Paul Sorvino, Anne Jackson, James Earl Jones, and Danny Aiello among others—not that many Jews. A woman working for Richard Brown came over and said I would be sitting in the audience until close to the time I'd appear and then be escorted backstage. I thought a moment, then said I'd prefer just to wait in the Green Room. She said there wasn't any Green Room. I explained to her I wasn't really comfortable being in the audience at an event where I was appearing. The way I see it, if I'm appearing I want to be backstage somewhere concentrating—not watching a show. Besides, I don't believe it's helpful for relaxation to be sitting in a large audience, looking at a podium where you'll later be. This may seem like a little thing, but I believe as a performer you do whatever it takes. I've read that next to fear of death, a lot of people rate appearing in public second in the fear department. I always tell people who ask me that the way to combat that fear is to spend your time beforehand thinking only about what you want to communicate, not about yourself. This is not best done by sitting in the audience looking at the podium where you'll later be standing.

When I told the woman I'd prefer to stay backstage, she seemed slightly thrown, but let it go. It turned out a number of the other speakers agreed with me, so there we were, milling around backstage in our tuxedos waiting for the show to begin. A bunch of penguins in a holding cell. I wanted to find Richard to let him know I wouldn't be talking about emigrating from Pittsburgh in case that would affect his introduction, and also to find out when I was on. If you're on twentieth, you're obviously in a different gear prior to the show's beginning than if you're on first. No one seemed sure of when they were on. There was no list posted. I eventually found Richard, who was running around backstage intermittently greeting people, and looking as if he was trying to keep track of a dozen different things. I quickly told him my talk would be different.

He said, "Gee, I thought the immigrant idea was really funny."

I said, "It's not that funny; I have something better. When am I on?"

He looked at me oddly for a moment, then edgily said, "Don't do this to me," and moved away. I think he was referring to the question about when I was on, which for some reason seemed to throw him. I realized that he was under a lot of pressure. He had earlier told me that putting this event together was one of the most difficult things he'd ever done. I felt for him, but not enough to let go of the question of when I was on. When he raced by a few moments later, I again asked him and he quickly scanned a list and quickly said, "Sixteenth." It really wasn't a big deal and I wouldn't characterize his impatience as another snap, but it wasn't pleasant either. When you go through life determined to treat everyone in a friendly manner and someone says, "Don't do this to me," it's time for a reality check. I couldn't figure out exactly what I had done except show up in a tux when I was asked. In fact, not that it matters all that much, but I had actually gotten a movie company to play with their schedule a bit, so I could fly in from San Francisco in time to make the event.

The program itself turned out to be more about the immigrant experience than the Jewish experience even though the audience was all United Jewish Appeal contributors. As I waited my turn to go on I watched the others on a monitor. Paul Sorvino sang an Italian aria, and about ten minutes later Danny Aiello came out and ad-libbed something like, "You can't ask one Italian man to sing and not expect another one to." He then proceeded to sing the entire song, "You Made Me Love You," to his wife in the fifth row. It's actually quite a long song, or particularly seemed so under the circumstances. I mean there's absolutely no mention of Jews or even immigration in it. When my turn to go on came, there had been about five gentiles in a row talking about their grandparents' immigration experience, so I began with, "Now, back to the Jews." It got a nice laugh and I'm sure the audience settled back for some more. Instead I spoke about the resurgence of anti-Semitism and said that while I wasn't a practicing Jew—I was a devoted one. Actually the more each generation turns their venom on Jewish people the more devoted I get. The speech was received extremely well by this largely Jewish audience. Amazingly I was the only person in the program who addressed anti-Semitism.

Richard Brown threw a party afterward at the Russian Tea

Room. He was filled with praise for my speech as were the people from the UJA, who asked if I'd be willing to appear on their behalf at other functions. I said, "I happily would." There was a sit-down dinner, so I looked around and spotted David Brenner and Richard Lewis, who had also appeared earlier and sat with them. Given an opportunity, I'll always sit near the funny people. Richard Brown then got up and made a welcoming speech to everyone. He expressed his gratitude to all of us for showing up for him and his wife, Zora. He said it a couple of times and I don't recall his mentioning the UJA. Then he called upon each of us to come up and receive a commemoration of the event. When I got up there, I took the microphone and most likely did something I shouldn't have done. For those of you who can possibly remember, I started this whole Richard Brown saga by saying I sometimes get out of line.

Here's what I said. You be the judge. "First of all, let me say I'm not here for Richard, I'm here for the UJA." That got a laugh from the crowd and an embarrassed look from Richard. It gets worse. "When I got to Town Hall this evening I asked Richard, 'When do I go on?' and he said, 'Don't do this to me.'" That got a huge laugh from the crowd and a long "deer in the headlights" stare from Richard. Then feeling a little bad, I went on to say something about knowing what a difficult evening this was for Richard and what a great job he did, and I got off.

Now that may not seem like much to you. It didn't to me at the moment anyway, but later Richard came up to me and said his son, who I think is around twenty and who Richard said was my biggest fan, had said to him, "Dad, why did Charles Grodin attack you like that?" Richard went on, "My son had tears in his eyes, but I explained to him, 'That's what Chuck Grodin does. It's all in fun.'" Well, "the tears in his eyes" thing got to me. For all I know Richard made the tears thing up, but even without tears it got to me. I sure never want to make anyone's kid cry, even if it *is* all in fun—which it wasn't entirely, and I especially don't want to make the kid cry if he's my biggest fan. Now that I think of it—maybe the "tears in his eyes" and "biggest fan" thing were Richard's effort to have the last word. Well, that night he did, and I felt bad—for a little while.

There was another odd event earlier at dinner. As I said, I was sitting with David Brenner and Richard Lewis having a lot of laughs; then Richard had to go, so a woman from UJA sat down with her husband. This woman had earlier given me her card, so clearly she was solicitous of me in hopes that I would appear in the future for them. Her husband sat opposite David Brenner, and I was turned to my right talking to James Earl Jones, who is a wonderful, warm man I had worked with when we both were starting out. I barely overheard the UJA woman's husband say to David Brenner, "You would have been great as *The Heartbreak Kid.*" I turned and looked at him, and he wasn't saying this as a joke; he obviously felt David would have been great as *The Heartbreak Kid*, which, of course, is a strange thing to say when the actor who played the part is sitting right there. Add to this I don't even think David is an actor. So the guy was weird. David found the whole thing as odd as I did, and we both were also kind of amused by it—me in a dark way, for sure. Now David said to the fellow, "Don't you think I would have been great in *Midnight Run*, too?" The guy was grinning from ear to ear like he could see David as the Godfather, too. I looked over at his UJA wife, and she was smiling a bit uncomfortably, I'm sure wondering if my future appearances for them were floating away before her eyes. I wanted to make sure this strange character wasn't fooling around, and we're not getting it, so I said to him, "You think David would have been great in my role in *The Heartbreak Kid?*"

"I really do," he answered gleefully. He was really enjoying himself, and I was basically trying to figure out if he was a wacko, hostile, or both.

I tried another tack. "What do you do?" I asked, hoping he'd say something like, "I'm a shepherd," or something so I could just write his observation off as kind of an "out of it" person's take on things.

"I'm a producer," he said, with a bigger than ever grin.

Finally his wife offered up that he has kind of a strange sense of humor and often provokes people to wonder what the hell is going on. I mean, he actually made me feel like I was middle of the road in the humor department, which isn't the part I generally feel on—more like off in the field somewhere, or as Albert Brooks said in an interview, "I wasn't born on earth." The interviewer asked, "Where were you born?" Albert answered, "Nearby."

All in all it was a highly eventful evening. The woman from the UJA has called, and we'll work out some appearances. Another Jewish organization called and asked if I'd be their honorary president for the next year. David Brenner has called and Richard Lewis gave me his number and asked me to call. The only person who hasn't called is Richard Brown, but he will, and I'll be back with him again probably acting a little nicer. If you don't get better as you get older, you only get older.

Presenting Awards

I have hosted an awards dinner in New York for the past two years. The award is called the Gotham. The first time I did it most of my laughs came from my saying I was thrilled and excited to be hosting the Gotham Awards, but "what the hell were they?" This material came from my actual experience leading up to the hosting.

Earlier I had appeared at a huge dinner given at the Waldorf's grand ballroom honoring Robert De Niro. It is probably the most star-studded, sold-out, major award event in New York. They have honored Mike Nichols, Sidney Lumet, Barbara Walters, among others, and I'm telling you, if you want to go see celebrities this is the one. It is really a tribute to the people who organize the event, because I bet you the majority of the people there couldn't tell you the name of the organization or what it actually does. It's called the American Museum of the Moving Image, and among other things, it preserves old television shows and movies, and they pack them in for this. Not that old TV shows and movies shouldn't be preserved, but still . . . the biggest event in New York every year?

When I spoke the year they honored Robert De Niro, I seemed to be the first one to take a comic tack, which is always a good idea if you're following an hour of, "Probably the finest actor of his generation," "Never before," "We haven't seen anything like him since . . ." etc. I said something like:

> "Earlier this week I received the D. W.
> Griffith Award, which I proudly accepted . . .
> > *(long pause)*
> for Bob.
> > *(long pause)*
> After the event this evening I fly to Los
> Angeles where I am getting the L.A. Film
> Critics Award . . .
> > *(long pause)*
> for Bob.
> > *(long pause)*
> Then I fly to Seattle where I proudly will
> accept the Actor of the Decade Award . . .
> > *(long pause)*
> for Bob.
> > *(long pause)*
> I was hoping when I did *Midnight Run* that
> there would be a Golden Globe nomination
> as Best Comedy Actor and there was . . . for
> Bob.

The audience really loved it. Everyone was very happy—except my wife, who said, "You didn't say one nice thing about Bob." I never run this stuff by my wife beforehand, because I know she'll shoot it down. Bob knows I think he's a great actor. He doesn't need to hear me say it at the Waldorf—I think. Since we became friends when working together and remain so, I know I'm on safe ground. If you want to pay tribute, of course, serious is generally better, but if you want to entertain—a little needle, at least, is needed. Since I see myself as an entertainer and not as a serious tribute guy I'm always a little at risk.

Back to the Gotham Awards. When a representative for them contacted me about emceeing, I said I'd be happy to, because I'd always seen myself as an emcee, but until that time no one had ever asked me to emcee anything. In fact, I had never been asked to have anything at all to do with the three major entertainment show business award events—the Oscars—the Tonys—and the Emmys. I had won an Emmy as one of the writers of a Paul Simon special, so there was a shot to appear on the Emmys, but I was making a movie at the time in Acapulco. There were a lot of us who wrote on that special, so it would have been me in a crowd anyway. I have never had the presenter's introduction, "Here's the star of movies, Broadway and television—producer, director, writer, actor, best-selling author—Charles Grodin!"—something modest like that, and I come down some steps with an equally illustrious gorgeous woman—me in my tux, she in her gown—to tumultuous cheers! Never happened.

There was a time in the past when various press agents for movies or plays have tried to get me on as a presenter on the Oscars or Tonys—but no go. Even when I was starring in a play I wrote in New York, the Tony people weren't buying—so now when I'm asked by people if they should pursue a presenter thing on my behalf, I tell them, "Save your time. It won't happen." I also won't ever be nominated either, because I almost always do comedies, and it is extremely rare for actors in comedies to be nominated. My response to all of this is simple. I don't get mad. I don't feel bitter. I just don't take it seriously.

The Gothams

Once more, back to the Gothams. The second one I hosted had a lifetime achievement award for Arthur Krim, who truly did deserve it. Arthur and his partners took over United Artists from Charlie Chaplin and Mary Pickford—so he has done a few things including founding Orion Pictures, which has made some of the best American pictures in recent years. We got a lot of telegrams that night, including one that I read from Woody Allen, which said, "Finally someone is getting what they deserve, and I don't mean me."

Like my Bankers Trust experience, it was really hard to figure out what the Gothams were for. As I've said, when I was first asked to host, I said, "Sure, what are they?"

The guy from the Gothams, a tall, lean, young attorney named John Sloss said, "They're for independent filmmakers."

I said, "So, the winners are people who work outside of the studio system?"

He said, "Not really, and we don't call them winners. We call them recipients."

I said, "Oh."

We looked at each other for a long moment, and I started again. Sometimes when you have the exact same question to ask, you try to find a different way to ask it, so you don't seem too pushy. I said, "So, the Gothams . . . uh . . . are they for people who work in New York?"

He said, "Not necessarily." Then he seemed a little uncomfortable, because, of course, as the Gotham representative he should be able to say what they are. He went on, "To be honest with you, we've gone round and round on this definition thing ourselves. Maybe you'd like to join the advisory committee? We'd welcome your input."

"Geez," I said, "I'm a little on overload here, doing a movie, having a family and all; I'm up for a one-night emcee thing, but

I don't know about any advisory stuff trying to figure out what the Gothams are."

Eventually when I did host, I talked about all this and came to the conclusion that you couldn't say they were for working outside the studio system—which they weren't, or for working in New York, because a lot of the recipients worked in a lot of places besides New York—no, I concluded they were for people who *lived* in New York. So we were giving awards for people who lived in New York—like you should get an award for that distinction alone—which maybe you *should. Really,* what the Gothams were doing, as I see it, was trying to publicize and to attract independent filmmaking to New York, because the people behind the Gothams all had businesses in New York and were looking for more business from more independent filmmakers in New York.

See, it's really hard to spot what an award is really for, and that's true for all of them.

I know a guy who was given a visionary of the year award by a group of eye doctors. They had a big banquet in the grand ballroom of the Waldorf. What really happened was he gave their organization a contribution so he would be visionary of the year. Normal stuff. Awards are peculiar, especially when they give them to people because they've been sick.

Anyway, at one point, John Sloss, the Gotham representative, suggested that maybe they were celebrating the independent spirit of people who work in New York.

"But what the hell," I countered, "can we really say—our spirit is more independent than a group of filmmakers in Indiana, for example? I'd hate to have to make that case. I'd have to look the guy from Indiana in the eye and say, 'I have a more independent spirit than you do.' I don't want the job." Besides, as I told the audience, it doesn't have anything to do with how independent or not our spirit is—we live in New York and we want to work at home. *We want to stay home.* Believe me, the whole thing is pretty complicated.

As I've said, I hosted two Gothams. The first went great—it started early, and wasn't long. The second one started late and *was* long. While I personally was received really well both times—believe me, you want to start early with a program: seven-thirty at the latest and end at nine at the latest. I know that doesn't sound like much, but you could show a good movie in that amount of time. I doubt most programs—I'm talking across the country in all fields—aren't as good as a good movie, so why should they take longer?

The Outer Critics Circle Award

At another event there may have been a casualty, albeit a deserving one. It was at a recent Outer Critics Circle Award ceremony in an upstairs room of Sardi's restaurant in New York. I had been asked to be the presenter of the award for best revival of the season to *Guys and Dolls*. When I accepted I didn't realize I would be doing my presenting close to 1 A.M. The show started after the theatres had let out. As the evening wore on, recipient after recipient (a lot anyway) accepted their awards like it was the second coming. I've won one of these, and it's nice to get it, but well, with only a slight exaggeration, here is what many of the speeches sounded like to me.

THE WINNER
(barely able to speak)
This is the happiest day of my life. Finally,
years of struggle have been rewarded. There
were times when I wondered . . .

And it goes on and on and on, thanking everyone with great emotion and excitement.

There is a trap in show business and its name is narcissism. Not to take anything away from talent, hard work, and perseverance, it's just that watching one person after another be overwhelmed emotionally because they got an award gets a little sticky at best. We are an entertainment industry, and it's certainly nice to be recognized, but even the best of us won't be discovering a cure for . . . anything, and the people who do are usually too busy looking for their next cure to be caught up *that* much in awards. As I go on in show business maybe the single hardest thing to endure is the super self-involved person who really believes the most important day of his or her life is the day he or she wins some award. It's not a pretty thing to watch.

Anyway, this awards ceremony was filled with that, and worse yet, the room was *hot*! I mean, people were wet. This had been going on for a couple of hours before I got up there for my *Guys and Dolls* presentation. I felt I had a chance to kill two birds with one stone. I said something like the following, speaking very seriously with considerable emotion, "I feel . . . so privileged . . . to have the . . . opportunity . . . to be here . . . because seldom am I able . . . to have . . . a sauna before bedtime." There was dead silence after I said it, and I quickly calculated the line was too oblique, and then I received about the biggest laugh I've ever gotten in my life. It was so big, I was almost tempted to make an emotional acceptance speech about it myself.

The Los Angeles Riots

I was on a tour for my second book *How I Get Through Life*, heading for an appearance on "The Arsenio Hall Show," when my faithful companion Clay turned to me and said, "They just acquitted those four cops in the Rodney King beating." I was amazed, but just looked at Clay as he went on. "There are the beginnings of some demonstrations in downtown L.A., maybe riots—I don't know if that's what Arsenio will be talking about or what." When I got to the studio things seemed normal for backstage at Arsenio. This was the second time I'd done the show, and it's the liveliest backstage area I've ever seen. It's an up, jazzy feeling, more like what you'd expect around a disco than a talk show. It's exciting, and this night you got no sense of what was beginning to happen in downtown L.A.

By the time I got back to the hotel after the taping, bedlam had broken loose in Los Angeles. I expected Arsenio to be pre-empted since all the networks were in live riot coverage, but he came on and there I was talking about my book. By the time the next guest came on (I was already gone), it was all talk of the verdict and the riots. The next day, naturally, all my other book appearances were canceled. I was having a meeting at Universal Studios when it was decided by all to stop everything and go home. I believe I caught the last plane out of L.A. to San Francisco where I was going next. I flew over a city that had smoke rising from hundreds of fires and into San Francisco which immediately was put on curfew as L.A. had been. No one seemed to have a sense of how San Francisco would react to the verdict. Reports were that the police there were prepared for anything. We also didn't know if it made any sense to come into a city on a curfew to promote a book when the riots in Los Angeles were all that was on anyone's mind. I was asked if I wanted to cancel my appearance at a bookstore that evening. It could still go on and be completed just before the curfew time. I said if they thought people would show up, then so would I. Race relations certainly wasn't what my book was about, although I had written about it and actually had for years expressed some strong opinions which had led to some heated arguments. I was in a car being taken to a radio appearance in San Francisco. The producer of the radio show had been inclined to cancel me, but the host with whom I'd appeared before said, "Let's have him on for five minutes. He's come all the way here." We were listening to the radio guy on his show as we headed to the station, and he was ripping the rioters. While no one was applauding the riots, some people like myself seemed to have a better understanding of the rage set off by the verdict. The radio guy was saying, "Any people in the streets were hoodlums and criminals" and generally was espousing the worst kind of right wing rhetoric: "If you don't like it here, get the hell out," and he was smooth and articulate as most radio people are. This is what I was walking into. I knew he'd ask me what I thought, and I knew it could be sticky, and I hoped I could be sufficiently articulate on the subject to hold my own. He welcomed me, and asked if I'd been listening to the broadcast. I said I had and here's my memory of what followed.

RADIO GUY

Don't you agree we're dealing with a lot of hoodlums and thugs here?

ME

I really don't.

RADIO GUY
(surprised)

You don't?!

ME

No, I think we have some, but to condemn everyone who's outraged now, I think, is overstating it.

RADIO GUY
(a challenge)

You think it's O.K. to be in the streets and burn and loot and vandalize!?

ME

I don't think it's O.K. to burn and loot, but I wouldn't say everyone in the streets is a criminal.

The guy was kind of looking at me like "You idiot. I didn't even need to have you on, and now you're going to give me some liberal bullshit."

RADIO GUY

How do you see it?

ME

I think this is a racist country . . .

RADIO GUY
(startled)

A racist country!?

ME

Yeah, there's no question this is a color-conscious country, and there's no question it's a hell of a lot harder to be a black man in America than white. People who understand that are never surprised when riots break out at times like this.

We went back and forth for about forty-five minutes on this, and I actually got him to agree that maybe not every person who took to the streets was a criminal. The phone calls started to come in in support of us both. The switchboard was jammed. It's interesting that when I've debated conservatives they will never yield that a liberal is more caring. If you put a question a certain way it forces conservatives into more caring positions that I think they feel anyway. If you ask a right wing person, "Do you feel it's O.K. that we have endless thousands of people sleeping in the streets?" or "Do you think that everyone should be able to get medical attention if they're sick?"—they will always say, "Yes." Then the differences get reduced to methods rather than goals, and that's what really happened in those forty-five minutes. I got him to soften his rhetoric, and we got some light instead of just heat. I believe in the future it would be helpful if partisanship became a bad word.

The only call that came through that took passionate exception to what I was saying was on my position on capital punishment. I'm sure you won't be shocked to hear I'm against it. At the time there was an execution happening in that area of a man named Robert Alton Harris, who had murdered some teenagers and eaten their cheeseburgers. Nobody could understand how I could be against executing this guy, and also none of these people had ever heard that when this murderer was a little boy, his dad, a deranged Vietnam war veteran, sent the kids out into the nearby woods and tried to hunt them down and shoot them—for fun. I'm talking real bullets here. In any case, later I showed up for the book signing that night where I again spoke for about a half-hour about race. My main point was that after all these years there still was a separation of the races in every way. I looked around and said, "I don't see any black faces here." Then a black man I hadn't seen raised his hand. I nodded and said, "There's one," and then another black man walked in and I said, "There's another black man." I had earlier been trying to make the point about this being a color-conscious country by saying *I* was aware of a person's color. It didn't matter that I thought everyone was equal and all that *really* connotes—I was aware of a person's color. It was virtually impossible to be born and raised in this country when I was and not be. Two interesting things happened at the book signing afterward. A black man I'd not seen appeared who had bought five books for me to sign. He said he'd never heard of me until he was listening to the radio in the afternoon. He said he'd never heard a white man express a black man's point of view that way and he appreciated it. The other thing that happened was the black man who'd come in while I was speaking wanted to know why I'd said, "There's a black man," when he had walked in. Not having heard the context, he was offended as was his white wife, who was standing next to him actually trembling with hurt. They had come, because they were fans of mine, and inexplicably I had attacked them, they felt, as soon as they entered. I tried to explain I wasn't attacking them. I was just making a point of color consciousness and what black people were up against. They said they felt they had to deal with this all the time, and to deal with it from me was a shock and hurtful. I tried to explain again I was only stating what they already knew. We went around in circles for a while, and they were somewhat pacified, not really because they got what I was saying, but only because they knew they weren't looking into the face of a bigot.

A Trip to Washington

I once visited the home of Donald Kendall, who was the chairman of the board of Pepsico and a leading Republican. He had actually been offered a cabinet position by President Nixon, who had visited his home shortly before I did. In fact, at one point Mr. Kendall pointed out to me that President Nixon had sat in the very chair I was sitting on. Years earlier when I visited Jason Robards, he pointed out that George C. Scott had recently sat in the chair I was sitting on. Since I don't value myself higher or lower than any other human, including President Nixon and George C. Scott, I never know quite what to say at those moments. I tried to look at the chair, kind of impressed to be polite, but not so impressed that I felt like a liar. Pressed to the wall I would probably admit I know stuff about President Nixon and George C. Scott for that matter that would make me respect myself more—pressed to the wall—but I wasn't about to say to Donald Kendall or Jason Robards, "Next time they're over, tell them Charles Grodin sat there."

Anyway, I was at Donald Kendall's for the christening of Jessica Lange and Mikhail Baryshnikov's daughter, Alexandra. Jessica was a friend of mine from working on *King Kong* and Misha had become a friend as well. Once I stayed up late drinking vodka with him. When I phoned the next morning, I said to him, "I don't know about you, but I'm not dancing today." When I took over the "Tomorrow" show I wanted to do a bit about running a ballet contest from just picking out three men in the street and have them come on, leap across the studio, and be judged by the audience. The third would be Baryshnikov, who could leap so high the camera would have to point at the ceiling. He agreed to do it, too, then at the last minute thought it might not go over that well with the board of directors of his ballet company. Today I bet he'd do it in a minute. He loves a laugh and can still leap out of sight. Anyway, I met Donald Kendall because I was there for Jess and Misha's baby's christening. Mr. Kendall and I became pals so quickly that when he stood up to make a toast to Jess and Misha and the baby, he made one to me first. It was a little awkward. Within a week I was flying alone with him on his private plane to Washington, D.C., to meet some people coming in with the Reagan administration. This was 1980. He really didn't even know me as an actor, and he was startled when some acquaintance of his he introduced me to went nuts when he met me. I was a little startled, too. Anyway, Don Kendall was the president of the U.S. Chamber of Commerce. I'm not sure what they did, but I don't think any Democrats belonged. I met a lot of people that day who told me all about "trickle down" economics and how they had to get the government out of the way of everything. I raised a lot of layman's questions about all this getting the government out of the way stuff that later led to things like the S & L scandal, increased pollution—things like that. Privately some of the people there confided to me that these were the kinds of questions nobody raised in their circles and it was good to hear them—meaning they had doubts themselves. I was feeling pretty good about the whole thing. I surprised myself with my political knowledge. I was being urged to come back. Jack Kemp told me he was aware of what I was doing and to keep up the good work. I had no idea what he meant, but said I'd try. Just when I was secretly considering announcing my own candidacy for . . . something, someone asked me, "What's it like to work with Miss Piggy?"

That night before I left, someone from the White House staff took me on a tour of the White House. We were out in the garden around midnight actually standing under President Reagan's bedroom window. This was the night before he was going to sign a major tax cut that many, myself included, felt would really be bad news for our growing deficit. I wanted to throw a pebble at the window, and whisper up, "Don't sign that. It's not good for the future." Actually, I believe that tax cut ended up being the reason George Bush had to break his "Read my lips" pledge and raise taxes later. If a Secret Service man hadn't suddenly appeared, shooing us away from the President's window, I could have thrown the pebble, awakened President Reagan, given him my advice, and years later George Bush might have been reelected. How history turns on such small things.

Night of a Hundred Stars

Several years ago during the first "Night of a Hundred Stars" special, the Academy Award–winning actress Celeste Holm approached me backstage and asked me to sign a petition to stop a group from tearing down some Broadway theatres. I asked, innocently enough I thought, "Why do they want to tear them down?" She instantly stiffened and said, "What difference does it make why?!" I said, "I never like to sign anything unless I understand the issue." She snorted or something and bounded away. I spotted Gregory Peck sitting in a corner, went over, and told him what had just happened. Before he had a chance to respond, Miss Holm was on him with the petition, which he signed without question—obviously responding to my story at the same time. I'm sure to Miss Holm and Mr. Peck it was like asking a Jew or a gentile to sign a petition to stop "them" from tearing down a synagogue or church. What difference did it make what the reason was? I'm sure the answer to my question wasn't going to be "They're going to put up shelters for the homeless, and also build more theatres in there than they were tearing down, which the homeless could act in." In principle, I just had to make *sure* that wasn't the answer. Besides, in the last twenty years, I haven't felt the theatres on Broadway have particularly housed abundant treasures. Between the costs and the critics it's often a big British hit or a hundred people roller-skating over your head while you sit there and hope they don't fall on you.

The first "Night of a Hundred Stars," which was the only one I participated in, was an extraordinary day. Whenever you saw someone who resembled a celebrity, it was in fact that person. There were actually close to three hundred stars there. James Cagney was present, wheelchair-bound. He was lowered to the basement on some kind of elevator platform and in error he was left there unattended. Oddly, the only other time I ever saw James Cagney in life was when an elevator door momentarily closed on his wife. Orson Welles was also there in a wheelchair. He was so startlingly heavy, his body totally concealed the chair. The most tragic event was the participation of Lee Strasberg, then in his eighties with a heart condition, in the big finale where he high-kicked arm in arm with countless others. He died of a heart attack within the next couple of days. Lee, ironically, started as a chorus boy.

There were several large dressing rooms designated by categories: male star dressing room, female star dressing room, among several others. I chose to hang around in the female star dressing room with, among others, Liv Ullmann, Carol Channing, Diahann Carroll, Mary Martin and Mickey Rooney. Princess Grace was part of the evening, and at one point I appeared in the doorway and said in a loud voice, "Ladies, excuse me, Princess Grace is now going to come in and change. Would you all mind stepping out into the hall for a few minutes?" The looks on all these ladies' faces were priceless, until they realized I was joking. Sometimes I feel someone ought to put me under citizen's arrest.

The most mischievous fun I had involved Carol Channing and Ethel Merman. I was standing backstage when Carol approached me. It went something like this.

CAROL

Hi, Charles.

ME

Hi.
                    (I see she's down about something)
Are you O.K.?

CAROL

Well . . . I've lost one of my contact lenses
in some lamb gravy.

A pause.

ME

Where did this happen?

CAROL

Upstairs in the rehearsal hall. I was having
some lamb, and it fell in.

ME

Are you sure?

CAROL

I think so . . . but I couldn't find it.

ME

Is the dish still there?

CAROL

Yes.

I'm aware through all of this that Ethel Merman is standing
several feet away, watching us intently.

ME

Why don't I get one of the production assistants to go with you to look for it.

CAROL

That would be wonderful!

ME

(calling over a male assistant)
Excuse me. Could you help Miss Channing
with something here? She believes she
dropped a contact lens into some of her
lamb gravy upstairs. Could you go with her
to help find it?

A pause.

PRODUCTION ASSISTANT

Sure.

CAROL

Thank you, Charles!

She goes off with the assistant. Ethel Merman comes over to
me.

MERMAN
(annoyed)
What was all that about?

ME
(as though it was the most ordinary thing in the world)
Carol lost a contact lens in some lamb gravy.

MERMAN
(annoyed)
What?!

ME

Carol lost a contact lens in some lamb gravy, and an assistant went with her to help her find it.

MERMAN

(rolling her eyes)

She *always* does that!

ME

What's that?

MERMAN

She always comes up with something.

Merman drifts away. After about five minutes, Carol comes over to me.

CAROL

(excited)

We found it!

ME

Great!

CAROL

It was there in the gravy.

ME

Good!

CAROL

Thank you, Charles!

I smile at her as she moves away. Merman comes back over to me.

MERMAN

What happened?!

ME

She found it.

MERMAN
(sarcastically)

Good!

She walks off. Carol comes back to me.

CAROL

Was Ethel saying something about me?

ME

She wanted to know what happened.

A pause.

CAROL
(calling over to Ethel)

I found it!

MERMAN
(dryly)

Great!

The two women eye each other edgily—then go their separate ways.

Personally I found them delightful, but they had both played the title role in *Hello, Dolly!* and these tensions are inevitable in such cases.

Goofing
with My Pals

Recently I participated in a two-hour television special celebrating Phil Donahue's twenty-fifth anniversary on the air. The producer, Jack Haley, Jr., called and asked what I would like to do. I thought awhile and said, "I would like to appear as Phil's friend and just talk about what he's like to hang out with, and I'd like to be wearing a dress." For those of you not familiar with it, Phil caused quite a stir a few years ago when he did his whole show wearing a dress. He wanted the audience to examine what feelings a cross-dresser brought out in them. The show, doubtless, was on that subject, but all anyone remembers was Phil in a dress. My idea was to sit there in a nice dress and talk about what it was like to hang out with Phil. We shot it. I was sitting there in a dress on a sofa and I said, "Nothing unusual, really. We're both sports fans. So we watch the Mets or the football Giants. Sometimes we throw a football around. No big deal." It was really funny, but it never made the show. I never asked why, since it wasn't my decision to make.

I had great fun at my friend Julian Schlosberg's fiftieth birth-day party. Julian is a film distributor. His company is called Castle Hill and he distributes among others a lot of art films. He also has his own radio show in New York where he interviews people in show business. At the time of the party he didn't have a show, but had had one in the past.

Once again I was amazed at what people will take seriously if delivered in a straight way. I got up—stood behind Julian, who was seated, put my hands on his shoulders, and said something like the following *totally made up stuff* about my, at the time, slightly overweight friend.

"I first met Julian in an acting class several years ago. Julian was quite frankly never much of an actor, but he was brilliant in ballet class. He was idiosyncratic in the sense that he always refused to wear anything under his tights. One night during a recital for a group of about one hundred people, Julian did a plié with his back to the audience and his tights split. There was no consoling him. He dropped out of sight after that, and emerged years later with his own radio show on WMCA in New York. He was so well liked that the owners, the Strauss family, couldn't bear to tell him his show was canceled after a month because of poor ratings. They chose to let him come to the studio and broadcast his interviews, even though they weren't actually going out on the air. Soon, word of this got out and Julian's guest list dwindled. He once again dropped out of sight for years only to later emerge having acquired distribution rights to several movies. Since I know movie studios control all rights to their films, I was curious to learn just what Julian was able to acquire. He has exclusive rights to all Ingmar Bergman's films for death row inmates as well as the rights to *Fiddler on the Roof* in Iraq."

Although most people there laughed throughout this, there were people later who were saying, "I didn't know Julian studied ballet."

116

THEATRE

Keeping Promises

The Roundabout Theatre in New York is run by a man named Todd Haimes, who, in the course of working with him, became a good friend of mine. I had written two plays, and I had an agreement with Todd that his theatre would produce them both. The first was *Price of Fame*, in which I appeared. It got mixed reviews—most significantly, as I mentioned, the *New York Times* didn't like it, but its three-month run sold out. The audiences really enjoyed the play. In fact, the people who sold subscriptions told me *Price of Fame* was the play the subscribers said they enjoyed the most that season, to date. What particularly interested me about all this is once the *Times* weighed in against *Price of Fame*, the subscribers who rated it the most enjoyable during its long preview run now found it "O.K." Worse, this put my friend Todd Haimes in an awkward position. As I've said, our agreement called for him to do my other play, which was actually written years earlier. That meant that the Roundabout, which is essentially a classic revival house which virtually never does new plays, was going to do two in consecutive years and both by me. Also, in the interim, the Roundabout had moved to Broadway and Todd was getting advice not to do *One of the All Time Greats*, my second play, after the *Times* didn't like the first one. "The *Times* will kill it" was just one reason. First Todd asked if we could delay a season, so we wouldn't be doing two by me in consecutive years. In spite of *Price of Fame* being a sellout, the perception was that it was a failure, simply because the *Times* didn't like it. The *Times*, of course, isn't even the *Times*, it's one critic who happened to review it. Actually other people from the *Times* had been down to see it and were enthusiastic, but all that matters is what that critic who reviewed it said. You can even get raves from other places, which we did, *and* be a sellout, and it's still considered a failure if the *Times* doesn't like it. In fairness, 60 percent of the audience at the Roundabout is pre-sold subscription, but believe me, if an audience doesn't like the show, you won't sell 10 percent more, let alone 40 percent. There's a problem here. The sensibility of most critics in the theatre and, as I've said, movies as well is much more elitist than the audience. A play about middle-class values and problems is often looked down on by the critical community. Because of this, many authors were no longer writing for the theatre—Paddy Chayevsky, for example, had stopped long before his death. Others like William Inge would never survive today's climate. My friend Herb Gardner weathered powerful critical abuse from the *Times* with his play *I'm Not Rappaport*, which ran for three years and won the Tony for best play, only because he started in a theatre where if eighty people came they could stay open.

Todd Haimes had a dilemma. He had an agreement with me to do *One of the All Time Greats* and, for a number of reasons, he saw it as not in his interest to do it.

A couple of years earlier I'd had a bizarre experience with the play involving the legendary Joe Papp, who ran the Public Theatre, which gave us *A Chorus Line* and free Shakespeare in the Park. I had sent the play to Joe. He liked it, called me in, asked if we could read it aloud in his office for his wife Gail, and his casting director Rosemarie Tichler. I read the lead and Joe played my wife. Everyone really liked it and Joe said, "Let's do it." I, of course, was thrilled. Then Joe said, "First let's do a full reading of the play to see what we can learn."

I said, "Fine, but for me to get ten actors and direct them is no small job. We *are* going to do it, right?"

"Absolutely," he said.

I got the actors, rehearsed them and put on a reading for about a hundred people. It went sensationally. Joe sat front row center, leading the laughter. Afterward he said, "Come to my office tomorrow and we'll get into it." Naturally I thought that meant set dates, etc. It didn't. After much going around in circles it became clear to me that Joe didn't want to do the play. From what I surmised, and I had to surmise because Joe never came out and said it, he felt if he did a play that was such a clear piece of entertainment it would be as though he was bowing to critical pressure. Recently he had been ripped for putting on two plays—one an adaptation of Genesis and the other a play with a lot of going back and forth in time that people had great difficulty in following. Joe felt that my play was more like a Broadway comedy. For him to do it he felt would be like selling out. In other words, if the reading hadn't gone so well there probably would have been a much better chance he would have done it. Since Joe had a penchant for doing plays by foreign writers out of political favor in their countries, one friend of mine cracked, "If *One of the All Time Greats* had been smuggled out of a jail cell in Venezuela, it would have been on in a minute."

Anyway, the word of mouth on the reading reached Todd Haimes, and he asked to read it and that's how we got to meet in the first place. Now two close friends had an issue. It was clear to me Todd didn't want to do it, so I said, "I understand. Don't worry about it." The problem came a day later when I realized that in my effort to be gracious to my friend I was once again nowhere with my play. This had been the case for twenty years, since an early version starring Alan Arkin had been done in a summer theatre to a wonderful reception.

I had offers from three different producers to take that production to Broadway, but I felt there was a big difference between a smash in summer stock and Broadway. I felt the play needed more to it, and in the interim twenty years I had added a second act which was better than the first. The play had almost come to production several times—once with the Theatre Guild, which didn't go forward when Terrence McNally's play, *It's Only a Play*, opened with a similar second act. So I had been up and down and around with this play that Helen Hayes had called "the best play about theatre I've ever seen." Forgive me for saying that, but I want to be clear we're talking about something really good that Todd is being advised not to do.

A couple of days went by and I realized it would be necessary to meet Todd face to face on this. I closed the door to his office as Todd looked up at me quizzically. We had become really good friends in a short period of time. I said, "Todd, I know you don't want to do *One of the All Time Greats*, but we have an agreement; and I need to hold you to it. I know in the short run, you don't see this as in your interest, but in the long run I feel it will be. I will never be your adversary if you don't do the play, and I honestly will wish you well, but we won't be friends, and I think that's more important to hold on to than anything."

Todd barely paused, then said, "O.K., I'll do it. I don't have that many good friends, and your friendship means a lot to me."

I was really moved by Todd's quickness of response. He had opted for friendship ahead of professional interest, which you don't run into a lot in show business, or I'd bet in any business.

One of the All Time Greats

A few days later Todd called and asked how I would feel if he could arrange for the show to be done in New York at a smaller venue. I said the venue didn't matter to me at all, I just wanted a production. About two weeks later Todd called and said he had given the script to some people who ran an off-Broadway theatre called the Vineyard and they loved it. It was one hundred and twenty seats and off-Broadway instead of five hundred and on, but I didn't care. *One of the All Time Greats* is about life behind the scenes in the theatre, and I actually preferred the smaller venue. It was booked for a limited run, which is the way these theatres do it, and I had Renée Taylor from the original cast of twenty years ago doing her role again. I got the actor Tony Roberts to make his directorial debut. He did a wonderful job and, miracle of miracles, we actually got an outstanding review from the *Times*, which according to the perception in the theatre, made it a hit. On opening night someone went out and got me a copy of the *Times*, which I read in the backseat of a car. There wasn't one critical comment in it, and this was a play that took twenty years to get produced in New York. Doug Aibel, our talented producer, stood up at the opening night party, thanked everyone for all their hard work—then announced, "And it's really something to be able to cap this experience with a great notice from the *Times*." I was watching Tony Roberts as he said this, and his mouth actually dropped open. I mean, no one—not even *Guys and Dolls*—gets totally unqualified praise from the *Times*, but we did. I asked Renée Taylor to read the review aloud. She said, "The whole thing?" figuring there had to be a couple of digs in there, and I had the great pleasure of saying, "Yeah, the whole thing." There was talk of moving it to a larger off-Broadway theatre when the run at the Vineyard ended, but Broadway for the first time in years was booming and off-Broadway was hurting, so I didn't press it. Besides, I had achieved what I wanted—a New York production for my play that was received with great enthusiasm. Being a bit in the vindication business, it was all I wanted.

There are so many "no's" and setbacks in show business that if I get any kind of "yes" I'm generally inclined to take my emotional winnings and go home. It's undoubtedly why I produce so much work and am active as a writer, actor, and producer. This way when things fall apart as they always do, I've got several other things going on so the negative feeling is diminished. It's called surviving in what has to be one of the cruelest professions.

One added note. The reviews for *Price of Fame* and *One of the All Time Greats* were similar—some raves, some good, some mixed, some bad, in about the same measure for both plays. But as I've said, because the *Times* liked one and not the other, one was perceived as a hit and the other not. Two different *Times* critics reviewed each of the plays. If you reversed which critic saw which play you might have had two hits or two pans. It's all very whimsical and, frankly, ridiculous.

The Audience Survey

The certainty with which critics express themselves—as though they alone possess the objective truth, can be tough to combat because people tend to believe what they read or hear. I learned a long time ago that my opinion of someone's work is only my opinion, and doesn't mean any more than that's what I felt. Criticism, of course, is extremely subjective and often tells you more about the person giving the critique than the work itself. I have a friend who's afraid to tell other friends he loves something, because we're all aware that virtually nothing he loves is successful.

Ironically, I think the people who have the biggest difficulty predicting what an audience will enjoy are professional critics. They are the most removed from the general audience's experience. Critics who see hundreds of plays or movies a year have seen too much. By definition they are in far too sophisticated a place to grasp popular taste. Not that that's their job, but it would be helpful if a slight reference to whether an audience might enjoy something occasionally slipped into a review. I believe the problem here is even more serious than a lot of my colleagues do and the real danger lies in the theatre. While reviews are important to most movies, they are crucial to plays simply because, in general, movies have massive advertising budgets and plays don't.

For a couple of years now I've been trying to get a plan off the ground for the New York theatre, which has been in trouble for years. Most of our best writers won't write for the theatre, because it's so critic-dominated. At this writing there is *one* straight play running on Broadway. My plan is to have an audience survey which is conducted by a reputable polling organization at one of the previews of a show before it opens, so the audience polled would be seeing the same performance as the critics who now come during previews. This is based on my observation, supported by many people, that an audience, with rare exception, enjoys a show more than a critic. Ironically, oftentimes when a critic chooses to champion a play, it is one he or she has much more interest in than the audience. Again because of the amount of things a critic sees, there must be an inevitable difference in taste. It doesn't mean audiences are nice and critics are mean, it's just occupational in the same way people least sensitive to illness usually are doctors. They've seen too much to reflect the widespread sensibility.

It is not unusual at all that a play can be previewing to enthusiastic audience response, then be reviewed in a mixed or negative way and close. This has been going on for years, and I believe it's one of the major reasons, along with rising costs, that the New York theatre, particularly with regard to new American plays, is in dire straits. For as long as I remember the people putting on plays have been tyrannized by the power of the *New York Times*, which is usually among the most sophisticated of our critics. I believe a reputable audience survey published in the *New York Times* the same day the review appears could help neutralize this power. The only thing I can imagine that would have any impact on the power of the *Times* reviewer is an established survey reflecting the opinion of several hundred people. I have met with the *Times* people and they've agreed to publish it, even if it contradicted their review. We are now living in a time of rising awareness of public opinion, and the theatre would benefit from this. I was in a restaurant in the middle of the theatre district about a year ago, and one of the waiters told me that the *New York Times* critic came in for dinner prior to seeing a show, looked around, saw the restaurant almost empty and asked, "Where is everyone?" He honestly didn't seem to be aware of what elitist criticism, among other things, had done to the theatre. More than ever Broadway theatres are unoccupied as the artists who could fill them flee to movies and television.

Of course, any play opening on Broadway has inevitably appeared successfully elsewhere, and audiences have liked it. Otherwise it would never have gotten to Broadway. This is another good reason to have a vehicle to express an audience's point of view.

I have had several meetings over the last couple of years championing this audience survey idea, and while there has been much support from various guilds and even theatre owners, I'd have to say at this writing my efforts have led nowhere. Here are some of the objections: "You'll be reducing the theatre to the lowest common denominator's taste!" When I asked who that was, the answer was, "The audience." Others doubted you could get a fair survey, because often at previews some people have gotten free tickets. I argued that I get invited to free screenings all the time, and it has no effect on my opinion. It's not as though someone would say, "I didn't pay, so I really like this." In fact, I believe people who pay are *more* determined to like something. Most of the objections oddly enough didn't come from actors or writers or directors, but from producers. One producer said, "Why should I pay for a survey that might be negative?" I argued that if the audience didn't like it, it's unlikely the critics would anyway, and if the critics did and the audience didn't, it might run but not for long. Even when I proposed no cost to the producer and that it would be his option to publish the result, the idea wasn't wholeheartedly embraced. People were afraid of negative word getting out, even though that's what happens anyway without a survey. I then began to contact potential corporate sponsors, at this writing without success, even though if it has the impact I believe is possible, the corporation would be seen as a white knight (as much as corporations could be seen that way). I've tried to engage other theatre artists to join me, but no one working in the theatre wants to be perceived as in opposition to the critics. I have worked in the New York theatre as a playwright, actor, director and producer. I can be hurt four ways by critics, and probably will be just by writing this, but I don't see this as anticritic, rather pro-theatre. I know many of the New York critics, and I've found them to be, with the exception of John Simon, reasonable, sincere, nice people. The vitriol of John Simon's reviews removes him from any civilized group of people. Ironically even the newspapers for whom these critics work are hurt by all this, as theatre ad revenue has plummeted.

People who argue against my point of view will point to the grosses on Broadway being as high or higher than in the past, but they are largely coming from musicals imported from London. The theatre should to some degree reflect the American experience, which overwhelmingly it doesn't.

I'm hoping for a day when the potential run of a piece of work is determined by how much the audience likes it. That is not the case at this time, certainly with straight plays, so I will continue my efforts.

Richard Watts, Jr.

Perhaps if more critics had the sensibility of the late Richard Watts, Jr., the audience survey wouldn't be needed. I knew Richard when he was the theatre critic for the *New York Post*. By the time I met him, he was in his seventies. Earlier he was a film critic for the *New York Herald Tribune*, and before that a foreign correspondent. He was a worldly, sophisticated man, and yet he retained his humility as a man and a critic. Dick expressed himself with a strong awareness that this was only his opinion, and he could be wrong. A lot of reviewers might argue that's implicit, but the arrogance in the language of many critics removes any implication of anything. I always felt that Dick approached anything involving me as a friend, but I didn't feel I was getting preferred treatment because that's how he approached everyone's work. His reviews of shows he didn't care for were always peppered with phrases like, "I'm sorry to say," "It's sad to report." Toward the end of his career he would actually acknowledge that his problems with a piece of work could be due to his hearing loss. Once he gave a mixed review of a show I produced, and a protégé of his, Jay Carr, gave it an outstanding review for a Detroit paper. I read Jay's review to Dick, and he exclaimed excitedly in his Mr. Magoo voice, "Why, that's a rave!"

He and I and our mutual friend the producer Alan Delynn, with a changing group of others, would get together most Friday nights for a drink at Twenty-One and then go out on the town for dinner. One night the writer Allan Oppenheimer walked by. Allan at the time was a man in his eighties who as a younger man had written for the Marx Brothers. Dick called out, "Allan, tell that story about you and Groucho." Allan said, "Oh, Dick, you've heard that so many times." Dick responded, "Yes, but tell it for my friend Chuck."

At the opening night of *Same Time Next Year*, Dick stood in the aisle, looked me in the eye, and applauded during the curtain call. I later said, "Dick, you can't do that," but he didn't care that he'd broken an unspoken critic's rule. My most cherished moment with him came at a lunch we had some six months after we met. He looked at me and said, "Chuck, you're one of my three closest friends in all the world." This was astonishing because Dick knew thousands of people. I said, "Dick, you don't know me that long." He said, "It doesn't matter. I can tell." I think of him a surprising amount of time.

Going Backstage

There are moments when it's difficult to be sensitive without feeling like a liar. Once on an opening night I saw something I was completely bored by. It was directed by a friend of mine—a man. I didn't want to go backstage, but my friends reminded me the director knew I was there. I never lie—but *never*—I can't—it makes me feel like . . . a liar. I had no idea what I was going to say when I saw him. You can't say what you *really* feel. That would be cruel. If you try to hedge it some way, you'll feel bad, and the director will know what you're doing since *he's* gone backstage many times and done it. All this was going through my mind when I spotted the guy. He gave me a big expectant grin. I immediately said, "I loved it!" hugged him, went to give him a kiss on the cheek and accidentally planted a big smacker on his lips. Oddly enough I was surprised to find I didn't feel bad I had lied. He was happy I loved it, and I was happy I didn't feel bad the way I would have if I'd told the truth. That would have caused some trouble—depression—resentment all around.

It's the only lie in life I'm O.K. with. The problem is if you engage me past that first expression, the truth of my feelings will come out—gently, but it will come out. It's a very delicate issue. Most show business people are smart enough not to press you after they hear, "I loved it."

I once went with my wife and Marlo Thomas to see Lena Horne in concert. At intermission someone representing the producers came to us and said, "Miss Horne would be happy to see you backstage afterward." None of us knew Lena Horne, and although she did a great show, it's unlikely we would have gone backstage, because generally speaking I wouldn't go backstage to see anyone unless I knew him. My wife's not in show business so she's not racing back, and I doubt Marlo intended to either for the same reason as me. However, now we were summoned. I didn't know if Miss Horne was aware of this, but in case she had been told we were there, we had to go back. She's a wonderful performer, obviously, so it wasn't as awkward as if we didn't like the show. After a considerable wait that was brought to an end only by my telling someone we had a dinner reservation, we were ushered to Miss Horne, who greeted us standing in the half-opened doorway of her dressing room while we stood in the hall.

Marlo, who is capable of as much genuine enthusiasm as anyone I know, launched right in. "You were wonderful! What an evening! Everyone knows you're a spectacular singer, but what a wonderful comedienne you are!" This went on and on, and Marlo meant it all, too, but how long can one person go on? Through all this Lena Horne didn't seem in any hurry to bring any closure, as she only nodded and smiled. Finally running out of words, Marlo turned to me and said (she was reaching now), "And this man was *sobbing*!"

I had earlier told Marlo I found one of the numbers particularly moving. Now Lena Horne looked to me to pick up where Marlo had left off, but I said, "Well, I was a little upset by something that happened earlier in the evening." I really had liked the show, but after a certain amount of praise for anyone (especially myself), I always feel the need for a joke. Miss Horne looked startled and said, "That's right, kick an old broad when she's down."

She sure didn't look old, and certainly anything but down, and I believe she knew I was kidding, but I'm sure she could have used more of Marlo and less of me. Anyway, she *was* wonderful, and I had to remind myself that backstage after a performance is not the time for that kind of a joke.

Walter Matthau once came backstage with Jack Lemmon after seeing me in a play, and after Jack carried on generously for a few minutes, Matthau said to me, "You're *too* good." I still don't know what that meant. At least he didn't say the equivalent of what I said to Lena Horne, "I laughed like hell but I was thinking of something funny that happened earlier in the evening."

Working
in the Theatre

My personal interest in the theatre, as regards my own work, is now only as a playwright. I've already written here why I've lost interest in directing. I've produced only out of necessity: when others abandoned a project of a friend, or when someone whose work I admired couldn't get anyone else to produce his play. It's never been anything I really wanted to do, although it's certainly a challenge. As a producer it's hard, in good conscience, to ask anyone to invest in a theatrical project since usually everyone loses all their money. As an actor I played a limited run in my play *Price of Fame* in 1990, but my interest in being in a long run came to an end when I did *Same Time Next Year* in 1975. I found around the fourth month, in spite of the play being standing room only, I was ready to move on. It was simply doing the same thing every night for eight months that got to me. The producers couldn't believe that I'd leave when my contract was up. I was making a lot of money, and they couldn't imagine anyone giving that up for nothing, which is what I was going to do, but I did, provoking their resentment as my co-star, Ellen Burstyn, chose to leave with me. We had to throw our own closing night party even though the producers ultimately made millions from the play running for three years using the reviews Ellen and I got, which, of course, is common. If that sounds like I'm bitter, I'm not—not even a little. When stuff like that happens, a little light flashes on for me that says, "Future anecdote." I find it a great way to deal with life's small bumps. I'm actually quite fond of the *Same Time Next Year* producer, Morton Gottlieb. He's devoted his life to the theatre in various capacities—first, I believe, in public relations. He tried to persuade me to stay by telling me how Eva Le Gallienne stayed with a play for years touring around the country. Well, I never met Eva Le Gallienne, she wasn't a friend of mine, and I'm no Eva Le Gallienne.

PERSONALITIES

Art Carney

It felt like wonderful good fortune to meet up with Art Carney. When we did *Sunburn* together in Acapulco, from day one I hung out with him. We used to go to this fancy French restaurant in the breathtaking Princess Hotel where Howard Hughes lived at one time. Art has a lot of Ed Norton in him, so if you can imagine going to a fancy French restaurant with Ed Norton you get some idea of why it was such fun. Just listening to Art read the menu aloud was enough for me. If it's not obvious by now, I always try to find some laughs, especially if I'm filming in some grim location like a Mexican waterfront at night. We had a scene in this picture where Art and I are supposed to swing on ropes, crash through a glass window and land on the bad guys. The way you do this is you hold the rope—take a step or two—then they cut to a wide shot of our stunt doubles swinging through the air and crashing through the windows. We had done our part, and they were filming the stunt men. It was about 1 A.M. and Art went back to his trailer to take a nap, as we'd have more shots with us in a few hours. Around 4 A.M. it became clear the stunt was going to take longer than expected and Art and I were free to go home. I got ahold of one of the assistants, and asked him to help me play a joke on Art. The assistant knocked on the door of Art's motor home (I was standing behind him just out of sight). Art groggily woke up and the assistant told him that because they could see it was a double on the stunt, they would need Art himself just once to swing on the rope the hundred feet and crash through the window. The look on Art's face as he processed all this was priceless—I quickly let him see me, before real upset set in, so he'd know for sure it was a joke.

This movie, *Sunburn*, was a nice movie for its genre but very hard to follow. It fell to Art's character in one scene to explain to me and Farrah Fawcett, and therefore the audience, what the hell was going on. The speech was something like, "In 1942 the Nazis sent a U-boat off the coast here and put Heinrich Mueller ashore to meet up with Von Helsling and the others to work out a counter plan to the Allies X482. Deitrich got word of this and called the Kreinmans in to send an LV680 to counteract . . ." and it went on and on. It was a son of a gun to memorize, and the day we were shooting it I could see Art pacing back and forth muttering the lines to himself. "In 1942 the Nazis sent a U-boat off the coast . . ." etc., etc., etc., etc. At some point a little later I learned we weren't doing that scene that day, but no one had told Art, who was still pacing and memorizing. I walked over to him and said, "You got it down yet?" He wiped his brow and said, "Barely." Of course when I told him we weren't do-ing it—he thought it was another joke. It would be a few more days before he could let the Nazis, the U-boat, Heinrich Mueller and X482 out of his mind. A couple of weeks later on the last day of shooting, the elderly Mexican makeup lady stopped in my motor home to say good-bye. I asked her to help me with one last gag on Art. I told her when she said good-bye to Art, to say to him, "Y'know, Art, in 1942 the Nazis sent a U-boat off the coast . . . " Af-ter a few minutes there was a rapping at my door. I opened it to find Art lying on the steps, sobbing with laughter.

Jackie Mason

I was once sitting in the lounge of MGM Grand Airlines when I spotted Jackie Mason. To me running into a favorite comedian is like for some people seeing a beautiful woman. I don't mean I can't appreciate a beautiful woman, but a comic, well . . . Being in show business as long as I have, you wouldn't think it would be so unusual for me to run into a comic, but it is. In the movies I usually work with actors playing comedy, not necessarily funny people, although Art Carney and Marty Short were certainly notable exceptions. Anyway, spotting Jackie Mason was special. I planned my approach like a guy trying to interest a woman at a party. First, prior to boarding, I walked by him in the lounge, letting him get a good look to see if he'd recognize me. After a moment, he did. He looked up from his paper, stared at me and said, with a slight smile but not much enthusiasm, "Oh, the actor." I shook hands with him, and decided I'd make my move on the plane.

Once we'd boarded, I saw he was seated forward of me, actually in another compartment, but we were in supreme grand first class or whatever they call it. There was free passage, unlike coach to first class, where if you try to cross the border a stewardess puts something like a citizen's arrest on you.

Before we took off, Jackie came walking by my seat. We nodded, and he asked me if I was working. I answered provocatively, figuring correctly I'd hook him with, "You don't want to know." He asked what I meant. I said, "In my experience people in show business, or maybe anywhere, don't want to hear how well another guy is doing." He said he wasn't like that, and we made a casual plan to chat once the plane took off.

Eventually he came back and sat in the empty seat next to me. First he reiterated that he wasn't a competitive person, and it wouldn't trouble him to hear I was working. I quickly moved the conversation away from me to him anyway. I basically was telling him that in the television show he'd been doing lately (it was him in a forum), there was too much audience participation and not enough of him. You can't go too wrong with that kind of criticism. We had some really good laughs. I should say, I did. When it came out that I was friends with Phil Donahue, he wanted to know if he jumped around at home like he does on his show. I said he didn't, but Jackie refused to believe me. He said, "I'm *sure* he jumps around pretty good at home, too." I said, "No, he's just like a regular person," but Jackie persisted, "I'm sure he jumps around pretty good."

The stewardess came by about three times and told him his meal was at his seat, but he stayed. When he finally got up to eat, a couple of hours later, he said, "You must be pretty good for me to sit this long." I really enjoyed that compliment.

Walter Matthau

I would love to work with Walter Matthau again even though he pulled one on me that is definitely in the loony department. He played the main role, along with me, in a movie I wrote and co-produced, *Movers and Shakers*. When the picture didn't test well we tried everything we could in the editing room to make it better. Finally it was decided, as a last resort, it should have a narration. It never occurred to any one of us working on it that Walter should do it. I was playing a screenwriter and the story was told from my point of view, even though Walter had by far the most interesting role. Besides, he was shooting a movie in Singapore while all this last minute work was going on. It turned out the narration, which I wrote and spoke, helped the movie considerably. Much later it got back to me that Walter felt I tried to take the movie away from him in the editing room. It was truly ironic, because no one loved Walter and his performance in the movie the way I, the writer, did. I loved working with him. He was devoted. He actually said aloud to everyone, "This is one of the best movie scripts I've ever done, and I'm going to learn every word exactly as Chuck wrote it." We became friends and I visited his home. I would quite honestly have removed my character from the movie entirely if it would have helped. I had given years of effort to this project and my emotional investment in it was as a writer and producer—hardly as an actor. In fact, one of the movie's problems was that I neglected to write myself a good role. I called Walter to set it right and he didn't take my call. He eventually took the director Bill Asher's call, who swore up and down to him that I was the person in the editing room who most protected everything Walter had done. Walter listened but still wouldn't take my call. Eventually I wrote him a note telling him exactly what I thought of his bizarre assumption. Still no response. A few years later we ended up being cast in the same movie, *The Couch Trip*. The director, Michael Ritchie, told me Walter was afraid I was going to be mad at him. Michael didn't know the details. Walter and I only worked together one day and when we saw each other we embraced. We sincerely like each other and we just let it all go. I, of course, was willing to because Walter was a dream to work with and what he attributed to me is totally out of my character, which he obviously didn't know.

He's an eccentric man. I took Peter Falk to his house once, so they could get to know each other. They had met but only knew each other casually. Walter pretty much stayed in one room watching some obscure World Football League game on a huge screen. I went in and said, "C'mon out, what are you doing?"

He said, "I'm watching a World Football League game. Watch it with me."

I said, "I'm not a fan of the World Football League."

He said, "Neither am I," and he wasn't, but he was an obsessive gambler.

For some reason he loves to tell people about his toilet habits. He showed us his bedroom, which was the biggest one I'd ever seen. If you woke up in the morning and had to go to the bathroom real bad you might not make it. Maybe that's why he likes to talk so much about his toilet habits. It's such a long journey to the bathroom you might be more inclined to talk about what you did once you got there. He was incredibly cooperative as an actor. He had a clause in his contract requiring him to work for only eight hours a day because he'd had a heart attack. When I said, "Someday that might put us in a spot," he said, "Don't worry. I'm not strict." He is a full-course meal—Walter Matthau.

Bill Murray

I hosted "Saturday Night Live" in the first season Bill Murray was on replacing Chevy Chase and, of course, he was a complete unknown. I was immediately impressed with him and asked him where he'd like to see his career go. He really had no idea. I asked him who represented him, and he had no agent. I said that shouldn't be hard to get, given how good he was. Bill, from what I understand, is a person given to dark moods. At the end of one scene on the show where he was part of a group of bees who were upset with me, he threw in the word "Parasite." He later came over to me at the postshow party, apologized, and said he didn't mean anything against me personally. I had no idea what he was talking about. We were doing a scene and he had ad-libbed something— period, but I got the feeling from that little exchange that he was dealing with demons of guilt. At a party recently, some fifteen years later, he was immersed in a conversation with some people; I went up and said, "I don't mean to interrupt, but just for a second, what's the meaning of life?" We shared a good laugh.

John Belushi

John Belushi was someone who went through life feeling besieged. Whether he was up or down, and I knew him during both periods, he often felt unfairly treated. When Carol Burnett and I were going on television espousing a need for us all to be friendlier, he approached us separately to see if he could become involved. This was ironic, because there were those who felt badly treated by John. I believe it was the deep feeling John had that he was being abused that drove him so far into drug use. I personally only saw him under the influence once. It was at "Saturday Night Live" producer Lorne Michaels's wedding on the beautiful grounds of his Easthampton home. John was dressed in a white suit and reminded me of the Godfather. I went over to him and whispered into his ear, "They got Sonny." He didn't laugh, but just looked at me uncomprehendingly.

Thinking of Bill Murray and John Belushi—performers whose brilliance seems to come from a deep well of . . . rage maybe, neurosis certainly—makes me think of Danny Kaye, as revealed in a recent book, posing as a customs inspector at New York's John F. Kennedy Airport and causing a strip search of his lover, Sir Laurence Olivier. The maniacal aspect of certain performers is a subject to be written about by someone other than me. To expect conventional behavior from certain kinds of entertainers is foolish, as foolish as trying to get a cat not to meow. People who have worked with Peter Sellers or Marlon Brando shouldn't have been too surprised to get that midnight call requesting scrapping the first three weeks of footage for them now to play their character as a woman or *anything* else. When you've been a performer as long as I have it's as natural to you as any profession, but let's not kid ourselves—it's not all that natural to stand on a stage relaxed in front of a thousand people, among many other things performers do that others would find frightening. We are a different breed, and sometimes it amazes me that you can get a lot of us together, and organized, civilized, creative stuff happens.

The subject of theatre "madness" has always fascinated me. In Jim Kirkwood's riveting book about the pre-Broadway tour of his show, *Legends*, he tells of Mary Martin being equipped with an earplug, to help with her lines. She was having a problem caused, as I read it, because of the people in charge constantly changing the script—a curious notion when you have an actress in her seventies. The earplug, along with Mary's lines fed by a prompter, started picking up 911 emergency calls. That's a different kind of madness, I know, but it's show business. I'm sure this profession attracts more active nuts than say, accounting.

Gilda Radner

As I knew Gilda Radner, it would have been hard to imagine her anywhere but in show business. She was like a playful, wild child on screen, and often off. I got to know her better when she married my close friend, Gene Wilder, who is not your average boy-next-door either. I stayed in touch with Gilda as she went through the various stages of her illness. There were times when she was certain a successful treatment had been found. I can hear her now as though it were an hour ago saying with great enthusiasm, "With this new treatment, I'll have to take chemotherapy for the rest of my life, but I'll get to live!" I never read her book, *It's Always Something*. I opened it once in a bookstore and read a paragraph and quickly knew I'd be unable to read it. I went to a touching service for her organized by the people at "Saturday Night Live" where a couple of the guys felt compelled to talk about their romances with her. Weird.

Chevy Chase

Chevy Chase has gone through a lot of changes since I met him in the 1970s. The first time I worked with him was when we were both on the Paul Simon special in 1977. Chevy loved to shock. At one point he entered the sound stage and in a loud voice announced, "President Carter has just been assassinated." We *were* shocked, until Chevy made clear it was a "joke." I let him know it wasn't one of his better jokes, and he seemed taken aback. The goal was to shock, and he did, so what was the problem? When I reminded him of this about a year ago, he cringed. Chevy continued in his "shoot from the hip" comedy style when he publicly referred to a male icon movie star as gay—touching off a great deal of backlash toward him as well as threatened lawsuits. It always struck me that Chevy was so detached it was as though all of his life was some sketch. What makes Chevy so interesting as a person is that privately he's unusually caring. He has given his name, talent and considerable money to many worthy causes. He's a devoted family man, and I believe over recent years has tried to put a rein on some of his more outrageous impulses. When we worked together around 1980 in the movie *Seems Like Old Times* with Goldie Hawn, we did a reading of the script at producer Ray Stark's house for the writer, Neil Simon. Chevy was great and funny. At one point Ray Stark sneezed and Chevy looked over at him in what I knew was mock annoyance and said, "Ray, please!" Nobody but me found it funny. He also ad-libbed a few lines here and there. The next day I got a call from someone connected to the production wanting to know what I thought they should do about Chevy. I had no idea what they meant. It seems there was a general feeling he was out of control and wouldn't stick to the script. I assured them there'd be no problem at all, and there wasn't. That was just Chevy's comic spirit. He's really witty and almost never unacceptably hostile in life now, and I find him a touching person along with everything else.

Chevy and I almost worked together on another project I had written that Warner Brothers bought for us to do when he was their six-million-dollar man. That's what his salary got up to— mostly based on the success of the vacation movies he did. So far we've ended up not doing it, as Chevy and I were at odds with the studio over suggested script changes. One afternoon we had a meeting with the Warner's brass where I was supposed to explain the relationship of our characters in the movie. I stood up and in an imitation of Mad Dog Russo, a radio sports personality in New York, yelled, "How do you think I feel? I've won all these acting awards, starred opposite people like Robert De Niro, and I'm going to work with this vacation movie guy. He's going to get six million dollars and I'm going to get a fraction of that!" The outburst was done to show them something about our relationship in the movie, but it just drew stares from everyone—including Chevy.

He is considered one of the best at the hostile put-down at various roast events, which I always find just an excuse to express venom in a socially acceptable venue. Chevy confided to me recently he has come to hate doing it.

Neil Simon

We had a situation on *Seems Like Old Times* that I'd never experienced before. While I've done three pictures where Neil Simon was involved, *The Heartbreak Kid*, *The Lonely Guy* and *Seems Like Old Times*, the latter was the only Neil Simon original, and there was a fellow on the set who was supposed to make sure we all said every line exactly as written. When it comes to setups and jokes, I agree that was completely appropriate, particularly given who the writer was, but this extended down to every prosaic "the." Movies are often shot in many different locations, and sometimes minor alterations of just functional lines are necessary and more natural. Eventually I spoke to Neil, who had the guy back off a touch.

A couple of years ago I attended a big dinner in L.A. honoring Goldie Hawn where Chevy was the host. It was in a huge sprawling banquet hall and there were some very funny performers including Chevy, of course. Because of the huge room and the noise, no one was really effective. When Chevy introduced me he used my most obscure credits, "You all remember how much you loved him in *Absence of a Cello*." There were no laughs for anything. I went up and said, "Chevy has proven it's impossible to get a laugh in this room tonight." That was the first big laugh of the night, because it spoke to what actually had been happening. I then quickly introduced Neil Simon. "Here is the only person who I know will bring the house down, and I'm so sure he can do it, I'm going to stay up here beside him and watch." Neil had some written, *serious* comments about Goldie and he read them while I stood beside him and looked at the audience as if to say, "See, wasn't that hilarious?" The audience liked that. At this writing, which is a few years after the event, I still haven't heard from Neil, but I'm sure that's a coincidence.

Actually I've really only had one run-in with him. We were rehearsing for *Seems Like Old Times*, and I asked him if he wanted it clear that Goldie should leave me, her husband, and go off with Chevy, or should she have a real dilemma? He said he wanted a real dilemma. I then suggested it might balance the scale if I had one scene with Goldie where I wasn't complaining about something. He said I could be complaining and still be appealing. I said I realized that, but I thought it still might be an idea to have one simply loving scene between us. Neil took umbrage and walked off the sound stage. He came back the next day and apologized, and basically I'm always real happy to see him. I find him warm and really witty. I've heard he's a fairly tormented guy, but I haven't seen that side. With all the great laughter he's provided, I wish he could be one of the happiest people in the world.

Herb Gardner

Herb Gardner, one of my closest friends, is one of a kind. He's the author of *A Thousand Clowns*, *I'm Not Rappaport* and *Conversations with My Father*—all hits. However, there were almost twenty-five years between *A Thousand Clowns* and *I'm Not Rappaport*. In that period he continued writing in his own way, in his own time. He never changed. He didn't become more, or less, anything. He took critical abuse, but continued doing what he was doing and eventually won a Tony and made a lot of money. He acted the same when he was rich as when he was poor. I mean exactly! Unlike most others, you wouldn't know what period you were meeting him in. Once, at a low point, Barbra Streisand asked him to do a screenplay of the famous Triangle Shirtwaist Factory fire. It would star her and Jane Fonda and bring Herb a lot of money. He said, "No." When I asked him why, he said he "didn't really have an angle on it." Anyone else I know in that position, including me, would have *found* an angle. He also turned down large sums of money, when he had none, to turn *A Thousand Clowns* into a television series, because he didn't see it that way. In the artistic community there are very few people who are respected and revered the way he is. Like Elaine May, he has given his time and talent to friends unendingly, flying out of town to help this one or that and for no compensation. He is so non "show biz" he once actually fell asleep on the panel of a talk show.

Oliver Stone

I've never worked with Oliver Stone, but I once had a meeting with him about doing the movie, *Salvador*. It was just the two of us alone having a drink one night. In the area where Oliver planned to film in South America, there was as usual a lot of political turmoil, ambushes, assassinations, etc. This didn't seem to faze him at all. He told me we could drive from L.A. right into wherever it would be in South America. That surprised me, but I didn't see it as a major enticement. It was clear as we talked that we were two people who had totally different senses of danger. I had a heightened one, and he didn't have one. At one point he mentioned that his liaison down there had recently been murdered. He expressed it casually as though it was just another piece of news. I said, "That doesn't concern you?" He looked at me as though he barely understood the question, then said, "They've got a lot more to do down there than to kill some actor or director. You're a real city rat, aren't you?" I wasn't sure what he meant, but I got the gist. We didn't work together, but I came away from the meeting enormously impressed with him. Later I spoke with James Woods, who did the picture. He said, "They were the roughest three months of my life." I'd love to work with Oliver Stone in some indoor movie set in Connecticut.

Robert Downey, Jr., with whom I'm working on *Heart and Souls*, told me yesterday he had a meeting with Oliver and Oliver told him he had wanted me to do the picture *Salvador* for him. That's the first I knew of this. Oliver told Robert they couldn't afford me. I never even heard he wanted me after that meeting. I wonder how lack of communication affects a person's career. My old friend Penny Marshall once told me the sense of me in Hollywood was "you won't get him." That sounds a little more exclusive than I like, but it does remind me of the apocryphal story of the producer who didn't want an actor.

PRODUCER

We don't want him! We don't want him!

PRODUCER'S ASSISTANT

He doesn't want to do it.

PRODUCER

We've got to have him!

Robert Altman

Robert Altman is another tough guy I've always admired. My agent once got us together thinking we were a really good fit, because he likes improvisation, which I love to do. We didn't particularly hit it off. Years later we were the only two people in this huge room where a postscreening party was going to take place. We were the only two there because we had both slipped out of the screening. He looked me in the eye and said, "I know I should like you, but I don't." I thought it was a pretty refreshing remark, and I just smiled at him, probably making him dislike me more. I have a theory on why he felt that way. Robert Altman is used to being treated with great deference by actors, and as I've said, I'm not that big in the deference department. Funny thing is I'm a lot more deferential in an actual working situation with directors than I am socially. In fact, comparably speaking, with other actors who have been doing this as long as I have, I could get nominated for most deferential. It's probably because I know directing a movie is one of the hardest jobs in the world, and I'm actually touched when I see someone doing it. A friend of mine who was laid up with a bad back disputed my take on Altman. He said Altman came over to visit him and stayed an hour, giving my friend his entire back history. I said that just supported my contention that he needed to be the authority figure. I'm actually not all that deferential when I'm laid up, so it wouldn't work if Altman saw me under those circumstances either, but as an actor he'd be shocked by my deference. In any case he's a remarkable talent, and every actor I know who has worked with him adored him.

Otto Preminger

The late director Otto Preminger was a rough character who is reported to have once kicked Paula Prentiss to get her to cry in a scene. Elaine May once took me to meet him about playing a part in his picture *Such Good Friends*. He sat behind the longest desk I've ever seen—it was more the length of a bowling alley than a desk. He spoke for about ten minutes telling me everything he felt about the role and the movie. I was completely unknown at the time so I must have startled him when I said, "I disagree with just about everything you've said." There was real tension in the room as he peered at me for a long time, then said, "That's why I make lousy movies." I got the impression you could talk differently to him if he wasn't paying your salary which, of course, is almost always true of everyone.

Diane Sawyer

About a year after my cancellation from "Good Morning, America" I was at a gathering in New York. I was talking to a number of television network executives when I was introduced to a woman who was the producer of "Good Morning, America." I was planning my next move when Diane Sawyer came over to say hello. The dialogue went something like this.

DIANE
(matter-of-fact)
Hi! We met once before at a party. You had a
lamp shade on your head.

ME
What?

DIANE
You had a lamp shade on your head when we
first met.

ME
(glancing at the network executives)
I think you have me confused with someone
else.

DIANE
No. It was you. Charles Grodin.

ME
(trying to find it amusing)
I've never had a lamp shade on my head.

DIANE
You did that night.

ME
A lamp shade?

DIANE
Right.

There was no way Diane was joking, and everyone including the "Good Morning, America" producer seemed to take it as a point of information—nothing all that amusing. If anything, the "Good Morning, America" producer might have been thinking of me for a lamp-shade-on-the-head booking. I knew I'd never worn a lamp shade in Diane Sawyer's presence, or even alone, but to protest further didn't seem all that graceful, so I just smiled at her and waited for the subject to change. Of course, the clear implication was that I'd had too much to drink, which in my memory happened once. *Once*, and Diane Sawyer wasn't there.

It was years later when Diane married Mike Nichols and I'd see her around occasionally that I asked her about the lamp shade thing. She smiled at me and said, "I was kidding. I thought you knew." In spite of that, in my limited social exposure to her, she seems like a totally charming, nice lady.

Dustin Hoffman

I was once walking with Dustin Hoffman down a remote country road outside of Marrakesh in Morocco. Dustin looked at the people staring at us and said, "Hey, more people recognize you than me." I said, "I've done a lot of community theatre around here."

Dustin is unique. When we worked together on *Ishtar*, he realized we were both New York Knick fans, and he decided he wanted to form a friendship, which was fine with me. I'd known him since around 1960, but we'd never hung out. Getting together was another thing. Here's how it went. I got a call from a guy in his office.

DUSTIN'S GUY
I'm calling for Dustin Hoffman. He'd like to
know what time you might be available to
take a phone call from him this week.

ME
What time?

161

DUSTIN'S GUY

Yeah.

ME

I'm here. I work at home. He can call me whenever he wants.

DUSTIN'S GUY

I'll get back to you.

ME

Fine. O.K.

The next day I got another call.

DUSTIN'S GUY

Would between three to four on Thursday afternoon be good for you?

ME

For a call?

DUSTIN'S GUY

Yeah.

ME

Sure. Fine.

The next day I got another call.

DUSTIN'S GUY

The Thursday time isn't going to work. Would the following Tuesday at 11 A.M. be all right for you?

ME
I'm here. Sure. Whenever.

DUSTIN'S GUY
You'll be available to take the call next
Tuesday at 11 A.M.?

ME
Yeah. I'm here. I work here. Fine.

This was seven years ago. I'm still waiting for the call. My theory is Dustin just went through a stage when he wanted to know my whereabouts.

Anthony Perkins

I became good friends with Anthony Perkins when I did *Catch 22*. He was very bright and always had a warm smile. A couple of years later I recommended him for a directing job of an off-Broadway show where one of the producers was a friend of mine. The play was *Steambath* by Bruce Jay Friedman. Eventually the leading actor was fired and replaced by another actor who was fired. They then asked me to go in. I became the third actor to be fired from the role with my friend Tony's compliance, thereby ending our friendship. I don't even think Tony saw me in the role as he was in L.A., fulfilling an earlier acting commitment. He returned to replace me in the part. Many people around the production thought it was a mistake to fire me, but by then the producers were in such a financial hole they felt they needed a star, which I wasn't, and which, of course, Tony was. The play, which I always felt was an outstanding one, didn't run very long. The critics felt Tony was miscast. A few years later he called me on New Year's Eve, I'm sure to make amends. My girlfriend at the time took his call in my New York apartment, and told him I was in Los Angeles working. She said it in such a removed way, that he never called me in Los Angeles or anywhere else ever again. It was almost twenty years later when I ran into him on a flight from Los Angeles to New York. In those twenty years I had gone on to starring roles in movies and, aside from his success with *Psycho*, he had struggled. He was very friendly, generous and appeared clearly happy about all that had happened to me, as though he had spotted something long before others did. It was a warm reunion. There was no mention of our upsetting experience. In the last year, a Broadway theatre company was considering doing a revival of *Steambath*. They wanted to put on a reading of it to see how it played in front of an audience. Ironically, they called me to play the lead. While I told them I wouldn't be interested in acting in a play, I couldn't resist once again playing the role in the reading, which went beautifully. It was around the same time that I read in the papers that Tony had died of AIDS. Sometimes life feels so short and strange.

Louise Lasser

Louise Lasser of *Mary Hartman* fame is an old pal of mine. Way past the age when people would think of doing such things, we would invent I guess what you'd call sophomoric games. There was a bakery on the East Side of Manhattan that would allow us to sit in chairs off to the side of the counter and make recommendations to the customers as they perused the cookies and cakes.

LOUISE
(to a customer)
I think you'd enjoy the apple strudel.

ME
I think the marble cake.

The customers would look over at us, find us vaguely recognizable faces and seem to consider what we'd say.

Personalities

> **ME**
> The apple strudel's too fattening.

> **LOUISE**
> No more than the marble cake.

> **ME**
> What about some nice pound cake?

> **LOUISE**
> I could go along with that.

Then we'd both nod at the customers, who'd usually smile at us, and then buy what they came in for in the first place.

Once I pulled a joke on Louise. I was about to do the movie *Heaven Can Wait*, and I pretended I was on the phone with my agent, whom Louise knew, as she walked into her living room.

> **ME**
> *(talking to no one)*
> Well, what's holding it up?

A silence as I pretend to listen. Louise is watching me.

> **ME**
> What billing problem? All right, I'll hold.
> *(to Louise)*
> There's some kind of billing problem.
> *(to the agent who I pretend has just come back on the phone)*
> Yeah. I'm here—
> *(a silence as I listen)*
> Wait a minute! Wait a minute! You're trying
> to get me billing ahead of Warren Beatty? I

never asked for that! I mean, it's *his* movie.
He has the biggest part!

Louise's mouth drops open as she watches me.

ME

No! I *don't* want you to try to get it. It's not
right. We have a misunderstanding. I *never*
asked for that!

LOUISE
(reaching for the phone)
Let me talk to him. You *never* expected to
get billed ahead of Warren. This is really a
misunderstanding!

She takes the phone and hears an off-the-hook recording and
realizes it's a joke.

I always found Louise one of the wittiest women I've ever met.
It's a shame that she, along with the brilliant Jeannie Berlin,
who played my wife in *The Heartbreak Kid*, do more teaching
than acting.

Danny Thomas

Danny Thomas was a friend of mine whom I knew through his daughter, my friend Marlo. Marlo's brother Tony was producing a new television series for NBC called "The Practice," which had an old curmudgeon doctor character as the lead. Danny wanted to play it, but the network wanted Jack Klugman. They saw Danny as a nightclub comic, not an actor. Marlo asked me if I would direct her father in a screen test she would produce without the network's knowledge. I got a few actors to be in scenes with Danny and we worked on it for a couple of weeks. Marlo and I then worked through the night editing it. When we emerged from the editing room at dawn, Marlo turned to me and said, "I'll never forget what you've done for my father." I said, "*Your* father? I thought he was *my* father!"

Marlo showed the test to the network and Danny got the part. I was struck reading Danny's version of this story in his book. He noted how impressed he was that I never charged any money for my services. Frankly it never occurred to me. What Danny didn't say was that a few years after that, when I was trying to raise money to produce a friend's play off-Broadway, Danny asked how much I had. I told him fifty thousand. He said, "You now have seventy-five."

Peter Falk

Recently I learned from Peter Falk that the only way I could get the New York Knicks basketball games on my satellite dish here in Los Angeles was through a special contact at Madison Square Garden in New York. I was able to get it. Then about a week later we had the following exchange.

ME

Peter, do you have the wine and cheese arrangement with your satellite?

PETER

The wine and cheese arrangement?

ME

You don't have it?

PETER

What is it?

171

ME

When there's a Knicks game on, a guy in a
white jacket comes to your house with a tray
with a bottle of wine and cheese and crackers.

Peter knows I'm kidding throughout all of this, but goes on as
seriously as I do.

PETER

Was this something that was offered to you?

ME

Yes. I assumed it was for everyone on their
VIP list.

PETER

This is the first I'm hearing of it. Is there a
charge?

ME

No, it's complimentary. You ought to say
something.

PETER

I'm not entirely comfortable bringing it up
now, but I have to admit I'm a bit taken
aback it wasn't offered.

ME

Frankly, I am, too.

I kept this up for so long after some other friends had joined us
for dinner, that Peter finally turned to me and said, "Y'know, at
first I was sure you were kidding. Now I'm not so sure."

Paul Simon

I've had a lot of fun with Paul Simon over the years. I met Paul through his then-partner Art Garfunkel when I was working on *Catch 22* with Art. We became friends when I directed the Simon and Garfunkel television special in 1969.

I fondly remember a lawsuit I brought against Paul and his subsequent countersuit. It was all a joke. I was reading a paperback copy of a book called *On the Street Where I Live* by Alan Jay Lerner, in which he wrote about the making of his musicals. Paul and I were both in London at the time. I was doing a movie, and Paul was doing concerts. I told Paul how much I was enjoying the Lerner book and said he should read it when I finished. Later, as a gag, I pulled something like the following on Paul in a phone call.

ME
Well, I finished that Alan Jay Lerner book.
It was really good. You should read it.

PAUL

O.K. Great.

ME

Now I paid three pounds for it, so I was
thinking I could let you see it—for say . . .
two pounds four pence. How does that
sound?
(a silence as Paul decides to go along with the joke)

PAUL

Well . . . I was really under the impression
that you were going to *give* me the book.
(a pause)

ME

Well . . . I never really meant to give that
impression.

PAUL

That *was* the impression I got.

ME

Well . . . let's say we have an honest misunderstanding here.
(a pause)

PAUL

Is it marked up at all or is it a clean copy?

ME

It's clean, but frankly a copy with my nota-
tions on it would be, in my opinion, *more*
valuable, not less.
(a pause)

PAUL
(dubiously)
Uh huh.

ME
But y'know, more importantly, I'm thinking
maybe we do a musical about the making of
his musicals, using your original music
along with his—we co-write the libretto, you
star as Lerner and I direct. I can see the
opening. Curtain goes up. You're pacing,
stuck, on a lyric.

PAUL
Chuck . . .

ME
The only thing is, I don't want to get into an
ugly thing with you over the billing.
(a pause)

PAUL
Well, what do you feel it should be?

ME
Well . . . you're starring. That's you. The
songs. That's you. I direct. That's me. We
co-write the book. I get first billing, because
it's my idea, and I'll write the first draft.
(a silence)

PAUL
Let me think about it.

This all continued after Paul went back to New York, and I was
still in London. In a subsequent phone negotiation he spotted a

hard-cover copy of the Alan Jay Lerner book in his library and called off the purchase of my paperback, provoking my lawsuit. I actually had an attorney friend serve him with papers, and he had an attorney friend serve me. We both claimed undue suffering, among many other hardships, and had a lot of laughs.

I remember a more recent encounter with Paul that I think amused me more than him. When he was concluding his *Graceland* album, he was having some difficulty with the lyrics being heard clearly enough and doing justice to the myriad of rich instrumental tracks. I went into the studio to listen and made a suggestion that would have put the lyrics much more up front at the expense of reducing the level of the tracks. Paul wasn't thrilled at what he felt was the extreme nature of my idea, but it provoked his engineer Roy Halee to furiously begin to adjust this dial and that. Roy then asked that I sit behind him and tap him on the shoulder if I didn't hear a lyric sufficiently. Paul knows I'm a fiend for clear lyrics—no matter what, but he tolerated the experiment. In the middle of all this, Cyndi Lauper, who was recording next door, stopped by to visit. She knew me as a comedy person from the movies and was understandably baffled as I kept tapping Roy as though I was in charge of everything. I got a kick out of the whole thing. I don't know how much I had to do with it, but after that session the problem went away. Of course, neither Paul nor Cyndi asked me to work on their next album, but who knows what might happen in the future?

The humorous connection that Paul and I enjoyed in our personal relationship was used to good advantage when we worked together in a comedic context. When I hosted "Saturday Night Live" Paul was the musical guest, and at one point the lights came up on the two of us sitting on stools—me wearing an Art Garfunkel wig. The audience cheered madly for a moment thinking it really was Art. The idea was we'd do "Sounds of Silence" together. The bit was that Paul would act very uncomfortable about the whole concept especially when it became

176

clear I really didn't know the words. At that point he stopped playing his guitar, and it went something like this.

PAUL
(irritated)
You don't know the words!

ME
I know the part that's coming up a little better.

Paul gives me a long look, then reluctantly resumes playing only to stop again almost immediately.

PAUL
And another thing! It's very disconcerting to
me to look out of the corner of my eye and
see that Garfunkel wig.

ME
I thought it would make you *more* comfortable.

Paul shakes his head negatively—then resumes playing and singing until, because of my lagging behind on the lyrics, he just can't continue.

PAUL
Why are you doing this, anyway?!

ME
Well, so much of my material has been cut,
and I . . . well, I don't have that much left to
do on the show.

PAUL

I'm really not comfortable here.

ME

I understand. I appreciate your effort.
(to audience—sending him off)
Paul Simon, ladies and gentlemen!

The audience gave him a hand and he went off, only to be called back out by me for another bow, which he attempted to take gracefully.

After Paul went off, I stood alone a moment, still in the Garfunkel wig and then I nodded to the band, which began to play "Bridge Over Troubled Water," which was essentially Art's solo. I got about three lines in, and of course, wasn't good, but not bad enough to get a laugh, until I hit the first really high note in a weirdly unacceptable way, which got a big laugh that was topped by applause as Art Garfunkel came out of the audience onto the stage and said, referring to the wig, "All right, Chuck, hand it over." I took it off sheepishly and handed it to him as we went to black. Of course there were hundreds of letters complaining about me forcing poor Paul Simon to sing with me.

Shortly after I hosted "Saturday Night Live," a group of us got together and made "The Paul Simon Special," which won an Emmy for its script, which was written by Paul, Lorne Michaels and me among several others. The show had Chevy Chase, Art Garfunkel and Lily Tomlin in the cast along with me and, of course, Paul. It was a fictional look at Paul preparing for a special much in the manner of the old Jack Benny show. We all used our own names, except I alone played a character, the incredibly aggressive and insensitive director of the special. Here are some of the show's exchanges between director and star as I recall them. We are sitting in a control room when I bring up the name of the special.

Personalities

ME

We've got to talk about the name of the special.

PAUL
(matter-of-fact)
"The Paul Simon Special."

ME

Bear with me a minute here.
(a long, dramatic pause)
"The Paul, Bridge Over Troubled Water, Simon Special."

PAUL

(confused)
I don't . . . why . . . I . . .

ME
(in explanation)
The recognition factor.

A pause as Paul thinks.

PAUL

Well, you wouldn't say "The Neil, I Am I Said, Diamond Special," or "The Barry, I Write the Songs, Manilow Special."

ME

Well, there's only one Neil Diamond and one Barry Manilow.

Paul stares at me.

ME

You have a Paul Simon who's in Congress. I think there's a Paul Simon who's a sculptor.

PAUL

Well, they would hardly have their own special.

ME

Well . . . I don't know . . . Nowadays just about anyone can get a special.

PAUL

Well . . .

ME

(interrupting)

Just think about it . . . you don't have to answer now. Just think about it.

The scene ended with Paul seriously mulling it over. I did everything on the show a director should never do. At one point I took Paul aside and said, "I want you to go home and get a good night's sleep. Tomorrow twenty-five million people will be watching every move you make, so relax." A director friend of mine wanted to use the tape in seminars to instruct about bad direction. It was shows like this, along with the kinds of movie roles I was playing in the seventies, that contributed to the perception of me as a jerk. Again I was playing an incredibly insensitive guy and worse yet I used my own name. My daughter used to come home from school and say, "Dad, people think you're really like that. Can't you play some other kinds of parts?" What made it even worse was I was a good enough actor for people to think that's what I *was* really like. Sometimes it was so convincing, even on the show there were problems. There was a musical group, the outstanding Jesse Dixon Singers, who were guests on the special. The idea was that I was going to watch them do a number with all their hand gestures and "Do Ops" or whatever little riffs they had and basically, in a very nice way, take them apart. The group knew exactly what I was going to do, but after about five minutes of "Why do you move your hand there? Do you need that 'Do Op' there? Why not take three steps to the left instead of four? Don't move your heads so much," you could see Jesse and the singers start to look at me like, "I know this is a bit, but it's getting on our nerves." That scene wasn't in the final cut of the show.

A sidebar to all of this. This was the third time I had worked with Simon and Garfunkel. Earlier I had directed their only television special about which I wrote extensively in my first book, and I never witnessed any problems between them. We were all three good friends and there was never anything but good times and laughs. My fondest memory with them was in 1969 when they wanted me to hear them sing a new song of Paul's, "El Condor Pasa." It wasn't recorded yet, so in order for me to get the stereo effect, Paul sang into my right ear while Art sang into my left.

MOVIES

Difficulties

Breaking Bones in Mexico

Sunburn was memorable for me because, among other things, I met two real characters, the producer John Daly and the director Dick Sarafian. It would be hard to imagine two more opposite people trying to work together. John Daly looks like a blond Paul McCartney. He is known as one of Hollywood's wildest wheeler dealers, to put it nicely. To me, however, he has always been a charming, endlessly cheerful English gentleman. Dick Sarafian is a large powerful swarthy-looking man. He seemed to relish anything that would fly in the face of authority. At a small gathering John hosted for the company, Dick arrived swigging a bottle of liquor with a woman who seemed to be a hooker on his arm. I remember John coming to my suite pacing back and forth and carrying on about Dick. Though he was agitated, he still held his good humor. We had a big shootout scene where mobsters tried to kill Farrah Fawcett and me in this house. John had complained to Dick that the tremendous amount of endless gunfire was overdone. Dick told John, "That's the best goddamned shootout I've ever shot!" That was the end of the conversation.

Dick generally seemed angry. One day I asked if there was anything I could do for him. He then told me he resented that the actors had air-conditioned motor homes and he didn't. I didn't know that, and told him he was welcome to use mine whenever he wanted. I was sitting with a friend there one day when Dick came in and, without a hello, went to the refrigerator and chug-a-lugged a quart of orange juice. While my sensibility was more attuned to John, I admired Dick's talent and commitment to the work.

Sunburn was also the picture where I had a scene with the accomplished Mexican actor Jorge Luke. After crashing through a window I was to scuffle with Jorge, and then he was supposed to knock me out. The action called for me to be lying on my back groggy when Jorge lets me have it. The way this is done is with the camera behind Jorge, who is straddling me, and he's supposed to punch across my face. If I move my head in reaction at the right time it looks real. I tried to discuss with him how he would do this, but he cut me off saying he had done over fifty action pictures and knew exactly what to do. On the first take Jorge chose to punch straight at me with the intention of pulling his punch just short of my face. He didn't quite pull it enough and broke my nose. My daughter, who was visiting, saw my blood spurt all over the place. Jorge was deeply apologetic. I decided after a few minutes to keep filming, since we were in the middle of the sequence, and I knew we'd have to deal with a lot of black and blue stuff shortly. Dick Sarafian said to me, "You're really showing me something here." I knew Dick would be impressed with that, so I milked it for all it was worth. "No, no, no problem," waving off all offers of help. "Let's just keep shooting." That night I had dinner with Art Carney and his wife Jean at our French restaurant. I was concerned I'd end up with a weird nose. Jean reassured me that she had broken her nose years ago, and it wasn't even noticeable now. I said, "Let's see." She turned profile. Her nose looked perfect, but I recoiled in horror and shouted, "Uuuuuuu!"

Roger Corman and Me

I had another exotic experience on a low-budget movie called *Last Resort*. This was a movie produced by the wife of the king of low-budget movies, Roger Corman, who was really behind it. My agent, Jim Berkus, tried to keep me out of this one. He felt Roger Corman and Charles Grodin could be a troublesome combination, but I liked the script and they said I could pick the director. Eventually they also hired me to do a rewrite. This was all before we started, and I had yet to meet Roger. Julie, his wife, the producer, had a darling little baby girl who she always held between you and her, giving a softening effect to anything she was saying.

There were four directors they wanted me to meet. One, a woman named Zane Buzby, seemed immediately unusual. I started to receive phone calls from various people I knew praising her, obviously at her instigation. She was essentially a talented comedy actress and had never directed a movie, but I looked at a tape of her acting she had prepared. In one clip, as a romantic move, she put her mouth over John Ritter's nose. It surprisingly wasn't gross, but funny. It was slightly disconcerting that, unlike any of the other directors, Zane was in the outer office while I was looking at her tape "to answer any questions I might have." I met with her and, over the objections of the original writers, chose her. It was a happy choice. She seemed to know where every undiscovered comedy actor in Hollywood was. She brought in, among many other talented unknown people, Jon Lovitz and Phil Hartman, both of whom later went on to fame on "Saturday Night Live." She put together an outstanding cast, and I was looking forward to the whole thing.

The story of *Last Resort* is a simple one. A family goes on vacation to some remote island resort called Club Sand, which turns out to be a terrible place. In fact, the original title of the picture was Club Sandwich, which I liked. My first inkling that this would be a "different" experience came when I learned the Cormans wanted to film this picture, which was set on some exotic island, in Los Angeles's Griffith Park. I wandered into a production meeting one day to hear Julie Corman say, "We can't send a location scout to Catalina Island. That would cost a hundred dollars." I knew this was a low-budget picture, but still . . . No one had actually told me *how* low budget the picture was, and I could never bring myself to ask. Anyway, we did end up making most of it on Catalina Island, and it was a strange but kind of magical experience. We also shot part of it in Griffith Park.

All through this I had yet to meet Roger Corman, even though we were working out of his offices. His spirit was dominating the production, though. The quarters on the island were a boys' camp out of season. This was supposed to be, for script purposes, as I've said, a terrible vacation spot, but this place was worse than terrible. In many instances, there was no water and sometimes there were no roofs on the buildings. The day we arrived, the actors took one look and from everywhere there were cries of, "I'm outta here!" My wife and I were put up in quarters a ten-minute speedboat ride away where some marine biologists were ensconced. Eventually we all kind of got used to everything the way people tend to do (I'm sure the Cormans counted on that) and proceeded to make what I personally believe is the funniest movie I've ever done, albeit a cheap-looking one. The Cormans truly redefined the words low budget for me on the day about fifty extras were sent over from Los Angeles. They were expected to sleep outside on the beach and bring their own food. They *did*, too!

My showdown with Roger came when we were back in L.A. finishing up. We were filming in a house in the San Fernando

Valley. The temperature outside was in the nineties, so inside the house with the movie lights it was well over a hundred. When I arrived I was told there was no air conditioning and one of the children had fainted. I said, "I'll just wait till they get an air-conditioning unit in there," and I sent word to Roger that the next time we shot in a hot location that had no air conditioning he should tell me in advance, and I'd pay for it. The next day he sent his production manager to see me. The guy said, "I'm really uncomfortable with this, but Roger wants me to ask you if you'll chip in for air conditioning on the sound stage we're working on next week." I looked at him and said my offer was for houses, not sound stages (which are huge). Roger had no shame. He even wrote a book about how he never made a movie that lost money. I don't think he ever made a movie where he paid profit to anyone either. He has been known to wonder why all the people who got their starts with him, Francis Coppola, Marty Scorsese, Jack Nicholson, etc., never returned to work with him. He must get credit, however, for giving these major talents their starts. No small thing.

When *Last Resort* was finished it was screened and the response was everything we hoped it would be. I knew that with Roger releasing it, because of the lack of marketing money available, its exposure would be extremely limited. In fact, one of Roger's own people confided to me, "He couldn't sell a steak in a famine." So along with two friends of mine, Edgar Scherick who had produced *The Heartbreak Kid*, and Julian Schlosberg, who, as I've earlier mentioned, has his own distribution company, Castle Hill, I tried to buy it from Roger. First he seemed interested, then probably figuring we knew something, he decided not to sell. Roger's plan was to open the picture in Seattle and see how it did. Along with Zane Buzby, I flew there, and was on what seemed to be every television and radio show in the city, along with giving newspaper interviews.

A local college kid working on the school paper wrote disparagingly that I could be seen or heard on most of Seattle's TV and radio outlets and even read about in their newspapers. Of course, the only interview I regretted giving was the one with him. I met him in the restaurant of the hotel where I was staying, and it was a perfectly pleasant encounter. I don't usually get that riled at this little jab or that one (emotionally, you can't afford to), but this one went to the heart of something I have a high awareness of—just how hard it is to make a movie and how virtually impossible it is for low-budget independents to compete in the marketplace—necessitating people like me to appear wherever possible. I actually wrote the kid saying it would be hard for him to understand what I was doing on all those TV and radio shows, because I'm sure he never worked as hard as you have to to make a movie, and if he ever did he would then know what it took to make people aware of it. In the case of these low-budget pictures from small, independent companies, all the effort in the world from people like me usually makes no difference—so we're not in the best frame of mind to be knocked for trying.

When the picture opened in Seattle it was the city's highest-grossing movie, outgrossing all the major studio releases. I feel if I had flown everywhere it opened, we might have made it a hit, but I don't believe Roger would have paid the travel expenses, and I wasn't inclined to fly to every city in America. Sometimes I wish I had. I'm sure the movie made money for Roger. I've really only met him once at some kind of gathering for the picture, but he made a point of leaving as soon as he realized I was there. Having said all I have about Roger Corman, I must admit the only two things I really dislike about the man is an apparent disregard about whether children faint, and his telephone calls to Zane Buzby during the filming telling her, "If you think we're using anything you're shooting, you're crazy!" Whatever that meant.

A strange thing happened with the writing credit on the picture. When I did the rewrite I, of course, kept the simple story—a family's misadventures on a vacation—but I rewrote every scene and added about twenty new ones. In fact, I would say I wrote over 90 percent of everything spoken in the picture. Julie Corman submitted the screenplay credit to the Guild with my name first—then the two original writers, only one of whom I knew, Steve Zacharias, who is a real nice guy. The original writers contested the credit. Steve called me and explained the only reason they were contesting it was because they'd be paid more if they didn't share credit, even though he acknowledged, given what I'd done, shared was appropriate. I said I understood, assuming the worst that would happen was that the Guild would reverse the order of our names, which was O.K. with me. I was startled when they ruled the original writers should have sole credit. The Guild acknowledged that I had written just about everything anyone said, but said I could have written 100 percent of what everyone said and not gotten credit, because the original story and characters were the same. I said, "In other words, I might have written every line of *Casablanca*, for example, and not gotten screen credit." "That's right," the guy said. (An interesting rule.)

The Cormans, true to their fashion, found a way to get out of paying Steve Zacharias and his partner Jeff Buhai the bonus due them for sole credit. There was a clause in their contract that said if the picture was first shown on cable, instead of movie theatres, there would be no bonus. The clause was there really in case the picture wasn't good enough for theatrical release and went straight to cable. The Cormans, to avoid paying the writers, had it shown once on cable late at night before it was released theatrically, and therefore technically avoided the bonus. Ah, Roger, what a guy!

Waiting

It was ironic that I went from *Last Resort*, the lowest-budget picture I had done since the early *Fun Lovers*, to the biggest-budget picture, *Ishtar*. I didn't want to be in *Ishtar*. It wasn't the script or the role—both of which I liked. It was going to Morocco, which was fairly close to Libya, at a time we were really having some stuff with them. The bigger reason I didn't want to do it was that I was really afraid of spending endless amounts of time over there waiting to film. After Elaine May, the writer/director, assured me she wouldn't do that to me, I signed on. Elaine once persuaded Frank Yablans, when he was the president of Paramount Pictures, to play the role of the villain in a movie she was directing. Frank was waiting to film in a hotel room in Philadelphia for several days before he realized it might look better if he was in his office in Hollywood, where Paramount Pictures is.

This waiting business is really the part of being a movie actor that puts all of us to the test. One of the worst times I had with this was on the picture I did with Lily Tomlin, who, by the way, I adore. It was *The Incredible Shrinking Woman* and there were a lot of special effects. By definition of the medium, a lot of time must be spent on lighting. All you can reasonably expect is that whoever is responsible for when the actors are called to work—the assistant director—makes a best guess on when the actors would actually be needed. On this one it seemed we were called first thing in the morning no matter when we might work. I remember sitting in the makeup room at Universal Studios being made up at 5 A.M. and the actor Henry Gibson sitting next to me saying, "We haven't had a call like this since *Hitler's Children* in '37." That, of course, was a joke, but unfortunately we had a lot of calls like that, and I remember on average waiting often four or five hours in makeup and costume before being called to the set. Not only is it exhausting to be waiting, but it's not that easy to maintain the appropriate energy and enthusiasm you want. Since movie days are at least twelve hours long, and often longer, it's really in everyone's best interest to give some attention to when performers are called. Actresses particularly suffer from unnecessary early calls. Generally they are called even earlier than actors and are expected to look beautiful twelve hours later. Once you're there and working, we all understand there must be waiting—so the real question is when are you called in the first place. We couldn't seem to get anywhere with the assistant directors on this so I went to the director, Joel Schumacher. This was at the beginning of Joel's directing career, and it was a very demanding picture. Joel looked at me like I was nuts, as I explained the situation to him. He said, "With everything I have to worry about, you expect me to worry about this too!?" I said it was no small thing, because the actors were getting drained by it, and all I was asking was that they give it some consideration, and do the best they could.

He said, "Do you realize you're making more money on this picture than Lily Tomlin?!"

I said, "I wasn't aware of that. Who's her agent?"

He said, "We pay you to wait."

I said, "No, you pay me to act. I'm not interested in getting paid to wait. By your definition, Burt Reynolds (who was our number-one movie star then) should wait longer than anyone."

We went round and round, and things got a little better after that, but not much. I think Joel and I actually liked each other in spite of all this. He could be very charming. On the first day of shooting he said in a loud voice, "My God, I'm directing Lily Tomlin and Charles Grodin, and they're listening to me!" He used to refer to himself as white trash and me as a Jewish prince. I don't think he meant the prince thing as a compliment. As the waiting situation continued I asked an actress on the picture how she felt about it, just to do a reality check on myself. This actress was actually convinced there was a conspiracy. She had continually been called at dawn and done nothing for so long that she came to believe they were actually having meetings to figure a way to drive her crazy. I didn't really buy the conspiracy theory, and I wasn't going nuts—completely, anyway, but it sure wasn't fun. I know it's odd to be paid well and complain about anything, but again, all we were asking for was an effort to deal with this. It didn't even have to be a successful effort. We just wanted someone to acknowledge it was worth considering. On most pictures they try to work with you on this, and it's really appreciated.

Ishtar

Anyway, back to *Ishtar*. I think the biggest problem the picture had was that by the time it was released it seemed like the cost of the movie was part of the title—*The Fifty-Million-Dollar Ishtar*. I mean, *Ishtar* alone isn't that hot a title but put Fifty-Million in front of it and well . . . a figure in front of anything isn't a good idea. There was a time when they were referring to Dan Rather as the two-million-dollar anchorman. Dan's ratings went down after that, even after he started wearing a sweater in an effort to look like the two-million-dollar guy next door.

The media jumped on the cost of *Ishtar* because it was a good story. The public seemed as outraged as if the money were coming out of their pocket. In fact, it was coming from Coca-Cola, which owned Columbia Pictures. I guess if you were a Coca-Cola stockholder you could be outraged. Since then so many pictures have cost more that it's no longer news in the industry. The brunt of all this cost seemed to fall on Elaine May, which was really strange because she'd be about the third person to look at. First, where was the studio? Then, the producer? Directors are commonly known to film and film and edit and edit until someone says, "Time or money's up!" You actually want a director to have his or her head totally into making the best movie, and someone else should be thinking about costs. What I observed in my limited exposure to the filming was a lot of people working long and hard to make a good movie. I didn't see extravagance, just an endless effort. Viewing something is a lot more subjective than people think. If the picture had cost half as much, I believe the reviews would have been twice as good.

There was a period of time that Disney Studios was getting a lot of bad press for being arrogant and too meddling. It wasn't surprising to me to see a number of their pictures come out and get bad reviews with some nice comments, rather than nice reviews with reservations. They too eventually understood that, I believe, and started doing business differently.

I am partial to *Ishtar* myself for subjective reasons. I am prejudiced on behalf of Elaine May, who I feel is largely responsible for my movie career. She insisted on me for *The Heartbreak Kid* when normally the role would have gone to a star. She urged Warren Beatty to get me for *Heaven Can Wait*, which she wrote, and she, as I've earlier mentioned, has always been a devoted, selfless friend to me and many others. I am also partial to the *Ishtar* story of two entertainers who are so bad they have to go to Ishtar to get booked. I am taken by their overwhelming need to be in show business. It's true I've never seen performers that bad get work, but I could believe they might get booked somewhere in Ishtar. Most people aren't interested in watching bad entertainers, but I find them touching and amusing and I felt Warren and Dustin were really good in the roles—also, of course, there is always originality in Elaine's writing. I, too, could criticize things about the picture, but I won't. Close friends shouldn't criticize each other in books, but the truth is I really liked it and felt it got a bum rap.

As it neared its opening all the talk about its budget didn't bode well. Elaine, Warren, Dustin and I attended a sneak preview somewhere in New Jersey before the picture opened. It seemed to go fairly well. There was a gathering at a restaurant afterward and Faye Vincent, later baseball commissioner, but then the president or chairman of the board, or one of those things, of Columbia Pictures, was expected but didn't show. I'm sure there was a good reason but I took that as a bad sign. The picture got blistered by the critics, but I never got more praise in my life. I sometimes felt all the carrying on about me was to legitimize a review, as if to say, "See, I didn't hate everything." In any case, it was a major movie disaster. I was the only one who benefited. All that praise couldn't possibly have hurt my chances of being cast in *Midnight Run* soon after. Strangely, at the time, I actually felt somewhat guilty, as if I were the only survivor of a car crash of friends.

MGM Grand Airlines

I'm writing this now on MGM Grand Airlines. I'm sitting in the Grand class. That's better than first class. I have no idea how much this all costs, because I don't pay for it. It's paid for by Universal Pictures. I'm going home for a Christmas break in filming to my family in Connecticut. After the first of the year, we should all live and be well (I always say that because I've learned you can't take anything for granted), I will bring my wife and son back to Los Angeles while I finish the picture I'm doing, *Heart and Souls,* and then do the sequel to *Beethoven* (we should all live and be well). Sitting directly behind me on the airplane is a man named Lee Rich who used to be one of the owners of Lorimar, which is a hugely successful television company responsible for "Dallas," etc. Lee Rich once offered me a huge amount of money to star in a television series for him. I declined. For years I've been offered my own television series, and I've chosen not to do it. Sometimes when you've taken a position for a long time as I have on not doing a television series—you can forget why you took the position. In my case I was working on Broadway and in movies and I told myself early on it was less desirable to be in a series than in the movies— I'm not 100 percent sure why, but that's been my position. That could change someday if my desire to work in the East and not travel would be stronger than my preference for movies over television. I hope I've saved enough money not to have to work anymore before that happens, as the idea of working in a medium where you could have millions of viewers and be unsuccessful is not particularly enticing. That—and all the preemptions, schedule changing and week to week waiting to see the ratings have kept me from television.

Anyway, Lee Rich, formerly of Lorimar, is sitting behind me. My seat can spin around, but I'm going to control myself from spinning and giving him what we used to call "a piece of my mind." The reason I'm considering spinning is years ago after I declined to star in a television series for him he called and asked me to come to his office to meet with him.

I said, "Lee, I'm not interested in doing TV."

He said, "No, this isn't about TV. I have a number of things I want to discuss with you."

Well, being a writer of screenplays, I'm in a perpetual state of looking for financing—so I drove about an hour to his office. When I got there he again asked me about doing a TV show. I said I really wasn't interested. He said he just wanted to hear me say it in person. (Since he had offered me a lot of money, he couldn't believe I really would turn it down. Business people think that way.) When I tried to interest him in financing one of my screenplays (they were also a movie company) it was clear he'd asked me to drive the hour solely for the TV thing, even though he'd denied it on the phone. I let it go then, but now I'm considering a belated confrontation. I probably won't do it, because I've had some champagne and I'm not feeling all that confrontational. Champagne makes me nicer, not rougher. It almost never comes up—but I'm one of the few people I know who doesn't mind a confrontation. I find them interesting, dramatic and doubtless material for a future book. Besides, if I was going to confront I should have done it then and not wait years and then spin on a guy.

Another thing about flying today is they now provide telephones, so you could be sitting there, in your God-knows-what-it-cost seat, basically listening to someone talking on the telephone, which is exactly what I'm doing while trying to write this. This guy in front of me (facing me) is buying some pet food company or something, and Lee is behind me on the phone wheeling and dealing. It appears that more passengers in first class and royal grand supreme or whatever they call it are telephone users, so all this luxury has its disadvantages too.

Spending Nine Years on a Movie That Shouldn't Have Been Made

When people ask is there any particular part I'd like to play, I can never think of anything. My take on the whole entertainment world is too much of what goes on isn't that entertaining. How about boring? I'm not saying there aren't wonderful things all over the place—I'm just saying too much is plain old boring—too slow—too uneventful. I get the feeling too many people are working too subjectively—too much in their own heads without any consideration of the basic question—Will an audience be interested in this? I know about this because I've been guilty of it myself. I spent considerable time over a nine-year period trying to get a movie made I wrote which ended up being called *Movers and Shakers*. It never should have been made. It wasn't worth the enormous effort, but I didn't know that at the time. I will say this: it made me a hell of a lot better screenwriter, as I learned plenty. The basic thing wrong with the movie was nothing happened. A number of people, particularly Peter Falk, pointed this out to me, but I just persisted with, "That's the point. People are trying to make a great movie about love and can't because they have no love in their lives and don't know much about it." If I were debating myself on it today, I'd say that's a passably interesting point for a short story, not a whole big movie. In the movies, trust me, something has to happen. For the millions of dollars it takes to make a movie, something *better* happen.

Today it amazes me that I got this thing on. I'm not saying it wasn't funny because to me and many others it was, but you really do need a story with some tension and twists and turns. I really got it on because the roles were great and we made it really inexpensively for about 3.5 million dollars. Most everyone in it was a friend of mine and worked for the least amount possible—Steve Martin, Gilda Radner, Penny Marshall, among others. The funniest scene in it is when a group of us—Walter Matthau, Gilda, Bill Macy and I—go in a big limo to see the legendary screen lover Fabio Longio, played by Steve Martin, made up to look like a spry eighty. The idea is Fabio is going to give us his counsel on love in the movies. As we head out in the limo, the dialogue went something like this.

MATTHAU

How old a man is Fabio?

MACY

He's got to be in his eighties.
  (a pause; he looks around; in a whisper)
Stays in this limo?

Everyone nods.

MACY

I think he's had his face sanded or something.

When we get to Fabio's mansion, he welcomes us. (Steve Martin contributed great comedy lines to this sequence.) He ushers us into his ornate living room and holds forth.

STEVE
  (in referring to one of his oldies)
That was the first movie in Technicolor.

MATTHAU

Really? I wasn't aware of that.

STEVE
(thinks a moment)
Second, actually.

He then goes to the mantelpiece and really becomes the authority on love, when from upstairs we hear a woman screaming in a shrewish voice. It is Penny Marshall.

PENNY
Fabio! Get your ass up here!

At first Steve and all of us pretend not to hear it, but finally it gets so loud, the meeting comes to an abrupt end, and we all hurriedly leave. It's a hilarious sequence and there are several others. Gary Franklin, the L.A. television critic who started the 1–10 rating system, gave it a 10. He also got a ton of mail from his viewers who rushed to see it. They complained (surprise) nothing happened!

So I've been as guilty of being too subjective as the next guy, but now I keep a keen eye out for the issue.

Who's in Charge?

I learned something else that was invaluable to me from *Movers and Shakers*. There must always be one person in charge of anything, and it must be clear who that person is. I partnered on this picture with a man named Bill Asher, who had directed me earlier in the production of *Charley's Aunt* I did for cable.

To digress for a moment. There was a bit during that experience that is one of my favorite moments in my whole career. *Charley's Aunt* is almost a hundred years old, and although we had a good cast, the first ten minutes or so of the play can be a little deadly—three Oxford undergraduates running around trying to figure out what to do about getting a chaperone as the girls are coming to tea. The idea is hatched that one of us—

me—dresses up like my aunt Donna Lucia D'Alvadorez. Here's the moment I love, and it's not onstage, but backstage. I come off to change into the woman's dress, but before I do I'd always look at the stagehands or whomever was standing back there and say, "God, we're dying out there. We need someone to dress up like a woman or something!" Then I'd spot the dress and as though I'd just gotten the idea, I'd say, *"Hand me that dress!"* The people who didn't know I did this bit regularly were startled and wondered what was happening. I loved doing that, even though most everyone had seen me do it before. That was also one of the several times I worked with the great character actor Vince Gardenia, who at this writing has recently passed away. Vince played Mr. Spettigue, who was ardently pursuing my Donna Lucia. It is times like that, working with Vince, that it's heaven to be an actor.

MR. SPETTIGUE
May I hope, Donna Lucia?

DONNA LUCIA
No, don't hope! I shouldn't hope if I were you!

Bill Asher is a veteran TV producer and director as well as a director of some of those early beach blanket movies with Annette Funicello and Frankie Avalon. To some we seemed like an unlikely pair coming from such different worlds, but I really like and admire Bill. He knows what he's doing, and certainly I would have had no idea how to make *Movers and Shakers* at the price we made it—so Bill became the co-producer and director after I had been shopping the project for about five years. Because I got the money and wrote the script and got my star friends to work for scale (as Bill and I did as well), Bill acknowledged that it was my project and he was there to help me. This worked remarkably well through preproduction and the actual filming. It wasn't until we got into the editing room that the trouble started. Now we weren't dealing with my star friends or shooting my script or thinking about who got the money to make it. (At least Bill wasn't.) Now we were jointly editing a picture Bill had shot and little by little the battle over turf started. I don't believe Bill has ever not been in charge, certainly in many years, and subconsciously it all caught up with him. He could no longer let me make all the final decisions or let me resolve whatever editing issue there was. Nothing was said, but for me you could have cut the air with a knife. One morning when Bill arrived kicking the door open and shouting, "Where's Grodin?" I knew it was time to have a chat.

We had been having our problems with the studio, and I asked Bill to join me on the second floor walkway outside the editing room. I said, "Bill, my biggest problem on this movie isn't MGM. It's you." Bill looked at me, genuinely surprised. He just listened, as I pointed out what I thought was happening. I said I thought none of it was deliberate—I just thought that he was in an untenable position, and he was "acting out."

Bill, to his credit, never blinked an eye and took full responsibility. He said, "Chuck, I love you. This has always been your project, and I'm here to help you."

Things got better after that, but the couple of weeks that led up to that confrontation were as uncomfortable a time as I've ever experienced in my professional life. It has taught me to never again have any doubt over who's in charge, and frankly, in most cases, I prefer it not be me. There are so many people responsible for making a piece of work that I would rather concentrate on finding ways to make it entertaining rather than protecting my turf, which is what often happens. Of course, if I were the producer, director, writer, star—I'd have to be in charge, but if I ever do that, it will be because that's what was necessary to get a project on.

Getting a director for a movie appears to be one of the more difficult tasks in show business. There are plenty of directors you can get, but generally the people putting up the money don't want them. They want the ones you can't get. That's a list of about ten directors who need a special room to stack all the scripts sent to them. One of the things wrong with these directors is they show serious interest in a number of projects—confusing a lot of people. When I'm asked to do something I say "yes" or "no" quickly. I don't have anyone read it. I just know. Period. That's not to say I'm right. It's just not a long process. I believe people who send you something that's already financed deserve a quick answer. Also I'm so impressed to see financed stuff, I'm always curious to see what it is—knowing how hard it is to get to that stage.

I once had a head of production of a studio tell me if I could get any one of five directors on a list he had he'd make a movie I'd written. I sent it to one of their guys. He wanted to do it, but the head of production's bosses wouldn't O.K. him. Clearly a lot more studio people can say "no" than can say "yes."

In movies where I am almost always an actor and sometimes the writer—I have a meeting with the director before we begin. I tell him I may have ideas for this or that. I make it very clear that as far as I'm concerned the director is in charge. All I want is for him to hear what I'm suggesting. If he or she agrees with me—great. If not, I will act the same way, as if the director *did* agree. In other words, I will never pout or sulk, because I hate that, and I'll never act unpleasantly if I don't get what I want. My experience is almost all of the time, if something really is a good idea—the director will embrace it. If it isn't, he won't. I've never felt artistic tension with a director aside from the one episode in the editing room with Bill.

The only additional proviso I should add is—I do not ever want to say something in a movie that's intended to be amusing that I don't believe is. This has almost never come up—maybe once or twice, that's it—and I have had an agreement with the director I won't be asked to say it. In those rare instances, I'll suggest an alternative, and if the director doesn't prefer that, we keep at it together to come up with something until we're both satisfied. It's extremely rare, but the understanding is important and should be taken care of long before filming.

With the exception of a few instances where I've seen deep insensitivity and abuse, my empathy on a movie lies with the director. There's no question he or she has the hardest job, works the longest hours, and has the most responsibility. For the good of everyone, the director should be approached with an understanding of this.

Another time I was in the middle of a painful situation where who was in charge wasn't clear was on *The Incredible Shrinking Woman*. This was a Lily Tomlin/Jane Wagner project. Jane was Lily's partner and the writer. Then Joel Schumacher came in to direct. It was never really clear who was in charge, and I don't believe it ever got defined, causing a lot of stress for Lily, Jane and Joel. There are thousands of decisions on a movie, and I got the impression Joel thought it was all up to him. It's certainly understandable why he would have thought that, since that usually is the case, but Joel was a new director and Lily was an established star, and it was her project. I doubt they ever had a meeting to thrash this out, and it was unfortunate. From where I sat it was a subtle but ongoing tug of war. Joel, in an effort to control what he saw as his terrain, decreed that no actors be allowed to come to see dailies (the film that was shot the day before). This was in a time where I used to go. I haven't wanted to in years now, as it adds at least an hour onto an already too long day. I assume an exception was made for Lily, as it was her project, but Joel was adamant I not go. I got him to agree to let me come once just to see what it all looked like. After one viewing I told Joel I thought the film was shot in too soft focus. He said there would be a lot of special photography later, and he didn't want it to look too different from the regular photography. Because of that one comment, I think he was thrilled I agreed not to come back. When the picture was released one criticism often heard was that it was shot in too soft focus.

My empathy during this picture was really for Lily, who is a friend of mine, but ultimately I felt for Joel as well. Lily, Jane and Joel brought such an enormous effort to the project as actors, writers and directors generally do, that it's just sad they didn't work out whatever differences they could before we started, and most importantly decide on who was in charge and how all that would work.

I even applied that question when my wife and I were looking for a decorator to work on an apartment we'd bought. I put the question this way at a meeting with a middle-aged, well-known decorator. "What happens when there's a disagreement?" Unless you've dealt with a decorator, you might ask why is that question necessary? The decorator answered something like this. "I had a client who bought an end table while I was away in Europe. I thought it was awful, but I let him keep it." (As you can imagine, he didn't become our decorator.)

Mike Ovitz and Sue Mengers

In the agency world, at this writing, CAA is considered tops—I became a client of theirs about seven years ago. Shortly after I joined them they said, "Come over and meet everyone." I said, "O.K., who would I meet?" They told me the names of a lot of their agents. I said I'd like to say "hello" to Mike Ovitz, who then and now is considered the most powerful agent in show business. I was told, "Mike won't really have time to meet." I said I understood he wouldn't be personally representing me, I just wanted to say "hello." I was told, "He has such a busy day that it's up to us to . . . " I didn't really hear the rest of it, and pretty much then and there knew I'd be at CAA a short time unless that stopped feeling offensive. I left after a few months. When I told this story to my friend Peter Falk, he stared at the floor for such a long time I thought he was considering buying my rug. Finally he looked up and said in wonder, "They wouldn't let you meet the agent?!" Later another agent at CAA told me if Mike Ovitz had known of my request, he would have been happy to meet me, and the person who said Mike was too busy was just being overzealous, but by then it was too late.

Years earlier when I was about to go to six cities to promote *The Heartbreak Kid*, I asked to meet Gordon Stulberg, the president of 20th Century Fox, who was releasing the picture. Some friends felt that was an inappropriate request, again because he was such a busy man, but I felt I should be able to meet the head of the company I'm traveling around the country for. Gordon was very welcoming and invited me to lunch with all his top film executives. They outlined plans for me to do several pictures for them, but when the first one, *11 Harrowhouse*, didn't make money, I never heard from them again. Not that I was shocked.

My most bizarre encounter with an agent came with the semilegendary Sue Mengers, who over the years has represented some of Hollywood's biggest stars. I had been signed by a large agency where she was a top executive. She opened our meeting by telling me what a big fan of mine she was and how thrilled she was to be representing me. She then quickly went on to say that since Hollywood was making fewer pictures it was unlikely I'd be working much. Not only that, but in regard to some of the pictures I had already starred in—I remember her mentioning *Seems Like Old Times*, she said that if they did that today a bigger star than me would play my role. She mentioned her client Michael Caine. I listened to her analysis, somewhat stunned. The next day I asked to see her again and rebutted just about everything she had said. Regarding *Seems Like Old Times*, I said Neil Simon wrote the role for me and basically, point by point, showed why I didn't share her pessimism. It was her turn to be stunned. She said, "God, what must you be like to live with?" Actually, I promise you, I'm not bad because I have a supportive wife, not a destructive one. The thing about people in some kind of authority telling you exactly how everything is, is that they are often wrong. Their sureness of tone intimidates a lot of people, but if I had reacted that way to negativity expressed with certainty—I would have been out of show business before I was twenty. Clearly, as I mentioned earlier, I'm not that big on people who present themselves as the ultimate authorities without just a tiny hint that they could be wrong.

Temperamental Artists

Thankfully it seems there is much less tolerance now for the tyrannical director as well as for the difficult actor. A little difficulty goes a long way. I once had a makeup man who had the temperament of a high-strung opera singer, which, as I understand it, is about as high-strung as you can get. This guy bristled if you ever asked anything. Everything was taken as a personal criticism. I lived with it, because he was really talented and conscientious, but one day I was compelled to ask if a five o'clock shadow he had put on me would match one he put on a few weeks earlier in the filming when it was supposed to be the same day in the picture. It looked too something to me. He bristled and said it was fine. I wasn't so sure, and frankly I was getting a little tired of the bristling. There are usually still photographs to double-check these issues of matching, but no one could find one. I asked the director for his judgment on it, knowing it would probably cause my makeup man to blow, but I didn't care. I didn't want to be held hostage to his moods, and I wanted the director to be aware it was in question. You can't appear in the same sequence with a dark beard in one part of it and a lighter one a little later. The makeup man's reaction to being questioned by the director was to tell me he'd be leaving by the end of the day. We'd been together for months, but now it was my turn to more than bristle. I went over and asked the director to get the guy off the movie, immediately. I had no choice. I can't work angry, and the guy had gotten to me. He was gone within the hour, a victim of his own temperament, which was already known to too many people. It was really a shame, because he is a talented makeup artist. I saw him a couple of years later, and we were glad to see each other. It hadn't hurt that I'd sent him a gift when the picture finished to show no hard feelings.

A similar thing happened on the Broadway show *Same Time Next Year*. Two people helping me never spoke to each other in my presence. Because it was during times I needed to concentrate I thought they were incredibly sensitive, until I realized they didn't speak to each other *out* of my presence. One had to go. It's not always who you think it's going to be who's temperamental.

The Still Photographer

The still photographs, or I should say the still photographer, has been one of the few banes of my existence while working in movies. These guys (with one exception, I've only seen men in this job) can be the nicest people in the world, but I often seem to be the actor who has the biggest problem with them, although I know several actors who won't even let them on the set. This is going to sound odd, considering what I do for a living, but I really don't like to have my picture taken. Anyone looking at family albums from my childhood might think the folks had one son, not two. Having my picture taken always strikes me as vain. "Hey, look at me over here standing by this camel," or "Hey, look at me" anywhere. I'm obviously asking people to look at me when I'm performing, but I'm doing something in an effort to entertain. That's O.K. with me. I'm actually amazingly comfortable with that, but look at me standing here or sitting there seems weird. My still photographer colleagues would argue that they, for the most part, are photographing me in scenes from the movie used later for promotional purposes. I understand that. I'm fine with that. The problem is *when* are they photographing? Anytime at all is O.K. with me except when we are actually shooting a scene. That means all through rehearsal of a scene is fine or I even offer to do it "full out" after we've filmed it. My problem is I don't like to see any movement around a camera when filming. Normal necessary movement by people responsible for getting this all on film is one thing, but an extra person moving around with a camera is a distraction, probably more so because I know it's not necessary to the making of a movie. An actor's concentration is essential, and some actors will regularly ask that *anyone* not absolutely necessary to the filming be kept off the set. I mean visitors of any kind. I know there are still photographers as well as publicity people who work for studios who would dispute something in what I've said, but no one ever said, "I heard it's a lousy movie, but the stills are great—let's go see it." If I had anything at all to do with a movie other than acting, and I have, I would do *whatever* necessary to keep the people in front of the camera relaxed and untroubled . . . which reminds me of an exchange I once had with a big movie star friend of mine. I said, "I'm very uncomfortable if I feel anyone on a set is unhappy with me. I feel a definitely distracting vibe." My friend said, "It doesn't bother me at all what anyone is feeling, because I already assume everyone hates me."

I've really only had two bad experiences with still photographers. The rest of the times, we've worked it out, I think, to everyone's satisfaction. The first bad one unfortunately lasted a whole picture, which would really be impossible today, because now having been burned twice I'd get to a strangling mode quicker. It was only my second leading role—in a picture called *11 Harrowhouse*. The leading lady was Candy Bergen, who had been a model, so she was really comfortable with being endlessly photographed. We were filming in London and this English still photographer, whose name I've long since blocked, stayed closer to me than Candy, with whom I had bed scenes. I was also the writer on the picture, so I had a lot on my mind. All these guys like to get shots of the actors talking to the director or each other, or looking off into space, or looking down or up or nowhere, but this guy could never get enough. It felt like he was recording every glance for posterity. He was also shooting like a maniac during filming. He was a little energetic guy, so he could really bop around. Snap, snap, click, snap, click, click—I'm talking endlessly every day for months. I tried everything to back him off. I took him to lunch and explained it was distracting. I offered to do whatever he wanted *after* the scene was filmed. He felt it wouldn't be the same, and he had a job to do. Thinking of it now I really should have drowned him in his soup—just pushed his face right down into the split-pea and held it there. I know that doesn't sound like me, but then I've never run into anyone so determined to do whatever he wanted no matter *what* he made me feel like. The director tried to get him to back off, but he was stopped by the producer, the dreaded Elliot Kastner.

I can't bring myself to revisit Elliot Kastner here, as I visited him about as much as I could take in my first book. Suffice to say, he's the only person I've ever met in an entire career I would sincerely describe as dreaded or dreadful—whichever. Okay, *one* new Elliot Kastner anecdote. This restaurant I frequent in L.A., Mateo's, has a dish that is a favorite of a lot of people, called Chicken Beckerman. Mateo's has Hollywood names after their dishes. Sidney Beckerman is a producer who somehow got his name on Mateo's top dish—maybe because he thought up the dish or always ordered it—something! Somehow Elliot Kastner, knowing how popular it was, got control of the dish and had the name changed from Chicken Beckerman to Chicken Kastner. This went on for a couple of years—then it went back to Chicken Beckerman. Either people stopped ordering it with Elliot Kastner's name on it (I did) or Sidney Beckerman wrestled it back in a behind-the-scenes kitchen fight. Anyway, lovely Elliot, of course, sided with the still photographer in my dispute, because that was truly the destructive position to take, and whether he knew it or not, that was Elliot's game.

The situation was never resolved. The guy kept popping away. I think, as I flew the hell out of there at the end of the shoot, he was even taking some shots of the plane taking off. Ironically, I saw him again when I was over in Marrakesh about twelve years later shooting *Ishtar*. He looked up and our eyes met, and he definitely had an "I hope he doesn't recognize me" look on his face. Because the people in charge of that picture were all friends of mine I could have had him tossed off the picture for old time's sake, but he kept his distance from me. I didn't even see him popping much when I had all my scenes with Dustin. Maybe he'd already been backed off by Dustin and Warren, because I'm sure those guys would have liked it even less than I did. Actually, as I recall we didn't even have a still photographer on *Heaven Can Wait*, where Warren was in charge. The picture managed to be a success somehow, anyway. Obviously if I ever want to write an essay, "Charles Grodin—the bitter side," this is my subject. Really because it interferes with the work, and I do get touchy if anything ever does that. Luckily, it rarely comes up. Another time it did was with another still photographer. This guy was on *Midnight Run*. He was sufficiently persistent that I had to have another one of those sit-down meetings. Two in twenty-five years isn't bad. Again I only requested he not pop while we were filming and even then I'm fine if it's a wide-open sequence—the rapids, etc. I told him I didn't want to think about it, I didn't want to check out his whereabouts just before the director calls, "Action." I really wanted to be thinking about other things. This guy was very understanding—an all-around sensitive response. We shook hands on it, and he even looked me deep in the eyes as we did.

Not that much later we were shooting the last scene of the movie. It's the scene where De Niro lets me go at the very end. Naturally I'm supposed to feel exhilarated, thrilled—stuff like that. Hopefully I don't need to say this, but I just don't smack some exhilarated look on my face for these occasions. Good actors are like emotional athletes. You have to actually tap into some real positive "light yourself up stuff" to deliver a scene like that. I was in the middle of lighting up in the first take when I looked around to see if anyone's watching when I take my money belt off to give some to Bob, and I see this guy clicking away, breaking our hand-shaking, look-deep-in-the eyes agree-ment. All exhilaration left to be replaced by . . . something less than exhilaration. I went over to the guy, and told him breaking a trust is no small thing—and a couple of other things. I had to walk around for a while to be able to get back to the scene. Bob De Niro actually helped considerably by telling me various things that had aggravated him on sets over the years. Ironically none of the things that bothered him had bothered me. I enjoyed hearing his stuff and, surprisingly, soon was O.K. Of course I couldn't work with that still guy again or the English guy I should have drowned.

The Movie Schedule

It gets clearer and clearer to me that the overall area where I have difficulty being friendly is when I feel someone is messing with my ability to do my best work. The twelve-to-fourteen-hour movie day was designed obviously to pack as much work as pos-sible into a day and limit the amount of months it takes to make a movie. In my experience the average movie is about three months long. If we worked from nine to five it would probably be four months long. The people who know about these things obvi-ously have calculated they are better off paying overtime than making a three-month schedule four months. Overtime doesn't go to the actors, by the way, but to most everyone else, which is real-ly O.K., since generally the actors are the highest paid. The actors' protection comes from something called turnaround. That means you are given twelve hours between the time you are released from a set to when you are asked to show up the next day. That in-cludes travel time. That's not too bad if you live next door to the studio or wherever you're working, but on average I'd say there's about an hour of home and back travel time, which gives you eleven hours to go home and try to do life stuff. Even if you don't need much time to sleep and eat and bathe, you're still not exact-ly going to write a book about your life between movie calls.

Scheduling for economic reasons is a must, as movies are already exorbitantly expensive. The problem with all of this is that it eventually wears out all involved. By the end of a movie the hundreds of people on it usually look hollow-eyed and shell-shocked. While everyone needs to be sharp, you really need to keep a special eye on those in front of the camera, and I say this as someone who's been worn out on both sides of cameras. To be sharp at the end of a long day I often need to go to bed earlier than my five-year-old son.

Nobody is allowed to get sick in show business. At least, that's the feeling. In all the hundreds of show business projects I've been involved in, I can count on one hand the times anyone missed anything, and I wouldn't use all my fingers.

I missed a performance during the run of the play *Same Time Next Year* because my back was in spasm. I could stand, but not move or sit. I actually played one performance that way, and the audience seemed to enjoy the show just as much—so much for inventive staging. At intermission of the performance I missed, my co-star Ellen Burstyn called me at home and in a threatening voice, told me I better be back for the next performance. This was a two-character play, and it was very difficult for an understudy to step in and blend with Ellen, with whom he'd never rehearsed. This was eighteen years ago, and because of a religious commitment to back exercises, I've never had a problem since.

In the movies it seems everyone is always sick. It's a given, because of the schedule, but it never enters anyone's mind not to show up. In a dark way it struck me as a kind of funny on *Heart and Souls*. There were bad colds everywhere, the director, the actors, the makeup people, the crew. A young actor in the picture, Tom Sizemore, stared at me the other night and said, "I'm really sick." I nodded sympathetically, but neither of us for a second thought, "Gee, Tom should go home and rest," the type of suggestion that would seem normal in most situations.

Show business quite simply is not most situations. The cinematographer on *Movers and Shakers* tried to quit after he got a cold, and we all looked at him as if he were insane. He actually missed a couple of days, which is truly unheard of. There is insurance in dire situations, but somehow no one wants to get near it. The feeling is anyone missing anything for any reason kind of gets a scarlet letter attached to them. I'm not sure why, but knock wood, I rarely have gotten sick, not even a cold. I also am probably the only one on this movie now shooting in San Francisco walking around with thermal underwear and drinking liquids and taking vitamin C, as *though* I were sick. I treat movie schedules with necessary respect. Years ago the director George Roy Hill told me he went into physical training prior to starting a movie. I had no idea what he meant. I do now. Making movies is a test of your endurance, and unless you realize that, you'll pay the price of working while sick seventy hours a week. Then the seventy feels like a hundred and forty. I'm going to take a break now and have some fluids.

A way to combat all this is to try not to be called earlier than you're needed. One of the assistant director's major responsibilities is to make sure a crew is never waiting for an actor to be ready, so naturally he will tend to err on the side of keeping the actor waiting—not the crew. It's logical, but it can be destructive to the film's chances for success. It's the bright assistant director who can find that middle ground for calling an actor so the crew doesn't wait, but where the actor isn't worn out after weeks of fourteen-hour days. At the end of the first day of shooting on the picture *Clifford*, I had the following exchange with the production manager over what seemed to me to be an unnecessarily early call for the next day.

P.M.
You wanted to see me?

ME
Yeah, I was wondering about tomorrow's call.

214

P.M.

Yes?

ME

I take these calls seriously. I actually come exactly when I'm asked to.

P.M.

Good.

ME

I'm afraid I'll be here alone.

P.M.

You won't be here alone. I'll be here.

ME

That's nice, but we don't have much business together.

P.M.

No, we don't.

ME

I'm happy to be here, if I'll be doing something, but I . . .

P.M.

You'll be doing something.

ME

Well, my experience on these kinds of calls is nothing really happens until about a half an hour later. I mean, it will be dark out. The crew will just be arriving, and I like to be fresh enough to come up with ideas twelve hours later. I mean, that's what I do.

P.M.

We're aware of that. That's why we hired you.

ME

Well, you can help me if you call me when you need me.

P.M.

We have.

ME

You'll need me to come up with ideas as dawn breaks?

P.M.

That's right. We're counting on you.

ME
(dubiously)

Uh huh.

P.M.
(pointedly)

So, we'll see you when you were called.

ME

Sure.

And they did. Of course nothing happened until about forty-five minutes later and by seven o'clock, some thirteen hours later, the only idea I could come up with was to go home.

This misguided production manager also thought it was O.K. to have Mary Steenburgen play a big love scene around 2 A.M. after she'd been up for about seventeen hours. There is a human element here, and people who consider it get the best out of the performers. On *Clifford* there was way too much energy expended by all on resentment.

I've just come from the movie set where someone told me that the Screen Actors Guild has negotiated a new agreement to allow the movie companies to reduce turnaround time from twelve hours to ten hours once every four days if they're filming in daylight. This must have been agreed to by someone who doesn't actually work in movies. It reminds me of a joke I heard Franklin Ajaye, a comedian I like a lot, tell years ago. It was during Jimmy Carter's presidency when he was asking everyone to turn their thermostats down. Franklin built the piece to the punch line, "Why have a house?" If the location is far enough from where you live—"why go home?" I feel self-conscious going on about this, because a lot of people would trade places with us who make movies, but it is strange. This is just one of the reasons show business people have a harder time having a successful personal life. The other is that most of us are nuts.

The Academy Awards

The only time I attended the Academy Awards was in 1972. It was the year of *The Heartbreak Kid*. I wasn't nominated, but my co-stars Jeannie Berlin and Eddie Albert were, and I was invited. At the party afterward I was sitting with the producer, Edgar Scherick, a flamboyant likable guy who used to run ABC or something like that. Edgar spotted Diana Ross, who had been nominated for *Lady Sings the Blues*, and said to me, "Now *that's* a star." It was a little peculiar to say to me at that moment, because there was a lot of talk I might be nominated and I wasn't, and well . . . you get it. Anyway, I looked over at Diana. She leaped out of her chair when she saw me, came running over and really carried on about what a big fan of mine she was while Edgar Scherick watched. I've always liked Diana Ross.

As I've said, I've won a few awards and it's always nice to get them, but to call all of that an inexact science would be a gross overstatement. It's almost impossible to distinguish how much the role had to do with it. I've always felt awards should go to actors who do outstanding jobs in mediocre roles, but movies with mediocre roles aren't seen all that much—for Academy consideration anyway.

Of course, the Academy Awards are an invaluable promotional device, but I was really struck by how silly this all can get when I realized that among the nominees for best supporting actor this year were David Paymer playing an old Jewish man and Jaye Davidson playing a young woman. Who was best?! At what?! Is the question whether David played an old man better than Jaye played a young woman? What a question!—not to mention Jack Nicholson, Al Pacino, and Gene Hackman and what they did. Who was best? The question makes about as much sense as best food. The nominees are Steak, Lamb Chops, Fish, Veal and Chicken, and the winner is . . . *Steak*!, or how about fruit? The nominees are Apples, Oranges, Pears, Cantaloupe and Grapes, and the winner is . . . *Grapes*! Give me a break. I promise if I'm ever nominated, I'll really try not to mention any of this, but just smile and wave.

I actually won a best actor award at some international film festival for *Midnight Run*. The studio notified me of this, but didn't seem all that excited about it. I guess because the festival was in what used to be called Yugoslavia and I shared it with some Russian actor. To me an international film festival was still an international film festival—but nobody wanted to take an ad out or anything.

I Screen Test
for *Pretty Woman*

Generally, when I have a chance, I try to cushion myself from anything negative. With rare exceptions I've never wanted to know what my representatives are trying to do for me, as I'd rather not hear about all the people who don't want me. Once I got a call about a script the producers wanted Burt Reynolds for, but, "If they don't get him they might be interested in you—do you want to read it?"

"No," I said quickly. I figured if it came to the point where Burt said no, and they definitely wanted me, of course I'd read it—but who had to go looking for rejection? If I ever stopped to think of all the people who obviously have preferred to have— you name them—it might cut into my basic optimism.

There was an exception to this when I was asked to screen test for the Richard Gere role in *Pretty Woman*. They had spent a long time looking for a leading man. My name had been mentioned, but some of the people involved felt, while I could be funny in the role, they didn't see me as a sexy leading man.

However, the casting director, Dianne Crittenden, an old friend of mine, assured the people at Disney Studios, "I know Chuck socially, and believe me, he's a very sexy man." I wouldn't have described myself that way, but I didn't send them a cable saying, "She's wrong. I'm not!" The last time I had screen tested for anything was *The Heartbreak Kid*, almost twenty years earlier, but this was clearly an opportunity to present myself more as a leading man, so I agreed to fly out and test. The first thing I did, really the only thing I did in preparation, in the week I had, was to try to get a tan. There was going to be some bare-chest stuff. I couldn't frantically start pumping iron for a week— besides, I felt I was passable in that department. I wasn't going to win any contests, but I also felt no one would say, "Why doesn't Julia just kick him out of bed." No, a tan was all I could aspire to. I knew they could use body makeup, of course, but I thought psychologically it would be in my favor if I was really a tan guy—not a body makeup guy. It wasn't the time of year where I could step outside and get one—so I sought out a local tanning machine place. I lay in a coffinlike thing for four days and basically got two strips of red down my sides—so I let it go and opted for the body makeup.

The truth is when you are known for comedy it's almost a contradiction for people to think of you as sexy—although certainly people like Cary Grant were both. It's not a long list. As many supporters as I had at the studio—no one saw me as Cary Grant—including me. The night before the test, the director, Garry Marshall called and said, "Feel free to do or say anything you want tomorrow." Well, I'm a good improviser, but I don't improvise sexy. I went in and tested with the unknown Julia Roberts. We improvised some stuff in a seedy hotel room. She was dressed like a . . . well, she didn't have much on. We hit it off extremely well and did some really funny stuff. The studio decided to go with a straight, sexy leading man, Richard Gere (who hadn't tested), but soon after offered me a three-picture deal. There were some people there who preferred having the guy be funny—but the prevailing wisdom was to let Julia be the funny one, and she was. I thought they both did a great job in a picture that always made me a little uncomfortable for its glamorization of prostitution. If they had offered it to me, I would have lived with my discomfort—rationalizing the picture as a fairy tale or something. I've never really cared that much about revealing the sexy side of me or any particular side for that matter. If the picture is entertaining and I help it—that's plenty. Someday maybe I'll play a sexy leading man, but in the meantime I'll just rely on the Dianne Crittendens of the world to spread the word of my sex appeal.

Attorneys

I've been involved in one lawsuit which I wrote about in *How I Get Through Life*. One lawsuit, but more and more attorneys and contracts have entered my life. It's better than no contracts or attorneys, but with all due respect to the personal attractiveness of the parties involved, the subject matter gets to me pretty quickly. Attorneys are either paid a percentage of my salary, or charge by the hour. I've opted for the hour deal. Eventually, as the negotiations drag on for months, I have to ask the dreaded question: "What is it you guys are discussing?" Basically when I sign on to do a movie I'm interested in how long the movie is, and what I'm going to be paid. In recent years I have had the great good luck to have an assistant, Clay, who keeps popping into these pages, so we need to make Clay's deal too. To me that's not a long conversation. I mean, you can go back and forth for a while, but *months*?! When I peek in, I discover they are disputing ("they" being my attorney and the business affairs representative for the studio) things such as "Can they put my face on flatware and fleecewear?" Of course my first question was the obvious "What's flatware and fleecewear?" Most of you may know (I didn't) flat-ware is dishes, bowls, silverware. Fleecewear is sweatshirts and tee-shirts. This flatware/fleecewear dispute can go on longer than you'd ever imagine. I've never in my life seen my face in a bowl or on a sweatshirt, so why are we arguing about this at all? It's not that easy though. Any astute counselor will quickly point out, "It wasn't *Batman* the movie that made Jack Nicholson ridiculously rich, it was all those plates and shirts, or let's really broaden it here, because you never know—they could put your face on vari-ous weapons." "Hold it," I say, "what kinds of weapons?! We're talking about a family comedy here." This starts to get pretty com-plicated so let me put this in script form—it's easier to follow.

MY ATTORNEY
We may be talking about a family movie now, but we're establishing precedent. You could be doing something involving weapons next year, and besides, aren't you aware of the millions of *Beethoven* tee-shirts and sweatshirts all over the world right *now*?!

ME
That's not *my* face on them.

MY ATTORNEY
It could be next time.

ME
Me and a big dog's face together on a tee-shirt?

MY ATTORNEY
Or a dish.

ME

I think it works better with just the dog.

MY ATTORNEY

Maybe it does, but do you want them to have the *right* to put your face on that dish?

ME

Do you think it will really come up?

MY ATTORNEY

It could.

ME

A dish?

MY ATTORNEY

A dish, a mug, a shirt, a jacket—flatware and fleecewear—they want the right.

ME

I've been making movies for over twenty-five years, and I've never seen my face on any of this stuff.

MY ATTORNEY

You're more famous now. You might.

A silence as I mull it over.

ME

From what I understand, theoretically what you're saying, they could have the right to put my face in a dog bowl if they chose.

MY ATTORNEY

That's exactly right. How do you feel about that?

A long pause.

ME

What kind of money are we talking about here?

MY ATTORNEY

It's percentages. It depends on how much flatware or fleecewear they sell.

ME

Percentages?

MY ATTORNEY

Right. We're negotiating. I'll get you a fair deal. I'll let you know. You're O.K. with all this?

ME

What kind of money did Nicholson make?

MY ATTORNEY

I don't know. You hear fifty million.

A pause.

ME

Maybe it *does* work better with me and the dog in the bowl.

226

Of course, flatware and fleecewear are just the beginning of it. You then get into approvals and consultancy issues. I believe I have an approval over any photograph taken of me, and in the course of a movie the still photographer may take thousands of them—not just me alone necessarily—but thousands I'm in, and I have the right to stop use of them. I have to let them use some, but I can stop most of them. The problem is if I studied all these photographs I wouldn't have time to make the movie. It also says in these contracts that I have to agree to travel around the country to promote the movie, if I'm available. I've always balked at that one, because if the movie turns out not so hot, I'm really not going state to state beating the drum. As I've said, I won't knock it, but I'm not wearing some sandwich board up and down Broadway either. My attorney told me to forget about that one because no movie company wants some actor out there tub-thumping if he really doesn't like the movie. Their understandable nightmare is that you have a couple of drinks with an interviewer, and suddenly you're trashing some fifty-million-dollar venture.

By coincidence I got a phone call from my agent, in the middle of writing this, telling me my attorney had just sent over a letter with a list of about eighty comments on different items regarding a current contract, even though I've been filming for weeks. This isn't unusual. Some movie contracts are *never* signed, because the different sides never come to an agreement on every issue, and almost always they are never signed until the filming is virtually over, because it takes that long to agree. That means throughout the entire filming of a movie, negotiation is going on. I just always hope never to hear about it.

Here's the ultimate detachment. I looked at the points in dispute in the contract and thought to myself as I perused them for material for this section, "Hmm, that's not funny." I'm now going to read on, looking for funny areas of disagreement. It's either that or get all worked up over something, and I'll leave that to the lawyers. That's not to say that if my guy tells me what's being proposed is unfair I can't get worked up too, but I fervently hope it doesn't come to that. I like to be very selective over what I get worked up about.

I have to be honest with you. I did not read this twenty-five-page contract. I didn't actually even peruse it. The important stuff I already knew, so I just perused my attorney's comments in the margins and then perused what they referred to. Even perusing this stuff can be exhausting. This agreement is with Universal Pictures, and maybe I'm still naive and optimistic, but I actually see the other side as being friendly to me. I mean, they have been hiring me for years, so I'm naturally inclined toward them. It's not like I'm trying to work out some treaty with Saddam Hussein where you have to watch he doesn't slip in a troop movement clause or he changes the language on fly-zones. No, in this one I just spotted a few things that caught my eye, and I'm prepared to fight to the end over them. First we must insist, as we do in our counterproposal that my name not be used in endorsements for laxatives or feminine hygiene products no matter how much merchandizing money they toss my way, and also (I'm not making any of this up, I swear) they must not be able to use my performance in this picture to promote other pictures. It's in there on page number eleven that the studio reserves the right to "exhibit . . . separate from the picture . . . throughout the universe . . . in any and all mediums . . . by any means now in existence or hereafter discovered or conceived . . . *for all purposes.*" I didn't reprint the whole thing because I didn't want to cause you to have to lie down as I'm now doing. If you're already reading this in bed, you're probably O.K., but it really does mean that theoretically they could use a scene with me from this movie to promote something else—not even a movie necessarily—and theoretically it could be on Mars. Actually now that I think of it, if the fellas at Universal want to do that someday—let them do it. I'm calling my attorney off right now. What am I going to worry about, that some people on

Mars who see me in a scene from this movie to promote an opening of a custard stand up there in 2147 will think I was a jerk for letting them do it? I can't worry about it. Maybe a little—but it's way down my list.

That reminds me of the story of the time we were negotiating with the Soviet Union during the Cold War over the seating arrangement for this big conference. It looked like the whole thing was going to fall apart, because we wouldn't agree to let certain countries allied with Russia sit at the table. Louis Armstrong's take on the whole thing was, "They want to sit? Let 'em *sit!*"

Working with a Dog

It's ironic that the biggest commercial success I've ever had in my career came from playing opposite a dog in *Beethoven*. A friend of mine called me recently and asked if I had seen a review of *Beethoven* in *USA Today* when the cassette was released. I said I hadn't. My friend said the critic really attacked the movie and me. I asked my friend why he was telling me this. He said, "I thought you'd like to know." I told him I never call anyone with bad news unless it's one of those terrible situations when you have to, and I really like it when no one does it to me. One of the ways I keep going is not seeking out bad reviews. They have a way of staying with you more than the good ones. Since they're generally abusive and not constructive, they only hurt the morale. A critic once wrote about a movie I did, "If you want to know what it feels like to die sitting upright in a theatre seat, go see this movie." That was only constructive for those readers who actually *did* want to know what it felt like to die sitting upright in a theatre seat. Anyway, this *USA* guy really hated

Beethoven. His explanation for why it became a big hit was that parents were too lazy to take their kids to something good. He said it used every tried and true formula from other dog movies and was old hat. I wondered, "Old hat to whom?"—the children for whom it was made? I mean, I'm no authority on dog movies, but *I* didn't even know it was old hat, or using tried and true formulas for that matter. I just knew it was very well done and mightily entertained the audience for whom it was intended, and wasn't that the point? I mean, as any parent can tell you, kids can be bored, too. Then the critic got around to me. He said something like, "It should be noted that Charles Grodin, the star of *The Heartbreak Kid*, the masterpiece comedy of the seventies, is the star of this, and it's sad to see him reduced to ranting about dog drivel." The truth is, I was thrilled to be in a movie that entertained millions of children all over the world. I didn't see anything even remotely sad about the whole thing. Another critic, Jami Bernard of the *New York Post*, made her whole review an open letter to my agent. She wondered what on earth I was doing in this movie that has a scene where I get into bed thinking my wife is there and get licked on the back of my neck by a Saint Bernard, and enjoy it, until I see my wife come out of the bathroom. Clearly Jami, too, thought the whole thing was beneath me. I wrote her a letter saying my agent had been desperately trying to get me roles where Julia Roberts or Michelle Pfeiffer would lick my neck, but they preferred to lick Mel Gibson's or Nick Nolte's neck and this was the best I could do. Jami wrote me back that she'd lick my neck anytime, but I take that as an idle promise.

I did a joke on David Letterman about my negotiation for *Beethoven's 2nd*. I said I was having difficulty because Beethoven wanted all the money, and while the studio wanted me, they knew they absolutely couldn't make it without the dog. I went on to say that unlike Lassie or Rin-Tin-Tin, where a number of dogs were used, Beethoven is one of the only "dog actors." The only other dog I knew who was actually an actor was Mike, the dog from *Down and Out in Beverly Hills*. The audience listened to all of this as though I were completely serious. I went on: "Almost all dogs or other animals in movies respond to their trainers' commands, but Mike and Beethoven work only with the director who explains the scene to them and they involve themselves as actors. For example," I went on with a straight face, of course, "in the first *Beethoven* movie the director told Beethoven the little girl was drowning, mightily motivating him to dig out of his kennel and run a good distance, then leap into the water to save my daughter just in time." Now the audience is starting to chuckle. Letterman didn't laugh until I said, "Mike the dog was in Lee Strasberg's class with me. He didn't do scenes, but just audited." Letterman liked that. With his big gap-toothed grin, he said, "He didn't do scenes?"

So-called dog humor can be dicey, especially in print. I wrote a piece for a magazine about my experience working with Beethoven. I said the following things. See if you can tell which is true and which is a joke.

1. The trainer told me not to form any relationship at all with Beethoven so he would only respond to *his* commands. This created some immediate friction between the dog and me, because I paid no attention to him.

2. I had a huge motor home, and he was sometimes kept in a cage where he could see me going into my lavish digs, causing him to softly growl.

3. He was annoyed by the media's attention to me, since he had the title role, but when was the last time you saw an interview with a dog?

4. When they installed a satellite dish on top of my motor home to bring in New York sporting events he would begin to bark, so I asked that they move his cage so he wouldn't see what I had going for me.

5. When he was instructed to jump on me and knock me down, he always did it brilliantly on the first take. I, on the

other hand, did some of my best filmwork when I'd scream and yell at him.

6. The producers gave me a surprise birthday party, but Beethoven refused to come out of his cage, and when I offered him a piece of birthday cake as a peace offering—he looked me in the eye and pooped.

7. At a meeting with the Universal Pictures brass to discuss a sequel, he attended with his newly signed personal manager—glared at me throughout—and at one point from across the room sent a sneeze all over my pant leg. In spite of his manager's apologies, I saw a small smile on the dog's face.

The magazine editor, believing all of the above, asked if there were any tender moments between us. It was an awkward moment when I explained the only thing that was real was the trainer telling me not to form a relationship. I do have a satellite dish, but Beethoven doesn't seem to mind.

Happy Times

Fun on Midnight Run

When I was making *Midnight Run*, I spent an evening with Richie Foronjy, who played one of the hoodlums in the picture. Richie had actually spent a considerable amount of time in prison for hijacking. He earlier had told me the best thing to hijack, if you ever went into the field, was a trailer-truck filled with razor blades. "Can you imagine how many razor blades you could fit in a trailer-truck?" he reasoned. Anyway, one night we decided to see Frank Sinatra, who was appearing in Las Vegas where we were filming. A girlfriend of Richie's flew in from L.A. to join us.

I had seen Frank Sinatra once before at a benefit for St. Jude's Hospital. This is the hospital founded by Danny Thomas, and I was there with my friends Marlo and Phil. That night Sinatra was surrounded by three guys who stood by his table where he was seated with his party. Before anyone judge that, imagine spending hours every day, most of your life, with people coming up and extravagantly complimenting you. I wouldn't want it. It would be exhausting. If I were approached as much as Sinatra, to be honest, I might have a few guys around the table. Luckily I'm approached an appreciated amount. Anyway, that night Marlo told Phil to go over and say hello to Frank Sinatra, who was appearing, because he was a close friend of Danny's. Marlo wanted Phil to thank him for coming. Phil looked over at Sinatra's table and said, "He probably doesn't even know who I am."

Marlo said, "You were on the cover of *Newsweek*, for God's sake," but Phil surveyed the three bodyguards, shook his head and stayed where he was.

Later Sinatra performed, and he was great, but for some reason our table was far away from the stage. This night in Vegas, Richie, his date and I were sitting up close in a banquette. Earlier I'd told Richie I'd meet him in the lobby at eight. This was the only time I'd ever been out with him. At eight o'clock the phone rang in my suite. He said in his ex-con voice, "Charlie, it's eight o'clock and I'm down here in the lobby." I got down there by 8:01.

Anyway, we were sitting up close. Sinatra came out and gave the most affecting show I had ever seen in my life. He was seventy-two. He was so alive on the stage, in the moment, he made me feel like I was letting life pass by unnoticed. He sang memorably, and he was funny. He told a story about him and Dean Martin being pulled over for speeding. It was a nothing story, but you hung on every word—delighted. He talked to the audience as though we were all intimates, which is the way to do it. I was overwhelmed, mesmerized. There aren't enough words.

What happened in the cab coming home really put a capper on the evening. For some reason, I guess to make everyone most comfortable, Richie sat up front next to the cabdriver, and I sat in the back with his girlfriend. The cabdriver started to tell a story about some stripper he'd seen "who waved her tits around . . . " Richie shot the guy a look and said, "We're not talking about that!" The cabdriver I guess didn't hear him or didn't get it or something, because he went on again with "she waved her tits around . . . " Richie again jumped in with a louder *"we're not talking about that!"* The cabdriver heard it that time and stopped talking altogether. My wife and I regularly do Richie Foronjy saying, "We're not talking about that!" when it suits our purposes. In my house it always gets the job done and a laugh to boot.

Steve Martin and The Lonely Guy

Working with Steve Martin on *The Lonely Guy* movie was special, as was my first evening out with Steve. We had met at a restaurant in New York. I was with some people, and we were leaving when I saw Lorne Michaels from "Saturday Night Live" with Steve. I went over to say hello to Lorne and he introduced me to Steve. I put my hand affectionately on Steve's shoulder. Later, getting to know him, I realize he must have been cringing. Most of us don't like to be touched—except on special occasions, of course. Anyway, that evening Steve muttered that he had seen me do something on "The Tonight Show" that really made him laugh. It was a bit where I likened the sound of the shark's theme in *Jaws*, "Uh Huh, Uh Huh," to the sound of a woman being angry at you on the phone if you called to say you'd be late or worse. Steve really thought it was funny and then he muttered even more softly, "I wish you'd write something for me."

Three months later I was in L.A. I had an idea for a movie I could write for him and me. I called him, and we made a date to go to dinner. I went over to his house. He opened the door. I went in. Neither of us spoke. I looked around his foyer and living room. It was about a full minute of total silence before I said, "How did you get the money to pay for all of this?" We laughed through the whole evening. We never did the movie we were talking about, but he asked me to be in *The Lonely Guy* with him. Nobody wanted me in the movie but Steve—not the studio, not the director. They thought Steve and I were too alike, but he persisted and I did the picture. He went around telling everyone, including me, that he thought I was the best comedy actor in America. Sometimes when we're negotiating a fee for me to do a movie, I wonder if there's a way to get Steve to call the studio to make my case.

The first day of shooting, we were doing a scene in a kind of pickup bar. I added some lines of advice to him on how to have a better life.

ME

You ought to get yourself a dog. Dogs love people. You come home, the dog will jump up and down and go crazy that you're there.
(a pause)
Hitler had a dog.

A pause. Steve stares at me.

STEVE

Adolf Hitler?

ME

Yeah. That dog loved Hitler.

That was just the beginning of stuff I'd write for us—or he'd write for us or we'd write together. A lot of lonely guy scenes. Just all these scenes of us on a park bench or at a breakfast nook or on a roof somewhere. None of this was in the script. I didn't think the movie was good, but the stuff with Steve and me that we wrote was some of the best comedy I believe either of us has ever done. Because these scenes don't advance the plot about a dozen of them never made the picture. Here's one Steve wrote that never got in. We're sitting in his living room.

STEVE

I was at a party once when I look across the room, and my eyes meet with this girl. We

stare at each other, and it was just special
... you could tell. I get up from where I'm
sitting and I walk over to her—our eyes
never leaving each other. I get over there
and I look at her—and she was dead.

I barely react.

ME
(softly)

She was dead?

STEVE
(softly)

Yeah.

We just stare into space.

Working with Steve then, and when he did a day on my movie
Movers and Shakers, was outstanding. Because *The Lonely Guy*
didn't make money, no one has suggested we work together
again, but we should.

The Muppets

The Muppet organization has a reputation for being an outstanding group of people, and they are. I had worked with them a couple of times and became friends with Frank Oz, who, among
others, is Miss Piggy, and Jim Henson, who was Kermit. One
morning I received a lovely note from Jim saying how much he
enjoyed our working together on a special we had just done. It
was the only time Jim had written me, and the note was filled with
generosity. I was in rehearsal for a play I had written, and when I
got to work, the stage manager said that "Entertainment Tonight"
wanted to come down and interview me about Jim Henson.

238

I said, "It's really not a good time, in the middle of a rehearsal."

The stage manager looked at me a moment and said, "Do you know Mr. Henson has just died?"

After a moment of shock I surprised myself by throwing my briefcase against the wall. The circumstances behind Jim's death were heartbreaking. He evidently was in extraordinarily good health, but also never chose to see doctors. He got something that could have been dealt with in a short time, but by the time he felt it necessary to seek help it was too late. He actually was able to walk into the hospital but was gone within twenty-four hours from galloping pneumonia.

I primarily worked with Frank Oz/Miss Piggy when I did *The Great Muppet Caper* in London. One night we were filming outside a castle. It was a scene between Miss Piggy and me that Kermit enters into. For those of you who might not know how this is done, Frank and Jim and all the muppeteers often work lying flat on their backs with Miss Piggy or whomever manipulated by their hands inside them. The muppeteers watch the action on little monitors by the ground. As an actor, if I don't look down, which I choose not to do, I'm simply playing a scene with Miss Piggy, who appeared to be standing beside me. This night it started to drizzle so people came with umbrellas and held them over Miss Piggy and me to protect us while we waited for the light rain to stop.

As we stood there I looked at Miss Piggy and said, "Y'know, when Kermit comes in, I think it would be better if you delayed your line a little."

There was a long silence and then Miss Piggy said, "Well, I don't see it that way, but I'd be willing to try it."

Everyone roared with laughter. Frank Oz, who of course had said the line, told me later that was the first time anyone had engaged Miss Piggy in a discussion of acting.

When the picture opened, the ad featured a shot of Miss Piggy and me in a romantic attitude. The copy line read, "The

Man. The Pig. The Romance." I went on "The Tonight Show" with Johnny Carson to promote the movie. I had given Bob Dolce a photograph of Miss Piggy and me huddled together romantically in a booth in a nightclub. The idea was for Johnny to question me on just what had gone on between us. This was in a period before Johnny and I really got on the same wavelength. When Johnny picked up the photo I looked over at it and before he could get a question out, I snapped edgily, "Where'd you get that?!" For a moment Johnny thought I really was upset. Then he saw it was a bit and proceeded.

JOHNNY

What's the story behind you and Miss Piggy?

ME

(irritated)

I was told by your staff I wouldn't be asked about that!

JOHNNY

I don't want to upset you.

ME

It's not a comfortable area.

JOHNNY

I'm sorry.

ME

We're really just good friends.

JOHNNY

Uh huh.

A silence.

ME

She *did* end up with Kermit, you know. I'd really rather not get into it.

JOHNNY

I understand.

Working with the Muppets was memorable, and I'd love to work with them again, but with Jim gone it will be a bittersweet experience at best.

John Guillermin and Dino De Laurentiis

I have talked about working with John Guillermin, the director of *King Kong*, in my first book, and fun is not the first word that comes to mind in describing John, but riveting is, and riveting is, well . . . fun.

I vividly remember a group of us actors offshore in a small boat completely surrounded by man-made fog. Ed Lauter, an actor friend, was attempting to pilot the boat out of the fog, so John in the camera boat could film us emerging. The problem was it was impossible for Ed to know which way to turn to get us out. You don't want to breathe that stuff too long, but I'm afraid I found the whole thing funny. There's John in the clear screaming on a loudspeaker at Ed to come out of the fog, and poor Ed just going around in circles. John was getting angrier, until finally Ed screamed back, "For God's sake, John, I'm not a sailor, I'm an actor!"

Ed is a brilliant impersonator and does a right-on Burt Lancaster. Once he saw Burt in a play somewhere, went backstage, and re-created a speech from an old Lancaster movie for him. Mr. Lancaster didn't comment for one second on Ed's ability but only said, "Christ, that must have been over thirty years ago!"

John Guillermin, a wiry character with an English accent was born in France, but raised in England, and was an RAF pilot.

One day he was directing a scene with Jessica Lange, Jeff Bridges, and me on a huge freighter out at sea. At one point John asked Jessica to cross somewhere on a specific line of dialogue. Usually these things aren't an issue, but it did seem an extremely awkward place to be moving. Jessica looked uncertain a moment, then wondered if she might cross a moment earlier or later. It was all pretty innocuous, but John just walked away in a snit. We looked at each other—then at the assistant director, who suggested we take a break. Jeff and I drifted off, and Jess went to speak to John. After a few minutes she came back and said John was really upset and chose not to discuss it. I was the only one who seemed to have a comfortable relationship with John, so I went over to him. He was staring out to sea. He looked up when I approached and said, "Oh, hello, Chuck," as though he was surprised to see me out there on the high seas. I said, "What's the problem, John?" He said he had directed the greatest actors in England. I believe he mentioned directing Olivier, Gielgud, Richardson, and according to John none of them had ever questioned a direction of his. I said, "Oh, c'mon, John, that can't be possible." John thought a moment, then seemed to realize I was right. He immediately relaxed and we resumed filming. There's no question John was eccentric. He was also one of the most arresting figures I've ever seen. John and Dino De Laurentiis, the producer, seemed to have a running disagreement over things during the nine-month filming. It was a tragic coincidence that they both lost their sons in accidents a few years later. They were in their twenties.

Dino is a colorful figure. I was invited to his home once—a mansion up in Beverly Hills. There were many luminaries there. At one point I was standing alongside Roger Moore (James Bond) and looking at the director William Wyler and Dino. Dino and Mr. Wyler were about five three and Roger is my height, about six one. I guess I wasn't mesmerized by the conversation, because I decided to see if I could bend my knees sufficiently to get down to Dino's and Mr. Wyler's size without Roger noticing it. Roger is one of these super erect people who keeps his head held high. So he didn't notice when I, standing to his side, kept my head up but bent my knees, getting first to about five ten, then five seven and finally five three, on a level with the two shorter men who could see all this but were containing their laughter. Roger glanced at me once at five ten and I believe at five seven. At five three he got the joke and laughed, saying, "I *thought* you were a taller man." This certainly was an example of one of the times in my life when people might have referred to my "inappropriate humor." To this day I am guilty of it, but somehow can't resist what I hope is harmless fun.

One of my favorite bits was on the last day of shooting on *Heaven Can Wait*. We were filming at Chasen's Restaurant in Beverly Hills. When I completed my last shot of the picture, I went to the costume trailer, had the costume people load me up with all my suits, robes, etc. Warren Beatty and Buck Henry were standing outside the restaurant as I ran up the boulevard almost completely concealed by my whole movie wardrobe, with the costume people in pursuit.

Also on *Heaven Can Wait* I was amazed how many times I got looks of astonishment out of people when I'd glance at my watch in the middle of a big scene and say, "Geez, I'm going to have to leave. I have a dentist appointment in fifteen minutes." Needless to say, in the five-week to nine-month periods I've spent making movies, you make no appointments without clearance from several people—clearance by the way which is virtually impossible to get because of the uncertain nature of how long it takes to film something. The first day of *Catch 22* we showed up at 8 A.M. and went home at 5 P.M. without filming anything, as the cinematographer was still lighting the first shot. By the way, it was a magnificently lit picture. The waiting on *Clifford*, the picture I did with Marty Short, was not a problem because, quite simply, Marty Short was there. When he wasn't shouting out in a perfect Katharine Hepburn imitation, "Spence, put down that drink!" he was Bette Davis or Jerry Lewis screaming something. I also knew I could do anything and he would "feed" the story. One morning coming into the makeup trailer while it was still dark out—a really necessary time for comedy—I launched into a story about how I had once sat behind Ronald Reagan and Jessica Hahn on a flight, and the hard time they had given me for accidentally bumping their seats with my foot. As amazing as it may seem, only Marty knew it was all made up, and, of course, jumped in with a lot of, "Well, what did you do *then*?!" as everyone else stared at us.

Hanging Out in L.A.

Most of the movies I do are made in Los Angeles because they're comedies and with rare exceptions they take place in regular-looking places, which L.A. and its surrounding areas— Pasadena, Long Beach, etc., can provide. Also the studios are there. Of course, I'd rather work in Connecticut where I live, but nobody seems to make movies there. I read a good script recently where you would have to go to New Guinea or someplace like that for the movie to be credible. It's about a family that takes a vacation in New Guinea. You can't film that in Connecticut or L.A. If I have to go somewhere, for me, L.A. is as good as any place, mostly because I have as many friends there as I do in the East. I am a sports freak—among other things I am a New York Giants football fan. You rarely can see a Giant game in Los Angeles unless you go to a sports bar on Sunday where they get a lot of games. I've often gone to one owned by Telly Savalas, called Telly's. It's in the Sheraton Universal Hotel. The first time I went there with my trusted lieutenant Clay, Telly himself was standing at the top of a flight of steps you had to go down to get to his bar. We looked around. He motioned us down the stairs. "Right down there, fellas," he said. He was wearing a robe and thongs and shaving his head with a small electric razor he cupped in his hand. I didn't notice it, but Clay heard the buzzing—only in L.A.

When I go out to dinner in Los Angeles, which is usually Saturday night, I generally go to a restaurant called Mateo's. I went there for the first time many years ago with Sugar Ray Robinson. I met him through a mutual friend. This was around the time of the emergence of Sugar Ray Leonard. Sugar Ray Robinson's only comment on Sugar Ray Leonard was, "There's only one Sugar Ray." As I sat down to dinner with Sugar Ray, which was also the first time I met him, I quickly asked, "Have you ever seen me fight?" I was really pleased when he laughed. As years went by and he started to have his mental difficulties, he would respond to most questions such as, "Sugar Ray, how ya doin'?" with "Hangin' in there." If I asked how his wife Milly was, he'd say, "She's hangin' in there." Of course, after a while you begin to realize that's what most of us are doing.

I remember seeing Milton Berle at Mateo's. I had first met Milton Berle at Peter Falk's wedding. At that time he told me that Don Rickles was a protégé of his. One of the things he had told Don was that when you insulted people in the audience, you should make sure the lights were up enough so that the audience could see the person who was attacked laugh—therefore making the audience more able to laugh. For example, he said, "I might say, 'In our audience tonight, ladies and gentlemen, that great star, Boris Karloff. Please stand up and take a bow. Oh, excuse me, madam.'" Then Milton looked at me and said, "For example, if I were going to introduce you, I'd say, 'Ladies and gentlemen, in the audience tonight, Charles Grodin—he has a wonderful career.'" Then Milton made a face like my career was well short of wonderful. I chuckled, but later that evening—about five seconds later—I found myself wondering, "Did I have a wonderful career—or how *would* I describe it?"

I know it may be hard to believe, but it's not a subject about which I've given much thought. Former New York Mayor Koch would always ask, "How am I doing?" I would only ask, "*What* am I doing?"—and not to question myself but just to address what I'm doing. As long as I've been engaged I've been happy. It didn't matter to me that friends or associates were working or even becoming famous, it mattered that I was engaged—doing a scene for class—getting better—getting more confident. As long as I was occupied I was doing fine. I barely thought about *how* I was doing.

To digress a moment, I recently read about a survey that was done of a number of people who were a hundred years old or older. They were trying to figure out what, if anything, these people had in common. It wasn't their eating or drinking habits. Some drank and ate whatever they wanted. What they all had in common was they stayed engaged. They had found a way to occupy their minds.

I had a friend who thought the ideal job was where he had the least amount of work. It was years before he realized doing nothing was the hardest job.

I have a wonderful role model in my mother, who at this writing is eighty-five. She is a volunteer for the blind. Sometimes she takes them bowling. There are a lot of gutter balls, but everyone seems to have a good time. I don't think my mother ever feels more needed than when she is with them.

The lesson learned by the hundred-year-olds seems outstanding counsel for those of us in show business where the dominant state is "at leisure."

I believe the increased happiness of my life in recent years has much to do with a constant effort to be constructively engaged. I highly recommend it.

I've also, for reasons I don't understand, never been particularly competitive. It's strange to admit that it was only long after the fact that I realized I had made on average about four thousand dollars a year in the first ten years of my career. It's interesting to me to note that at that time I thought I was doing just fine. I was a regular on a soap opera, *Love of Life*. I played a large role on a live, hour TV show. I was a success on Broadway, but I still made about four thousand dollars a year. I never suffered from it—I loved my work, and I knew I was always getting better. That's all that was important.

Back to Milton Berle. When I saw him in Mateo's, he showed me a small box that when he opened it said, "F—— you. F—— you." It really cracked Milton up. As for me, I've always just been happy to be anywhere near great comedians even if what they're doing is opening a box that says "F—— you," or saying, "Charles Grodin, he's had a wonderful career," and then making a negative face. Of course, I may not be bothered because I know I've had a wonderful career. I've been making a living, for several years an outstanding one, in my profession of choice, and better yet I've always done only what I wanted to.

I was in Mateo's the other night when an older man came walking in holding the arm of another older man. He wasn't shuffling, but close. It took a second look before I realized it was Gene Kelly. It reminded me of a line I heard in a movie once. A rich guy says to another rich guy, "You know they don't have a cure for cancer if your daddy died from it." My first thought was, "God, if that's what Gene Kelly walks like when he's older—will I be moving at all?" I tried to console myself with the knowledge that Fred Astaire walked like that too in his later years, so maybe this is all about old dance injuries catching up—maybe.

One night Dabney Coleman and I were at Mateo's while Frank Sinatra was with a group at one table and Nancy Reagan at another. I always leave earlier than Dabney because, basically, Dabney never leaves. When I spoke to him the next day the phone conversation went something like this.

DABNEY

Well, you missed it.

ME

What?

DABNEY

After you left, Nancy Reagan came over to tell me how much she loved me in *Buffalo Bill*.

ME

Yeah?

DABNEY

She was going on and on, and after a while Sinatra came over.

ME

Uh huh.

DABNEY

He was just kind of hovering back there waiting for Nancy to finish, so he could see me.

ME

Yeah.

DABNEY

Eventually she went on for so long, he kind of drifted away.

ME

(disappointed)

Ah . . .

(a pause)

And what time did you wake up from this dream?

248

That got a good laugh from Dabney, who's not an easy laugh. Recently I was in Mateo's waiting for Dabney and his friend Kathy Carter when a television tycoon sat down and joined me. He was flying to Vegas on his own plane and wanted me to join him for company—all the while telling me how much he loved me in the movies. When Dabney arrived he shifted his attention, trying to form a TV deal with Dabney right on the spot. Then he offered us each four thousand dollars to keep him company and fly to Vegas. I was working, so I declined, as did Dabney. Eventually the guy left, taking the maitre d' with him for a thousand.

One night Dabney and I arrived at Mateo's around 10:30 P.M. Dabney looked at his watch and refused to go in.

I said, "I've called, they're open till 12 at least."

Dabney just sat in the car and shook his head. "They don't want us in there, believe me. It's too late. They're winding down."

I said, "I'll go in and check it out."

"They don't want us," he called after me as I went in.

There were people sitting at about four tables when I walked in. I was greeted warmly. "Is it too late?" I asked. "No, no, absolutely not," the maitre d' and captain exclaimed.

"You're sure?" I persisted.

"Please, please, come in! The kitchen's open for another hour. Come in!"

I went back out to the car and reported all this to Dabney, who just shook his head negatively. He refused to go in, saying, "If they really wanted us in there, they would have grabbed your arm and pulled you to the table. Let's go to Guido's," which is another place Dabney frequents. I went back in and explained to them that Dabney felt it was too late. They protested vehemently, but nobody grabbed my arm.

At Guido's where we arrived around 11, the place was more empty than Mateo's, but Dabney confidently marched in and, as I understood it, stayed till 3 A.M. I left after about an hour for sleep purposes, and also I didn't want to wait around for what I knew had to be some Guido's waiter dirty looks.

One night I was at Guido's with Dabney and his friend, the ever patient Kathy, when suddenly I heard softly from somewhere the theme from *The Godfather*. I didn't mention it for a while, but when I started to get a little edgy I called everyone's attention to it. Dabney quickly observed we really didn't have to worry until it got to a certain part of the theme where the gunfire usually occurred.

Later he said his most nervous moment in show business was when he was at the Ali-Spinks heavyweight championship fight waiting to hear Joe Frazier sing "The Star-Spangled Banner." He was extremely tense over what would happen when Joe got to the high notes of "the rockets' red glare."

A Movie Day—
The Early Hours

If I'm lucky, the alarm wakes me. Early calls, which most movie days have, tend to get me waking through the night. If I have to be awake by 5:30 A.M., I really like to be asleep by 8:30 P.M., but never am. It's more like 11, and you notice it by late afternoon. I always sit down early in the day, even if I don't feel like it. It pays off later. That reminds me of eating scenes in movies. Kids or people of less experience start wolfing down those cheeseburgers or whatever as soon as they're put in front of them at the first rehearsal. Of course, by the time they get to shooting their close-ups, they're ready to throw up.

I do back exercises every morning. It's been about fifteen years of this now, ever since I let some former actor turned "trainer" into my life who helped put me into the hospital. I'm actually in better shape than I've ever been, because, as I've said, I do them religiously. They build up my lower back muscles, so I also stand straight without effort, and am my actual height of six one instead of five nine, which I used to appear to be. This height change really startled Anthony Quinn, whom I ran into twenty-five years after we worked together. He wanted to know, "How'd you get as tall as me?!"

On movie days that means the first thing I do is roll out of bed and onto the floor in the dark and start exercising, and since I'm anti bad thoughts—try not to think of the "trainer." I particularly remember lying on the floor in London taking note that every radio station seemed to be talking about their economy. America caught up on that one later.

In the last five years or so the aforementioned Clay is out in front in the car waiting. Imagine what time he gets up?! Clay is who anyone would like to see anytime, but particularly on a dark, cold morning. He has an outstanding disposition. It's not like he's a cheerleader. It's just that he's always in a good mood. I remember once when he brought me home at the end of a day. As I got out of the car, I made reference to a few nice things that had happened that day and said, "Well, this was a good day." He turned around. (I sit in the back—not out of elitism—but for safety and comfort.) He turned around, looked at me, and said with a big smile, "They're *all* good days, Chuck." My wife says Clay is the most informed person she's ever met. He's a graduate of Yale, and seems to know whatever you might want to know about anything. If you put together the disposition and the intellect, you get an idea of what I have going for me here. Clay's college classmate Geoff Taylor was the producer of a picture I did, *Taking Care of Business*. Clay had been an actor for about ten years—had always made a living, which is almost a miracle, but now wanted to get into producing. Geoff felt putting him with me might be a route, and hopefully it will be. In the meantime he just generally makes life a lot better for me and mine. Driving is the least of what he does. Imagine having someone in your life who takes on everything you don't want to confront or can't solve. That's Clay.

It wasn't until I did the comedy mini-series *Fresno* that the idea struck me to ask for a driver. It occurred to me because sometimes I was spending about three hours behind the wheel a day. I probably could have had a driver years earlier, but I never thought to ask, and then it wouldn't have been Clay.

I had a driver on one movie who told our baby-sitter that my wife and I had to get married. Our son is five, and we've been married for ten years, so the guy wasn't a math whiz—but, of course, worse, it sounded mean-spirited to me. I'm really nice, until someone else isn't. Then I either go away or see that they do.

Another driver in Mexico liked to drive at high speed on the open road about a car length behind the car in front. Otherwise he was a terrific guy. He even participated in jokes with me. Once Carrie Fisher, who is an old friend of mine, came to visit me in Acapulco. Oscar, my driver, and I did a variation of an old Jack Benny-Mel Blanc joke on Carrie. Carrie and I were in the backseat, and Oscar, of course, was driving. The following had all been rehearsed by Oscar and me as a put-on for Carrie.

ME
Oscar, you made a dinner reservation for eight?

OSCAR
Sí.

ME
You think we'll like this place?

OSCAR
Sí.

ME
They have a band and dancing there, right?

OSCAR

Sí.

Carrie glances at us for a moment.

ME
You have a large family, Oscar?

OSCAR

Sí.

ME
All brothers and one sister, right?

OSCAR

Sí.

Now Carrie is staring at us.

ME
What's your sister's name, again?

OSCAR

Sue.

ME
Sue?

OSCAR

Sí.

CARRIE
(laughing)
You guys! You guys *did* that!

Anyway, once in the car with Clay we usually, on average, have about a thirty-minute drive. First we generally cover any sports news of note. He's a West Coast guy, so he's a fan of different teams from mine, but he roots for my teams as well—a supportive gesture that I really appreciate. Then I usually get to any philosophical or psychological problem on my mind, and he generally lightens that load! In this job where movie companies pay his salary, he's not covered for health care, so I take care of that. As you must understand by now, his health is very important to me.

Generally, I arrive at the studio or on location as the light starts to come up. Usually the crew is arriving around the same time. If a rehearsal is called, I head for the table where there's coffee and bagels, etc. If not, into the makeup trailer while Clay gets me whatever I want—most often an egg and cheese sandwich, using only the egg whites. I'm one of those nuts who has french fries and diet Coke and thinks I'm cutting back. Since I've done a lot of pictures, there are always guys on the crew I've worked with more than once over the years. I'm friendly to everyone, and everyone is friendly to me. Some actors aren't, and everyone hates them. Some production people aren't, and everyone hates *them*. If you have any control over your choice, choose nice.

When I head into makeup over these last few years I see Jim Scribner, whom I request. Jim is so thorough and professional he makes it possible for me to *never* look in a mirror for the entire day, which is something I really love to avoid. I'm sure, at least sometimes, I might be startled by what I see, and I'd rather not deal with it. Jim is an old pro, so I look as good as I can, and I'm willing to leave it at that. In the last year I've even gotten him to back off from his penchant for studying me like a lab specimen for any tiny hairs I might have missed in shaving. It's true, as a rule, I only see a movie I do once, but I've never spotted any tiny hair that wasn't supposed to be there. I've had a running gag with Ken Chase, the makeup artist, working along-side Jim. Ken made me up once years ago, and every time I see him I feign shock he's still in the business. Sometimes I'll get startled two or three times a day when I see him. I created a sce-nario where there's always a production meeting going on to decide whether Ken stays or goes and, miraculously, he stays. The gag is now done without words—a startled look from me and a sunny smile from Ken.

If we haven't had a rehearsal before makeup, we have one afterward. This is often the first time the cast and director go over the script, unless there is a rehearsal period prior to start-ing the movie. I have never gotten over how many actors and actresses seem outraged and indignant over their lines, whenev-er this rehearsal takes place. It is as though this is the first time they've noticed what they have been hired to do. I've worked with two actors who were aggressively hostile toward the text. They were shocked and outraged that anyone would even dream they'd say such drivel. Directors, in my experience, are magnifi-cent at these moments, as they look at the offending dialogue as though they too just spotted it. One actress I worked with years ago seemed taken aback by her every line. I was constantly hearing, "My character would *never* say that!" I keep waiting for someone—a director, a producer, *someone*—to say, "If you think it's such crap, why'd you sign on?!" I've never heard it. I think people are afraid of upsetting actors because that could cause costly delays in filming. Being an actor, I, of course, am a big one for being sensitive and supportive to the people in front of the cameras, but being a screenwriter, I'll probably be the one to eventually say, "Try acting instead of complaining." As I've said, if I ever have a problem with anything in a script, I'll dis-cuss it with the director *before* agreeing to do the picture. Also I let the director know I will be suggesting this and that—dia-logue mostly—comedy mostly—which I hope he uses, but if he chooses not to, I vow to always behave the same way whether my ideas are accepted or not. I mean nice. That way I feel free to make suggestions in a tension-free environment, where no one has to worry if we're a minute away from a problem. I was once asked by the producer Ray Stark to replace another actor in a picture. I read the script and said, "If I said those words, you'd want to fire me, too." He and the director encouraged me to change them, and it worked out really well. Particularly in comedy, words are everything. With all due respect to directors, I believe the script is the absolute one irreplaceable essential element. Without that it doesn't matter who's directing or acting. Of course, directors have a lot to do with supervising the script. The brilliant Ivan Reitman, for whom I've just written a script, supervised me to an absolutely new higher level. A lot of things have to go right before a movie can be successful. I think aside from the script the most important issue is having a smart person in charge—smart in the sense of taste and judgment about what's entertaining—smart enough to get the right screenwriter and actors. Then there are still a thousand things that can go wrong, and you have to be smart about almost all of them. That's why the percentage of really good movies is small.

Back to rehearsal. The best directors I've found are the ones who can listen as well as talk. That's not to say they can't do an outstanding job and not be all that interested in listening. Roman Polanski, who directed my first big picture, *Rosemary's Baby*, proved that. Roman didn't seem to be interested in hearing what anyone had to say and even filmed the picture with very little "coverage" (different angles on the scene) so that the studio wouldn't have much of an opportunity to alter how he had done it.

Mostly in rehearsal prior to shooting, the director is interested in setting up his shots with the director of photography. The actors are concerned about what they have to say and *everyone* is interested in food. The days are so long that there's kind of an ongoing eating throughout the day. There's always at least one person working on a doughnut or the equivalent. As I'm writing this on a hill in San Francisco, a man suddenly appears with a tray of carrot and celery sticks and a dip. It's 9:55 A.M., but of course, we've all been up since 6, or in the ladies' case obscenely earlier.

For some scenes there's just no rehearsing—like the rapids sequence in *Midnight Run*. There you just trust that everyone has scoped out the situation, and you go gently into the water. I lost some innocence on that sequence. They lowered me over the side of a boat into the freezing Salt River in Arizona, and if you associate Arizona with warmth—think again—not in the river in January, anyway. I had on a wet-suit under my pants, shirt, sweater, and overcoat, and all I can say is wet-suit, shmet-suit. Bob De Niro and I almost froze to death in a hurry, and the whole sequence had to be moved to New Zealand. Back in my camper a half-hour later, I was still shivering and about to have some brandy when the director, Marty Brest, burst in saying, "Don't drink that brandy!"—something about even worse stuff would happen if I did. It wasn't true in the Yukon movies *I'd* seen!

I have, in passing, mentioned several times that I am writing this book prior to and during the filming of *Heart and Souls*. I would like to describe the movie experience by selectively describing the experience of *Heart and Souls*. Any references about waiting to film need to be multiplied hundreds of times over to give a true description. I cannot bring myself to write, or worse yet, ask you to read a literal description of that wearying aspect of moviemaking.

Heart and Souls

I first heard of the picture when a script with a letter attached was sent to me from my representatives, United Talent. My agent is a man named Jim Berkus, who is married to one of my oldest and closest friends, Ria Nepus. I went with Jim after they wouldn't let me meet Mike Ovitz at CAA. All I knew about him as an agent was that he was married to my friend, who would probably give him hell if he didn't do his thing for me. I had no idea what his thing was. He seemed like a bright, knowledge-able guy with a more than average touch of cynicism which would probably balance my more than average optimism. That turned out to be true. Right now we are having conversations with a producer about me acting in one of my favorite scripts I've written called *The Junta and the Rebels*. Jim is sure it won't get financed by this guy, and I'm sure it will. He's probably right, but I enjoy my point of view more.

Anyway, the script of *Heart and Souls* arrived with a letter telling me what role they wanted me for. It's in a genre I really like—the *Ghost/Heaven Can Wait* genre. I would play someone who's killed in a bus accident early in the picture, and for the rest of it I'm invisible, seen only by the bus driver, David Paymer, and the other three souls who died with me—Alfre Woodard, Kyra Sedgwick and Tom Sizemore—and by Robert Downey, Jr., whose body we later inhabit. To the rest of the world we souls are invisible. It strikes me as the kind of movie a lot of people would enjoy, which, of course, is important, because it will cost thirty-five million dollars to make and probably another twenty-five to publicize. I read very few scripts I believe will interest a wide audience or, for that matter, a narrow audience. I tell Jim I'd like to do it, even though I have serious reservations about how much sitting around and waiting I will do. Along with being an ensemble picture, it also has a certain amount of special effects. As I've said, I realize several times by now, it's not the work, but the waiting that scares me. We make a deal, and then I hear the schedule is about six weeks longer than I was first told—a total of about nineteen weeks. No one was misleading anyone. It really was some lack of communication. Suddenly the thought of six weeks more of a little filming and a lot of waiting got to me, and I decided I wanted out. I had never done this before, but I didn't feel I was going against my word, because of the additional six weeks. I had a surprisingly comfortable talk on the phone with the director, Ron Underwood, whom I'd never met. Ron directed *City Slickers*. He has a reputation for being a class act, and he exhibited it with me, expressing only regret. "You were the studio's and my first choice for the role. You were the first person we got for the picture. I'm very disappointed, but I understand." I finished the call and had a great sense of relief. I told my wife getting out wasn't nearly as hard as I thought it would be. I had just settled into a relaxed state about the whole thing when the phone rang and it was the president of Universal Pictures, Tom Pollack. The call went something like this.

TOM
You can't do this to me!

ME

Tom . . .

TOM

You don't do this! Other people do this, but not *you*!

ME

Tom . . .

TOM

This is your studio! I'm your biggest booster!

(This is true. I mostly work for Universal. *Midnight Run* and *Beethoven* and the sequel are all Universal, and Tom *is* my biggest booster.)

ME

Tom, have you read the script!?

TOM

Of course! What are you talking about?! I've read the script a dozen times!

ME

So, you know this is not like Bette Midler pulling out of *For the Boys*.

TOM

This is a big picture. I need you in it!

ME

Tom, it's six weeks longer than I was told, and I'm scared of all the sitting around.

TOM

You're afraid of being bored?

ME

Right.

TOM

I want you on the screen. I'm asking you to
be bored off-screen for me. I'm calling your
agent! Think about it!

He didn't exactly hang up, but he didn't invite me to lunch,
either. I thought about it and realized two things. I was not going
to refuse Tom Pollack, if for no other reason than he said he'd
make *Midnight Run* with me when the president of Paramount,
where the picture originally was, wouldn't. I also realized that if
I wrote a book during the filming I would *never* be bored during
the sitting around, and once I figured out what I would write
about, I was able to make Tom and me happy. Before getting into
the details of the filming of the picture, let me say I'm also very
happy Tom made the call, because I (optimistic me) believe
we're making a very enjoyable picture.

I went to the Pittsburgh Playhouse School of the Theatre with
Bob Downey, Jr.,'s mother, Elsie Ford. She married the filmmaker Robert Downey. I had met Bob once on a flight from L.A. to
New York. He introduced himself as "Robert Downey, Jr., actor,"
and seemed like an enthusiastic, nice kid, which he is. I had
never met any of the other actors, which isn't unusual when you
realize Katharine Hepburn met Henry Fonda for the first time
when they did *On Golden Pond*. Most of us, contrary to what
newspapers and TV seem to imply, stay home and lead our own
private lives almost all the time—those of us not in our twenties,
anyway. This group blended beautifully. There were also some
small children in the movie who played Bob as a baby and
young child. There was consideration given to showing his char-

262

acter at the age of three, but an effort to rehearse a written scene with a three-year-old led to the chaos you might expect. The boy was a doll, who was interested in playing, not playing a scene. It was sad to watch his anxious father observe all this sitting a short distance away. Now we first see Bob's character at infancy, then about ten months, then five years. The five-year-old is played by Eric Lloyd and with the director and his mother's help he was able to do outstanding work. Of course, his main interest when I met him was to get me to go on the *E.T.* ride at the studio, but I've long since discovered things like roller coasters and Ferris wheels are better when you're a kid, not an adult like me, who always imagines the worst. In other words, my optimism doesn't apply to amusement park rides.

The first day of shooting was at the breathtakingly beautiful Santa Anita racetrack. One of the nice things about being in the movies is you get to go places you would never go. Because of my gambling experience at the dog track while attending the University of Miami, I've vowed to stay away from tracks. Actually I attended the dog track as much as I attended the university in those days. The Santa Anita track was closed, but we had the horses and jockeys hired for the scene in the movie. Because of the amount of time we take to shoot a scene in a movie, the horses eventually got exhausted, and we had to stop. The horses had an option actors don't. It reminds me of the director Marty Brest asking me, after going down the rapids in *Midnight Run* a number of times, "Do you have another take in you?" I was exhausted and a little faint. Not being a rapids guy I had no idea what my rapids tolerance was, but I did one more and was fine—just.

I'm writing this in mid-February 1993. We shot at Santa Anita December 1, 1992. It feels like a long time ago. Movies so dominate your life, because of the time and effort involved, that if you'd say a year I could tell you what movie I did that year. As I've said, it becomes an endurance contest. I'm just talking about avoiding fatigue and colds. The first day went well, and I was particularly struck by the sweet temperament of our director, Ron Underwood. It's one thing to be a lovely gentleman on the phone, or even in a rehearsal with four or five people, but now Ron was dealing with half a dozen actors, a couple of hundred extras, and a lot of horses. He was very easygoing, although he couldn't possibly have felt completely that way inside. Impressive.

The company's children are starting to show up. Ron has three girls, Alfre one baby daughter and Kyra an infant daughter and a three-year-old son, plus of course the children in the movie. For me it's a joy. I've always adored kids. One little boy who was an extra came over to me and said, "Are you the man from *Beethoven*?" I said I was, and he then asked, "Can I be in the movies with you?" He honestly thought that's how you got in. My own son at four ran onto camera while I was shooting a scene for *Beethoven*. I later asked him why he did that. He said, "I wanted to be in that scene." It's a concept that does leap over the agents and producers and everything. Most kids on movies begin shy and silent and within a few days the director is wondering if he's allowed to call the police for help.

The second day we were shooting in a hospital that had been closed down, I think because of rising costs. Evidently they found they could make more money pretending to be a hospital than being one. This day there was some screaming and yelling on the set. I heard it, but I don't know what happened. As I've said before, there were firings and quittings on what seemed like a daily basis on *Midnight Run* and Bob De Niro and I never raised our heads from the script. It's called protecting yourself. It's probably why I've stopped watching the news. After a while it beats you into submission. I do know what's going on from newspapers and magazines and the Sunday morning shows, but somehow it feels once removed, which is about how I can take it.

We next traveled out to San Bernardino, California, to shoot at Norton Air Force base. Heading out to San Bernardino around

5:30 A.M. in the dark, it's amazing to see how many people are already on the road heading to work. When we arrived it was still darkish and raining—pretty grim. This is why I like to "goof" on sets—to try to keep depression from setting in. I kidded around a lot on the set of *Heaven Can Wait*. When it was over, Warren Beatty said to me, "Do you know what percentage of all your kidding was helpful on the picture?" I said, "What percentage?" He said, "One hundred percent." Then before I could start to feel too good, he said, "But even *you* aren't liked by everyone." I said, "Oh, yeah? Who doesn't like me?" He said our cinematographer, who was an award-winning artist and a hell of a nice guy. I was surprised to hear that until Warren reminded me that early on when we had to reshoot something I "jokingly" said to the cinematographer, "Why don't we throw a little light on Dyan and me to see what we're doing over here." You don't tease someone about a mistake. I meant to make light of the need to reshoot, but it wasn't funny, certainly not to a great cinematographer.

I think Warren told me that because I had just busted him about something. It might have been about our lousy, tiny little dressing rooms or that he was keeping Julie Christie, James Mason, Dyan Cannon, and all of us waiting unnecessarily for hours every day (that again). Anyway, the truth is we've always had a remarkably friendly relationship in spite of the fact that he seemed to blame *Ishtar* running over budget so much on Elaine May, and not take responsibility himself as the producer, which he should have.

When I produced my own picture, *Movers and Shakers*, I constantly offended one guy on the movie. This came under the heading of "No good deed goes unpunished." I had gotten him the job. The problem was this was someone who used to give me his hand-me-down clothes when I first came to New York. He could never get over that I had gotten to a position where I could hire him. He used to actually snicker at me in production meetings—open, out-loud snickering. It was really aberrant. He would apologize and then keep doing it. It was a mess. If only I hadn't given him his first opportunity to work in a movie, we would have continued to have the extremely friendly relationship we'd had for twenty-five years. Another friend to whom I've loaned a great deal of money over the years is positive I hate him for not repaying, but I don't hate him. I just miss him, as he makes his whereabouts largely unknown. There was a music editor on *Movers and Shakers* who, if you even asked a question, would sulk and pout and almost quit. It's amazing these people survived their first week in show business, which is such a collaborative effort.

Anyway, in San Bernardino we filmed in a huge airplane hangar that housed a 747 from Japan Air Lines. They were repairing it. It was startling to realize the door seemed about a mile off the ground. I mean *that's* jumbo. On the second day out there we were having sound problems, because the Japanese were running the 747 engine constantly and wouldn't shut it off when we shot. I was starting to get annoyed, until I learned they couldn't shut it off to run the proper test. Also I remembered the Japanese own the studio now. Throughout all this, cargo planes were taking off with supplies to Somalia.

Next we moved to a sequence where we souls, for reasons too complicated to go into here, have to say good-bye to the little boy we have become so attached to. The scene, which was filmed from several angles over a three-day period, reminded me why years ago I became so interested in comedy. This was a deeply emotional scene where all of us had to be on the verge of tears or actually crying. The makeup people can put something in your eyes to cause the effect, but I've never used that. That meant I had to get myself to that state several times over a three-day period—not a lot of fun. I had done some work like that many years ago when I was starting, and I received a lot of praise. All I could think about though was—I want to get into comedy. It just takes too much out of you to tap into those sources that provoke tears.

I had a conversation with Sir Laurence Olivier when he came backstage after seeing me in *Same Time Next Year*. There was a woman with him, and she just listened as we had the following exchange.

> ME
>
> Do you enjoy doing a run in a play, because
> I don't.

> SIR LAURENCE
>
> Oh God, no! It's not for us to enjoy!

> ME
>
> It's hard work.

> SIR LAURENCE
>
> Oh yes! It's for the audience. I don't enjoy it
> at all.

> ME
>
> Yeah.

A couple of days later an agent who had spoken to the woman who was with Olivier told me how much she had been offended by me. I don't know why, but it was only two weeks ago, some eighteen years later, that I wondered exactly why she had been offended. Maybe she was a producer who was trying to get him to *do* a run in a play, and my conversation served to remind him he didn't like to. Maybe it had nothing to do with that at all. Maybe she was offended because I didn't pay homage to Olivier. I was respectful, but as I've said, I'm not much of an homage guy.

I had some fun today with Tom Sizemore. Last night our director sent the other principal players and me a Christmas gift—an exotic jar of candies.

When I came into the makeup room this morning, I saw Tom sitting down at the other end and began to talk in a voice loud enough for Tom to hear about "the beautiful briefcase the director sent me. It's not leather. It's soft as butter. What is that exactly?" I asked with a wink to my co-conspirator and makeup man, Jim Scribner.

Jim said, "I think what you're talking about is elk."

Out of the corner of my eye I see we've got Tom's attention. "Yeah," I went on, "beautiful inscription, *Heart and Souls*, my name, then '92–'93.' " It's the details that sell this con.

Now Tom is on his feet. "The director gave you a *briefcase*?!"

"Yeah," I say. "You got one too, didn't you?"

"No." He shouts, "He sent me some candy!"

"Candy?" I say, surprised. "I just assumed you got the briefcase."

"No. Candy!" he again says, getting increasingly frustrated.

When I saw it was really getting to him, I laughed and he saw I was playing with him. Then he laughed even harder than I did. As I've said, movie days are long, so you look for your fun where you can.

This seems to be a picture with a very pleasant atmosphere. We've had our moments, mostly people being upset because they've had to wait eight hours or so, but overall it's a nice place to be. Our director always seems to have a smile (a sincere one, too), no matter what's going on. He may be the best actor in the picture. He asked me the other day if I was happy I'd decided to do the movie, and I was surprised he asked. He said I seemed really happy, which I was, but I guess he wanted to hear me say it. Today I told him the main reason I was happy was it was so pleasant working with him. He said he is thankful every day that I am in the picture. Before this gets sickeningly sentimental, I'm reminded of the time I overheard Dick Sarafian, the director of *Sunburn*, tell his assistant, "Let's bring our hero to the set." It clearly implied some negative feeling for me on his part. I went to Dick, told him I overheard him, and asked him if he had some problem with me. He absolutely spoke with a different tone for Art Carney and Farrah Fawcett than he did with me. If he wanted me to do something with more energy, instead of saying, "Give it more energy," he'd say, "You're coming off funereal." Aside from admitting earlier he was envious of my motor home, he just generally acted as if he admired me, liked me, and resented me all at the same time. He never admitted to anything other than the motor home thing. For example, it was obvious I was rewriting the dialogue of each scene I did. He thought it was an improvement and liked it, but was somewhat startled that I just did it. He said, "Are the producers aware you're doing this every day?" I said, "They asked me to." One of them was one of the writers. I didn't want credit, because I certainly didn't write the story of *Sunburn*. I not only didn't write it, I couldn't understand it. I don't think anyone could. It was what some people called a Riviera picture. You got to look at Farrah, gorgeous in her gowns, good guys, bad guys, action, adventure, beautiful locales, and whatever Art and I could bring. It would have helped to have a great story, but if it was *that* great, probably none of us but Art would have been asked to be in it. Farrah had just gotten out of her contract on "Charley's Angels," and a couple of friends of mine said it would be a long while, if ever, before the public would support her as a movie star. I don't know the details of her leaving her TV show, but it appeared as though she'd left simply for bigger and better things (movies), and that appearance usually is the kiss of death. More recently Shelley Long seems to have paid that price by leaving "Cheers." Farrah, at that time, was managed by Jay Bernstein, who was quite a character. When I was cast opposite her, he phoned me to say he felt the movie had just skyrocketed in its potential gross, as all their choices ahead of me (who had turned them down) were straight leading men. He felt by having a comedic person play the guy, everything was better, and the picture would gross seventy million dollars. It was a nice thing to say, but he added something like the following: "If you or I walk into a bar, we really have to work hard to get the girl, as against

Clint Eastwood, who just has to walk in." I'm not sure what his point was. I certainly didn't see myself as Clint Eastwood, but I didn't see myself as Jay Bernstein, either. I saw myself as somewhere in between, hopefully leaning more toward Clint than Jay. Jay had a penchant for those kinds of observations. At a party in Acapulco, prior to shooting, he went over to the cinematographer and told him, "You know I didn't want you for this job, but since you have it, I want you to take special care lighting Farrah!" I asked Jay why he found it necessary to tell the cinematographer he hadn't wanted him. He stared at me like he didn't understand the question and just said, "It's the truth." There are people who feel compelled to offer their "truthful" observations, whether asked or not. They're usually not the most popular people.

Anyway, it turns out Farrah took some bad advice from Jay in leaving "Charley's Angels," and it was years before she regained her popularity—on TV. As I've written elsewhere, I found Farrah to be one of the nicest people I'd ever met.

Sunburn actually tested very well in its sneak previews, but as my friends predicted, the public didn't rush out to see Farrah in her first movie after leaving her popular TV show. Today people like John Goodman manage to have thriving movie careers as well as staying with their TV shows—a better idea, if you don't mind working longer than humans should.

Joan Collins played a supporting role in *Sunburn* and was with us for a short while. I really appreciated her right away. We were once waiting to film a shot at night. Dick Sarafian walked by, and Joan asked how long it would take before they were ready to shoot. Dick answered patronizingly, "It's a tough shot to light, sweetie." Joan responded even more patronizingly, "It's a tough scene to act, *sweetie!*"

Playing a soul is a first for me. I initially recognized this was going to be an unusual experience in an early conversation with the costume designer, who said, "After you die, the director would like . . . " I didn't really hear the rest of the sentence. One of the differences in this role is the other souls and I "fly." We worked on this during the rehearsal period. They hook you up to a harness under your clothes, and somehow get rid of the wires in postproduction. In any case, you fly. Your physical well-being is under the control of people you just met. You have to have faith. There was a scene in *Taking Care of Business* where Jim Belushi was supposed to hang on my back as we slid down a cable from the top of Anaheim baseball stadium to the ground several hundred feet below. The actual stunt was, of course, to be done by stunt men, but the director, Arthur Hiller, normally a sane man, asked how I felt about going out on the wire a few feet—just death below—no net. I looked at him for a long enough moment for him to say, "You've answered the question." Stunt men are another breed. I've never seen injury or death statistics on the job, but I do know my stunt man in *Midnight Run* was later killed in a helicopter crash in a scene for a Chuck Norris movie. He was around thirty, with two small children.

When I finally got around to "flying" in *Heart and Souls* I was standing on a ledge between Alfre Woodard and Kyra Sedgwick. At a certain point we were just supposed to step off the ledge into space—no fun. At first, mistakenly, Alfre and I flew down, and Kyra sideways. Then we banged into each other. Eventually it worked right. I never got to the point where I did any better than tolerate it. This was 3 A.M., after being there fifteen hours. I wouldn't complain, though, because I knew I'd be doing it when I signed on. Of course, in my free time at home I'm in a Stratolounger, not skydiving or bungee-jumping.

We're also supposed to do some singing and dancing for a couple of scenes in the picture. Since my character is an opera singer, obviously there will be a dubbed voice, and also since my character is *not* a dancer, my own lack of ability in dance works nicely for me there. Sometimes it's good not to rehearse, but I was asked to attend these dance rehearsals. I believed I shouldn't even be there since my character couldn't dance, but I made a token effort to emulate the other dancing souls. Eventually I asked Clay to jump in to pick up some steps—

representing me. Clay has more zest for this type of thing than I do. When we shot it, I emulated poorly, which the director and I felt was just right, and which I would have done exactly the same without rehearsals.

I had to appear to be playing the flute in the movie *Thieves*. They brought a flautist on the set which interested me about as much as the dance rehearsal. Clearly they'd have to film the brief sequence in some way other than me actually playing the flute. All I remember about my encounter with the flautist is he pointed out two or three little levers on the flute I wasn't supposed to ever touch, which, of course, begged the question, "What the hell are they doing there?" I don't remember the answer.

They announced the Academy Award nominations today, and two of our actors were nominated—Robert Downey, Jr., for Best Actor in *Chaplin*, and David Paymer for Best Supporting Actor in *Mr. Saturday Night*. I've seen *Mr. Saturday Night* but I haven't seen *Chaplin*. I guess that means I'm more interested in seeing a movie about a Jewish comic than an English genius. I will, of course, see *Chaplin*. Bob has been trying to arrange a dinner with me, and I want to, but, as I've said, I don't like to go out after a day's filming, so we haven't done it yet. This morning when he came into the makeup trailer, I said, "Bobby! Let's have dinner tonight! I've just come from an early breakfast with Davey!"

Back to the filming. I had my first night shoot, riding around a rough part of Hollywood on an old bus. Eventually after riding around at one, then two, then three in the morning, the locals started throwing things as we drove by. We weren't making any unusual noise, but you could see it was a bus for filming because of all the lights. There are a lot of angry people out there, and some of the angriest are awake at 3 A.M. in poor neighborhoods.

In the movie story, after he is killed in a bus accident, my character is given a chance to go back through Robert's character's body and fulfill the one thing in life he never got to do. My character, Harrison, wanted to be an opera singer, but was always too nervous to get up in public and sing. In this sequence we get into a B.B. King concert. I had appeared with B.B. a couple of times on "The Tonight Show," so it was a treat to see him again. Also in this picture I get the best exit I've ever had in a movie. After I "sing" the audience goes wild—the bus I was killed in drives through the wall of the theatre to take me up to heaven. As I go off on the bus, B.B. steps forward, plays and sings "The Thrill Is Gone." I didn't know that was going to happen until B.B. did it. It wasn't in the script I read. The people I asked said that was the old song, "The Thrill Is Gone," but I couldn't tell. Jazz versions don't seem to use any notes from the songs as originally written, but it was great, anyway.

I'm writing this sitting next to Alfre on top of a large Chinese cabinet called a Tansu that's close to seven feet high. We are rehearsing a sequence where Alfre and I have no lines but are required to sit up here for hours and watch the boardroom proceedings below. We have a break, and I go in the rain to my trailer to watch President Clinton's State of the Union address. Just as Peter Jennings said, "The President will be entering the chamber any moment now," there was a knock on my trailer door and Shawn, one of the assistants, said, "We're ready for you, Charles." That meant that as the President entered the chamber to a standing ovation and strode to the podium, I strode in the rain to my position on top of the Tansu. Different careers lead people in different directions.

For promotional reasons, there is a "behind the scenes" crew filming on the set today as there has been on several days. If I wanted to discuss something with another actor or the director, they wouldn't hesitate not only to film it, but to put a microphone close enough to hear what we're saying. This has seldom gotten to me, but it's starting to. Alfre just took a drink from a bottle filled with vitamin juice that's the color of scotch. She said, "The behind the scenes crew could ruin me."

273

My character is a great lover of opera and chess, and I am neither. Harking back to the first chapter of this book about how people assume you are what you play, it makes me wonder again just how different our movie actors are from their roles. There's no question that years ago Ingrid Bergman was ostracized for having an extramarital affair because her image was that of a saintly person, and some of our current rougher movie actors haven't been hurt by admissions of using drugs. The lesson here is that if you're playing in "Father Knows Best" you can't be caught shooting heroin.

We filmed a sequence where we're chased by a big dog, a Rotweiller. Because of *Beethoven*, people assume I don't like dogs, but I do. I just don't like dirt and hair and mess. My son would like us to get a dog. Actually he wants two dogs, and a Rotweiller has been discussed. My position is, I don't want an animal in the house who's tougher than I am—noisier, yes, but not tougher. I don't want to go through life worried about what would happen if my dog got mad at me.

We were still up on the Tansu. It has been a couple of hours. Alfre has started to hum, and I'm checking my watch. Ron has tried to inject some levity into these increasingly grim proceedings by saying to Kyra, who's down below for a special effects shot, "Kyra, you could do a whole movie of this." It didn't work, though. Kyra, who has been watching a monitor trying to perfectly step into Robert's image, answers "I'll kill myself first."

We're using an extraordinarily expensive camera to get this effects shot where only my legs are seen. They could use a double, but Ron has asked me to do it, so here I sit. Referring to my "work" in the last take, Ron has just called out to me, "Nice legs up there." I answered, "Yeah, it felt good," and everyone laughs.

You do sense a little tension in the air, but not *tension* tension. It will be nice to get back to acting as we all know it.

We just got the shot. Everyone seems relieved. They've brought over our ladder, and Alfre and I are saying good-bye to our Tansu.

One of the weird things about waiting to work in movies is that any questions about "how much longer," or "will we work at all?" are looked at as though we're anti-art, and the work at hand here has to do with saving humanity from some dread disease. Kyra is nursing a baby. She particularly should be welcome to ask. Everyone in production is always very nice when asked, but there is that tiny anti-art thing.

We have started shooting at night on a street in San Francisco. This is after the bus crash where we die, and we're going to "fly" over the bus. I don't really know exactly how or what, and I don't ask until I have to. I figure it will only give me something to think about I don't want to think about, and I'd rather be writing this book.

One of the producers, Nancy Roberts, just stopped by my trailer, which earlier in this book in a passage I read to my agent Jim Berkus, I referred to as a camper. Jim asked me to refer to it as a trailer, which it is. I don't know the difference between a trailer or a camper, but Jim said he negotiated for a trailer, and it makes him look bad if I say I have a camper, so it's a trailer. Jim said this all with a slight chuckle, but I think he meant it. Guys who know the difference between a trailer and a camper are good agents, if you know what I mean.

Anyway, Nancy Roberts, one of the producers, stopped by my trailer. She's filled with sincere enthusiasm for what she's seen of this movie. She's been involved with the project for five years, and with that much time invested you try to *wish* it a success! I'm not saying she's wrong. I'm not shocked to hear it looks really promising, but I've never heard a producer say otherwise—to me, anyway. Why should they? You don't go to a guy who's going to fly outside on a cold night and tell him things aren't looking good. I mean a certain amount of energy and enthusiasm is called for.

I've been waiting in the trailer for a couple of hours now. I'm fully dressed and wired for sound. I have two sets of thermals, and I'm waiting to fly. After being in the freezing rapids in Arizona, harnessed flying seems like . . . walking.

They've just broken for what they call lunch, even though it's night. I've been here for over three hours and shot nothing. Neither has the company. They've been preparing the shot for three hours. That's not unusual. For a night boxcar scene in *Midnight Run* they spent the whole day preparing the shot before calling Bob De Niro and me to the set. There was a little fire Bob's character had made, and they had to vent the car. Stuff that doesn't sound like it should take hours to do, but it often does.

This was the one scene in *Midnight Run* where there actually was a dilemma as to how or if it would work. The writer, George Gallo, simply hadn't written this scene, or if he had, the director, Marty Brest, chose not to show it to us. In the scene that preceded this, De Niro is enraged at me for trying to escape and handcuffs me around a pole in the boxcar. This scene begins a little later. He's squatting, warming his hands over a little fire, which is also the source of light. I'm sitting on the floor, cuffed around the pole. He still looks furious and, within a few minutes or so, I'm supposed to get him to open up to me in a personal way for the first time. It seemed a huge jump. What do I do to get him to do that? After several weeks on the picture, Marty Brest's solution was that when we get to the scene, "Chuck will improvise something to loosen Bob up." That was a high compliment for what I'd done improvisationally in the picture to that point, but this was a different situation. It was one thing for Marty to say, "Make more out of the counterfeit money scene in the bar." That was taking an existing scene and elaborating on it. Here there was no existing scene and a situation that had kept one from being written. Nonetheless I was flattered that Marty handed it over to me. I wasn't, however, going to trust I'd come up with something when the moment came. I wrote about twenty "comic dig" lines my character could say to Bob when the moment came. I ran them by my wife and daughter, and about half survived.

On the day of the boxcar scene, after several hours passed and we were ready to shoot, when Marty said "Action"—I hit

Bob with my ten best lines, which everyone there was hearing for the first time. They were funny, but made no dent in Bob. He grimly hovered over the fire warming his hands, acting as though I hadn't even spoken. Marty eventually yelled "Cut," came over and knelt next to me on the floor where I was cuffed to the pole and said, "I love you. You know that. You're brilliant, but that stuff you just did only irritated him. You need to loosen him up. Let's go again." He then got up and started away, I guess, believing I had just made up ten irritating lines, so I could just as easily come up with ten "loosening up" lines. I only said, "I'll need a minute." There was a full crew standing there. The cost of this whole sequence had to be more than a couple hundred thousand dollars, and unless I come up with something good—it's lost money. In this case, necessity really was the mother of invention. I'm not sure exactly what I did next or how it came to me, but on take two, I played both our roles. Bob wouldn't loosen up, so I played Bob and me, which got him to lift his head and look at me, and then I hit him with, "Did you ever have sex with an animal?" Remember, I had to jar him out of his mood. I went on, "Because I saw you looking pretty good at one of those chickens on the Indian reservation back there." Bob smiled at me and said, "I was thinking about taking a shot at one of them." That opened the door for what had to happen in the scene, and we got it. I love to come up with stuff, but I wouldn't want that particular kind of challenge too often.

It's three and a half hours now, and I'm still sitting in the trailer. The makeup starts to feel cakey, if that's a word. I've come fortified. Along with writing this book, I've got all these cassettes a friend of mine who's a member of the Academy (of Arts and Sciences, which is what I think they call the Academy Awards) gave me.

If you vote for the Academy Awards, producers send you their movies on cassettes in hope you'll nominate something from their picture. I've got these cassettes—none of which were in stores at the time I was writing this: *Patriot Games, Husbands and Wives*, *White Men Can't Jump*, *The Crying Game*, *Basic Instinct*, *My Cousin Vinny*, and *Bob Roberts*, but my VCR isn't hooked up. It's a quarter to eleven at night, around the time I'd like to be turning in—maybe watch a little "Nightline" and call it a day, but the company is still on its lunch break. Gordon Smith, a lovely gentleman with white hair, just came in to hook up my VCR. He calls me "Sir." I always get uncomfortable when someone says "Sir," but luckily, it's a momentary thing and passes quickly.

It's after 1 A.M. I've just watched *My Cousin Vinny*, which I really enjoyed. I've been here close to six hours and haven't worked. The director and crew have been here two and a half hours longer than I have. Clearly things haven't gone as expected.

At 1:30 A.M. they called me to the "set," which is a 1950's bus lying on its side, appearing to have crashed. This is in the middle of a busy area of San Francisco on the edge of Chinatown and Nob Hill. We are at the end of a tunnel. They tell me people on other buses pass by and shudder, not realizing right away it's a movie. I have to crawl out a part of the bus and stand on the side and say, "Are you O.K.? I'm O.K.," to Alfre. That's it. Kyra and Tom have to stand perilously close to the edge of the bus, which is slippery. I'm more nervous for them than they are. Tom tells Ron Underwood, "Charles is nervous for me. Am I O.K. here?" He is told reassuring things, but I wouldn't want them perched there long. I'm not in a much better place—a little more space to stand, but no bargain, either. When we actors came on the set, the powers that be were checking to see if anyone was upset about waiting so long. There was some low muttering, but the actors did the shot. On a break, Clay and I found an all-night pizza place, and now the stunt men are "flying." We have to finish by 4:30 A.M. to reopen the street to traffic.

It's now raining off and on. Clay has put on *Husbands and Wives*, while we wait to be called again. It's 3 A.M. We've now watched *Husbands and Wives* until 3:30 A.M. when they tell me because of the rain I can go home. Because of watching *My*

Cousin Vinny, and two pair of thermals, I've had a surprisingly pleasant night.

It's the next night. I was called to be here at 6:45 P.M., and we're going to "fly" tonight. Mostly I'm thinking about none of us slipping off the bus. There's a light on and off drizzle. They've just told me they'll need me in fifteen minutes, so I should get dressed. I don't want to get dressed, as two sets of thermals under a wool suit is hot indoors, so I said, "Tell me—when it's five away, which will probably be in about a half hour." Now they're saying, "Ten away!" They often get us down on the set, and we mill around for another half-hour while lighting adjustments are made. That's the way it is. It's fine if you expect it. *You can't constantly be surprised by stuff that happens constantly*—like people who complain a line in a big market isn't moving fast enough—or about cable people not showing up. We're now in a holding area over near the bus. The first shot is actually the bus driver, David Paymer, flying. They tell me it will be his stunt double. David's being made up and will fly later.

It's now nine-thirty, and we're being hooked up to harnesses, so we can fly. We souls are all a little edgy, even though I'm confident it's safe. The problem is I'm never 100 percent confident about anything of this nature, so it will be nice when it's over.

It's over. We've flown! I loved it! We were hoisted by wires which, of course, you won't see in the finished film and taken high above the street well above the telephone lines. We were told we'd be taken up ten feet, but it seemed like a hundred. Whatever it was, it reminded me of a frequent childhood dream—even a sometimes adult dream of flying over the neighborhood. I was able to have complete trust in the wires holding me, which is really against my basic character, but I did. It was glorious. I think the reason I relaxed with it was there were a whole lot of *serious*-looking technicians working on this whole thing. I mean they were *focused*, and that made me O.K.

It's Saturday. We work six days a week when on location, which is anywhere other than home base, which, in this case, is

Los Angeles. We're asked to report for work at 5:00 P.M. There's a heavyweight fight on ABC's "Wide World of Sports" between Michael Moorer and Bonecrusher Smith which I'd like to see. I'm for abolishing boxing, but until they do I watch it. I get through the rehearsal in time to see the fight in my trailer. It's a dull fight, but reminds me of a Bonecrusher Smith story.

Phil Donahue, who is, among other things, a sports-watching buddy, is fully aware that I am more knowledgeable in these areas than he is. It's not something he likes to talk about. He is able to handle it, but he was very anxious one day to tell me who he'd run into at the airport.

ME

Who?

PHIL

Bonecrusher Smith! I was walking through the airport and I hear a voice call out "Phil!" I turn, and it was Bonecrusher Smith!

ME

Had you met him before?

PHIL

No! He sticks out his big hand. I said, "How ya doin', Bonecrusher!"
(a pause, with humor)
I bet *you've* never met Bonecrusher Smith!

ME

No, I haven't.

Around this time, Bonecrusher was going to fight Mike Tyson for the title. A few weeks later I was sitting around, and a fun idea

280

hit me. One of the unusual aspects of being Phil Donahue is that a surprisingly large percentage of people he meets either want to be on his show or want to suggest someone to be on. Phil, of course, has a large staff that handles all this. He's been on the air for over twenty-five years, so it's quite understandable if socially this is not his favorite subject. Barely able to contain myself, I called his office. A man answered.

ME
(in a Bonecrusher Smith voice)
Phil Donahue, please.

MAN
Who's calling?

ME
Bonecrusher Smith!

A long silence.

MAN
Hold on, please.

There was a wait of about a minute, before Phil got on.

PHIL
Bonecrusher! How ya doin'!?

ME
Great, Phil! Great running into you at the
airport the other day.

PHIL
(totally buying the voice)
Great seeing you, Bonecrusher!

ME

Phil, the reason I'm calling is, I have a new
book and my publisher thought it would be a
good idea to be on your show to help sell it.

A pause.

PHIL

Uh, gee . . . Bonecrusher, I don't know if I
can make boxing fly for an hour.

ME

It's more than about boxing, Phil. It's about
life!

A silence.

PHIL

Uh-huh. Well, let me give it some thought,
Bonecrusher. Have you got a number where
we can get back to you?

ME

Sure, Phil. By the way, don't you think I
sound a little like Charles Grodin?

A long silence.

PHIL

You son of a—!

Phil later told me he was actually considering maybe doing a
show with Bonecrusher and Tyson. He loves to tell the story as
much as I do.

It's now eight-thirty. We're doing a shot outside a theatre, which is taking a long time to prepare. As I've said, you can't be constantly surprised by something that happens constantly—

We got the shot. There were a lot of extras involved, as it was supposed to be taking place outside a theatre where there was a B.B. King concert. One young woman with a girlfriend came up to me—said she read both of my books in two days, that she showed up at another location of a picture I did, but missed me, wanted to have her picture taken with me. She was twenty-five. I asked her what she did. She said she was (what else) an actress living up in San Francisco. She said she'd been doing it for about five years, and she was surprised by how hard it was. When I asked how she got the impression it wasn't this hard, she said because she was from Hungary and had a slight Hungarian accent she thought that would open some doors. It seemed silly, but when you listened to her talk, you could see where she got that impression. It was a nice sound.

A young man came over to me and told me he grew up a couple of blocks from where I grew up, and he went to the Pittsburgh Playhouse, like me. I asked him about a former teacher. He said he had a heart attack and retired four years ago.

I forgot to mention I watched the rest of *Husbands and Wives* today. If it wasn't Woody Allen's current predicament that kept so many people from seeing it—it makes me nervous that a movie that good could interest relatively few people.

Earlier in the evening I was working in the backseat of a car next to Kyra for a shot. Kyra was really sick with a temperature; as I wrote earlier, everyone was sympathetic, but, of course, no one suggested she go home. It's really cold in San Francisco at night. Now as our day off came, I started feeling a little coldy and stayed in bed, wondering if I picked up Kyra's bug.

It's Monday now. I didn't get sick—a little, maybe, but I'm O.K. Today we're doing a sequence where I go to audition in a large opera house. I realize it's thirty years since I've had to audition in a theatre. That's one of the main benefits of being recognized. Many years ago I foolishly tried out for *Fiddler on the Roof* on Broadway. Not being a singer, that was clearly a mistake. Now doing an audition scene in a huge theatre brings back many memories—none good.

I have auditioned endless times and held them many times. I'm always struck, when seeing others, by how little thought or preparation most actors and actresses give to an audition. While I had great difficulty in the early years getting an audition, I often got the role when I did. I think this had something to do with my amount of preparation. I always tried to get the material ahead of time to look it over. Most of the people I've seen seem to almost be giving a "cold" reading—meaning they may have briefly perused it in the waiting room. It shows. It's amazing that so many people feel that's sufficient. Most often the job goes to someone who really gave the reading some thought. People conducting auditions want to see a performance level. It's true that sometimes it's downhill from there, but unless you really show something, it's virtually impossible you'll stand out from the dozens of people being considered.

There is also, I believe, a deeper understanding called for by the people conducting the auditions. Often you will hear people say "We saw over a hundred actors and no one was good." Part of that surely has to do with the actors' lack of preparation, but also sometimes it's the fault of those in charge. I was holding auditions once for a play I had written. The casting director had set up a chair behind a desk for me and a chair for the performer in the middle of the room. I helped the physical imbalance of power by putting the desk in front of the actor and letting me sit out in the open in the chair. I know it helped the performer's security, and I got better auditions.

I cringe when I think back on how I once badly screwed up auditioning a young woman for a play reading I was going to do for a piece of mine. The role called for a sexy actress, and after spending a long time reading this woman, I privately felt that, while she might be possible when we were to do the production—for a reading, a more obvious sex appeal was needed, since it's not all that easy to project sex appeal sitting in a chair with a script on your lap. I had worked with her so long I felt it was fair to share my thoughts with her. That was a mistake! She got very upset and didn't believe that while I wouldn't want her for the reading—I would consider her for the role. I realize that it sounds illogical, but it was what I felt. It got worse after she told me she is known for playing sexy roles. It was a mess, and I was wrong. Sometimes it's better not to try to be so forthcoming. Looking back, I did a kind of a Jay Bernstein (Farrah's manager) on her.

I heard earlier today I'm being offered another good movie. The producers of this new movie are saying if I do it they will film close to my house. The lesson here is to never underestimate the power of a dog. *Beethoven* took in almost sixty million dollars in America and almost ninety million elsewhere, plus selling four million cassettes.

I have another week of work in San Francisco during the day, then two more nights. I definitely am always interested in knowing how many nights. One good thing about the nights, I must say, however, is they tend to bring out the silly humor in me. Someone asked me the other night how many shots we had left. I answered, "Three. We have one shot of us standing on the bus—one shot of us watching the bus driver fly out of the bus, and then they want us to take a tetanus shot." I get my biggest laughs at night, too.

After we complete San Francisco's work, we go back to L.A. for a few days of what's called blue-screen. It's special photography at the studio of us "flying." Then I will have about six weeks before *Beethoven 2nd* starts.

I was reading and enjoying Michael Caine's book, *What's It All About?* He says the reason actors are paid so well is to make up for all the years we all made nothing. That's an interesting sentiment, but I think it's more that so few are in demand, like boxers or ball players. I consider myself extraordinarily fortunate, particularly because so many really talented actors don't even make a living.

The people on the picture now pretty much know I'm writing about this movie and them. Everyone hopes to be in the book. I guess they trust I won't trash them—not that there's anything here to trash. It's a group of people I genuinely like. That goes for the crew, too. It makes a huge difference, obviously, to work in a friendly atmosphere.

They've just put out a new schedule which adds an additional night. This has been a long schedule. It is now March 1, and we started rehearsing last Thanksgiving. It's long, but it's not as hard as some I have done where the time seemed longer. I'm sure that's because I'm writing this book.

One of the ladies working in the makeup trailer tells me this morning she worked for years in the San Francisco Opera House and opera singers pretty much grabbed women for a squeeze or a pat as naturally as they vocalized. I said, "Well, those times have passed." She looked at me and said, "Not so much around the opera." To produce those sounds must put people on enormous edge, but an uninvited squeeze these days and you could end up singing in the street, which is how it should be. I don't mean to impugn opera signers. I'm just reporting what I hear.

One of our hairstylists is undergoing tests for cancer. Life does have a way of working itself in there. I chose not to mention it earlier, probably wanting not to deal with it myself, but Alfre's mother passed away around a month ago. Alfre was in a daze for a while but now appears "back to normal." Of course, you never really are.

Gordon Smith has been adjusting my satellite dish on the trailer for months trying to bring in the New York Knicks games. He approaches this with the same focus and intensity as Ron does the direction of the movie, which is considerable. The other day Gordon told me he had pursued an acting career. "I was really good in summer stock, but never got anywhere in New York." That's not an unusual story. I wonder if he'd had the opportunities, what would have happened. I wonder that about a lot of actors.

This is another one of those sitting around days. I've actually done all my work in this scene, so I'm a background figure in most of today's shots. We get out the cassette of *Bob Roberts*, which I started watching the other day. It was very interesting, and, of course, points out how much of politics is show business. Great communicators, as we know, can become President. Who these people are, or what they really think, remains elusive.

Someone has called and asked me to read "Jack and the Beanstalk" for books on tape. I love "Jack and the Beanstalk," even though I don't really know the whole story. I know there's Jack and this beanstalk that goes into the sky, and a giant lives up there. I don't really need to know any more than that, so I said, "Yes." "It will only take a couple of hours," they say. They call my agent and offer me a thousand dollars to do this, plus 2 percent of the profits. If they had said no money and all profits go to charity, I would have done it, but 2 percent of the profits begs the question, "Who gets the other 98 percent?" It's not the author of "Jack and the Beanstalk," because that's in the public domain. So again, the question is, after all recording and packaging and promotional costs are recouped, who gets the other 98 percent? They tell my representative that Lily Tomlin and Dudley Moore, among other notables, have done it for that. Even if that's true, it's irrelevant to me. As in *The Incredible Shrinking Woman*, I'm compelled to again ask, "Who's Lily Tomlin's agent?" Unless there's some answer to the "who gets the other 98 percent" question that I can't presently fathom— you'll have to get through your life without hearing me read "Jack and the Beanstalk." As I've said, since I'd do it for nothing, this isn't about money—but fairness. I'm already a little wary because in the past these same people called twice to "ask" me to read my second book, *How I Get Through Life*, on tape, and I said I'd love to, but they never called back. There wasn't even a discussion of terms.

Without talking about myself, if somebody wants to buy a tape of Lily Tomlin reading "Hansel and Gretel," for example, and there's ultimately a dollar in profit involved, shouldn't Lily get more than two cents? I mean, who's going to buy a tape of "Hansel and Gretel" read by say, Jane Smith? Most moms probably feel *they* could read it as well as Jane. You buy it because Lily is reading it—period. She's got to get more than two cents on a buck, and so do I. I guess behind all of this is the non-follow-up on *How I Get Through Life*.

Another time I got a call from some producers who had earlier pulled the rug out from under a project of mine. My wife wanted to know why I was dealing with them again. I said, "They may be jerks, but they're *my* jerks"—meaning there were so few people calling. Happily that's no longer the case, so I suffer jerks or broken promises less easily. It's a nice feeling but, of course, if things take a turn for the worse in the future, I'll grab the thousand and run. The ironic thing about this profit stuff is, of course, you'd never see it anyway—so it really doesn't matter if *I* have ninety-eight and *they* have two—it's just the principle. That old devil-principle.

I am suddenly called out for a retake of us souls dancing across a hilly San Francisco street with Robert. It's the kind of sudden action that could make you throw up if you've just eaten, which I have. They really liked it the first time we did it a week or so ago, but the light in the sky is more attractive now, so we do five takes dancing across the street and get it. One more shot and it's home for the day. It's another retake because of better light. In the shot we're walking down the hill toward our trailers. Once Ron is satisfied, we can just keep walking, because we're finished for the day.

After the fifth try, Ron is satisfied. I keep walking to my trailer to Clay, the car, and home—I mean the hotel.

Another day is beginning. Kyra is still sick and on antibiotics. A doctor will be coming to see her. I have stayed just this side of O.K. The hotel people were really nice last night and sent someone out to get me lozenges and matzoh-ball soup. This is a day of just picking up loose ends in car shots. After today we move to split days—meaning part day and part night. I'll work only in the day, which means from about 10 A.M. to 5 P.M. That's the best you can ask for. It turns out we have about four more nights in San Francisco, then back to L.A. for three more days, and that's it. I'll get about four to six weeks before *Beethoven 2nd* starts. At first I was hoping it could start right away, but now I'll happily take the break.

I stay in touch with my agent, Jim Berkus, who tells me, in all likelihood, Universal will be asking me to direct my screenplay of *The Secret Life of Men*. It's something I wrote for the incredibly successful producer/director Ivan Reitman and Universal. Ivan said write something about three men in their forties, and it ended up being *The Secret Life of Men*. As I've said, at best I've had mixed feelings about directing a picture, even though I've had success directing on Broadway and television specials. One of the attractions here is I could film it in New York and Connecticut, where I live. Also we are now in negotiation for me to act in *My Summer Story*, which would start right after *Beethoven's 2nd*. This is based on the work of Jean Shepherd, who was a radio personality on the air in New York for several hours in the night when I first came to New York. I used to listen to him religiously. About ten years ago, MGM made *A Christmas Story*, based on a novel of Jean's, and because of the continued interest in that one—here comes *My Summer Story*. They've got Macaulay Culkin's brother Kieran to play the boy and want me to play his "old man." It is a period piece set in the forties. This is the picture they said they'd try to do near where I live in

Connecticut. I somehow don't believe economically they can do that. I'll just wait to see what develops.

We're now on my last shot of the day. I'm sitting between Alfre and Kyra in the small backseat of a *little* sports car, chastising Tom, who's yelling at Robert—only, because of all the necessary equipment, Tom and Robert aren't there. Ron Underwood says Tom's lines (Robert doesn't speak in the scene). Ron is on the camera truck where all the cameras are mounted. We hear his voice miked into our car. We are being towed quite conspicuously through San Francisco at rush hour. We are lit up. People are staring at us. Kyra is coughing and being advised to change her antibiotics. Alfre is noticing places she can take Kyra where they can get clothes. There's plenty of time to check out windows in stores, because in car shots most of the time you're being towed to where the shot begins and back again after you shoot it. Alfre also has a piece of material between her dress and my wool suit jacket she's trying to conceal from the camera. Wool is rough on her even through her dress. Every five minutes or so, we yell at the imaginary Tom Sizemore. If Robert and Tom *were* there, they'd have to crunch themselves into little balls in order to fit in the available space, and Tom particularly isn't going to crunch that easily into a little ball. Anyway, we yell at air for a while, and it's a day.

I came back to work today and immediately one of my jokes caused some momentary trouble. Two young women were walking by with four dogs. As they passed, I said to one of the assistants, "Those dogs didn't recognize me!" The assistant understood the joke, but the women turned and said with an edge, "What?!" I quickly said, "I did a movie with a dog. That was a joke." They stared at me for a moment and moved on. I haven't even gone into my trailer yet, and I'm causing trouble.

All of us actors are wandering around the top of a hill with our cellular phones cutting out. We're trying to stay in touch with our families and agents, among others. I even tried a phone interview, but all over the hill you hear, "Oh, oh, I'm losing you." "The line's cutting out." "I can't hear you." "Hello,

hello." Oh well. It's a beautiful day. I'm surprised to hear we have to do some more flying, but I hear it's a moderate amount, so I'll just look for some laughs—off-screen, I mean. We fly so quickly on-screen there's no time for a joke.

A little while ago I was standing on the hill talking on my phone when a woman drove by and asked me if I knew where the Russian embassy was. Clearly, I give the impression of someone who might know that kind of thing—with my cellular phone and all.

We've finally flown. It wasn't bad. The harness was tight, but other than that—fine. That's it for the flying until a couple of days in Los Angeles at the studio in a few weeks. Alfre actually asked if she could be taken up as high as possible just for the fun of it. I looked at her and headed back to my trailer. That's some Alfre—that Alfre.

I put *A River Runs Through It* into the VCR. It seems like a very good movie, but it causes a feeling of melancholy in me. Since I watch these cassettes to avoid melancholy—I stop that one. Under different circumstances, I believe I would appreciate it more. I search my mind for comedies to rent, but so far I haven't come up with anything. More and more I realize fun— comedy—and more fun is my blood transfusion.

The assistant, Shawn, gets word from the set on his walkie-talkie that I'm finished for the day. It will be like this for the remainder of the picture. I hear as I'm ready to leave that MGM has made their offer. It suggests we will make a deal to do this picture, *My Summer Story*, that will begin immediately after *Beethoven's 2nd*.

I once got an offer to do a picture from a producer who told my agent, "This is what we'll pay him. Take it or leave it!" The agent left it without even telling me, properly figuring I wasn't going to want to work with someone who had that style. It wasn't the money that was off, it was the producer, as I was paid exactly the same amount for my next picture, but they were very nice about it.

It's Saturday morning. We are working on top of a big hill again. It's a gorgeous day, and as happy as I am that we're winding down here, I know I'll miss this group when the picture comes to an end. I will have my makeup man with me on *Beethoven's 2nd.* Jim Scribner has been with me for three in a row now, and of course Clay will always be there, I hope, as long as he wants to be. He continues to excel whether he's dealing with the intellectual or the mundane aspects of the job, and, of course, there's always that excellent disposition—a very big item.

We're waiting across the street for our shot. Tom Sizemore leans against a wall and paint comes off on his jacket. We weren't told it was freshly painted. It's impressive what the scenic designer and set decorator achieve. We show up to film at these perfect-looking places, and after a while you tend to forget a lot of time and effort has been put into finding locations and fixing them up. They are constantly wetting down the streets with water trucks. It doesn't look like it rained but gives the streets a glistening quality. On the interiors, it's often *all* movie furniture and set-dressing.

A journalist from *Premiere* magazine is on the set. The actors take note of this and are a bit wary. From experience we know, in general, it's the journalist's job to ingratiate himself and then write whatever is compelling, which isn't always in the actors' interest. I don't really concern myself with that. There have been a few occasions over many years where I read stuff I didn't like, but very few, and this feeling passes quickly. In a book about the making of *King Kong* a journalist wrote that I complained there was no bathroom in my, I guess, camper. Maybe *that's* the difference between a camper and a trailer. Anyway, it was written as though I was out of line, but reading it, I felt the company was— not me. When you're in a movie for nine months, which is how long *King Kong* took, you're entitled to a bathroom of *some* kind. The main thing about all of this is, unless it's something heinous that's written—nobody cares or remembers—so you just have to stay away from heinous behavior, which isn't a bad idea whether a journalist is present or not.

I'm standing on the corner talking on the phone, and a man comes over and starts to tell me how much he enjoyed my first book. I try to nod politely, then indicate to him I'm on the phone, which, of course, he can see. I feel a little bad, but justified. He probably feels snubbed. I, on the other hand, am wondering if he didn't like my *second* book. Just a passing thought.

We are finishing a shot riding on the back of a tow truck that is traveling fast up and down a hill. The shot is over, but the truck speeds bumpily on as Tom Sizemore says, "This is making me nervous. Let's sing a song." He gets a good laugh out of me.

Michael, the wardrobe fellow who looks after my clothes, is called back to L.A. as his roommate has gone into a coma. We hear the next day he has died of complications from AIDS. As I've said, the longer the schedule, the more all elements of life get in here.

We're about to do a scene where we're chased by that Rotweiller dog from earlier in the picture. I can't help myself from asking, "How can we be sure the dog won't bite us?" I get joke answers like, "He has no teeth." "He's a professional dog." Once again I'll be glad when the sequence is over. To me people running away from a dog may make the dog forget he's acting.

We get through one shot with the dog chasing us with no harm. We have several like this today. The dog rehearses too, of course, but less than we do. In a shot as we run away from the dog up the stairs, the dog is supposed to bite Robert's coat and rip it. I see Robert's double waiting to do the shot. He's nervously chuckling as he discusses it. He says, "I worked with the dog before, but he wasn't supposed to bite me," and then come more nervous chuckles. Personally, they couldn't pay me enough money to do that job. The dog, Brutus, is just hanging out having some water. He's one of the only performers not wondering what time we'll finish on this sixth day of what must be around our eighteenth week. Before the shot where the dog "bites"

Robert's double, we run down a hall and up a flight of stairs with the dog in pursuit. We each guess how many times we will need to do this before Ron is satisfied. After four times Ron and everyone are happy, especially me. One more shot of us from up above, and the week is over. I'm perspiring from head to toe, it hurts when I swallow, and my legs ache, but I'm pleased we're close to finishing. I'm sure I'm imagining it, but Brutus, the dog, seems pretty pleased, too. I'm hearing unofficially we've finished *without* the last shot. Clay goes to check it out. "We're wrapped," Clay announces with a grin as he bounds into the trailer.

On location, which is what San Francisco is on this picture, as I've said, we work a six-day week, so we have Sunday off. Generally if you've really put in the hours, the day off seems to consist of a fair amount of staring into space. This Sunday, however, Clay has asked if I will come and meet his family—about fifteen people who live in the Oakland area. I agree, because Clay is Clay. This will be unusual, of course, because I will be the only person there who will know no one but Clay. Actually I did meet Clay's five-year-old nephew Steven, who came to play with my boy when he visited me here. My son, Nicky, had told Steven that I was real mean and drank blood, so Steven on first meeting me had approached cautiously. In a short while he satisfied himself that the mean and blood thing was a joke, and we had a good time, but still I would be meeting a house full of strangers.

The only other time I'd done anything even remotely like this was when I went to a rug merchant's home for dinner in Marrakesh. The language barrier there actually created some laughs, as the evening developed into a necessary form of charades.

When we arrived at Clay's family's house most of the clan was standing in front. It was quite a range of people from Clay's mother, Big Red, to a darling little baby new to walking. There was Steven, who happily greeted me like his long-lost soul mate and immediately showed me everything he owned. Grown-ups, including me, like to do that, too. We just attempt a casualness about it. There was Big Red's husband and a number of brothers and sisters and one friend of Clay's named Chuck, who preferred to be called "the other Chuck" rather than "the second Chuck." This Chuck it turned out had been a clown with Ringling-Brothers Circus in the seventies. He told me the pay was $150 a week with no expenses. They slept on the train in the rail yards. They didn't have beds but those chairs that tilt back. Brother! I'm going to try to talk less about the waiting in movies. Anyway, Chuck told me something I'd never heard before in my life. He'd had his date of birth changed on all documents but his birth certificate. He got a witness to convince the necessary people to change it on his driver's license, etc. The reason for all of this wasn't to qualify for the service or anything like that. His birthday was around the same time as some other birthdays in his family, so he hadn't gotten all that much attention. Also he had experienced some personal setbacks around that birthday time, so he chose another one a couple of months later. He said with the new date everything was noticeably better.

Everyone was very nice—very warm. The food was great. Even the young Dalmatian seemed sweet. I knew Clay had a brother, Frank, who is a high-powered used car salesman. I had never met him, but Clay had put my daughter, Marion, in touch with him to get some information about a car she was interested in buying. Marion reported to me that Frank was most helpful, but talking to him was a unique experience for her. That's really saying something, because some people have said the same about Marion. Let's just say Marion doesn't lack in energy, and for her to find someone unique in that department was, well . . . unique. When Frank entered with his understandably subdued wife, Carol, we were halfway through dinner. His appearance alone caused me to shout out, "O.K.! I'll take the Pontiac!" He was big and even in repose the energy exuded. When he started talking I realized the only other time I'd seen a force like that was, coincidentally, years ago on a used car lot—certainly never in a moderate-sized dining room. He was a phenomenon, and it was easy to see why he had won Salesman of the Month a record number of times.

Driving home over the Bay Bridge, the one where a portion collapsed during the earthquake, we spotted a woman who had stopped her car in the middle of the highway and was rummaging around on the floor of the backseat. Since we were approaching a toll booth, Clay surmised she couldn't find her purse. He sprung from our car and handed her a dollar. The look of joy and gratitude on her face was a wonderful capper to the evening.

It's a quarter to one A.M. Tuesday morning. I was asked to show up at 11:30 P.M. We've been getting the twenty-minute warning for an hour now. All I do is sit on a bus tonight, probably for a few hours once I get on there. There's something about coming to work just when you'd be going to bed that's . . . different. My body seems to be saying, "What's happening? Why are you getting dressed to go out?!" It's fun to see everyone, though. Kyra is still coughing a lot. She's really struggling, but she hangs in there beautifully. I've got *Patriot Games* with me, but I'll probably head out toward the bus before I put it on. Tomorrow I'm off completely, so I'm either going to visit the estate where we filmed *Heaven Can Wait* or San Quentin, which, of course, is a maximum security prison. Given the choice, I'll take Quentin. I don't know what that says about me. Maybe it's because *Heaven Can Wait* was filled with *so* much waiting that the estate is scarier to me than the prison.

At one point during the making of *Heaven Can Wait* I did something to this day I can't quite believe I did. I must have been so bummed out by the extraordinary amount of waiting. As I wrote elsewhere, Warren Beatty believed in having everybody made up and in costume for what seemed like just about every day. He had worked with Robert Altman, and Altman did it because he might at any moment decide to put one of the actors into a sequence where the script didn't have them. Warren, on the other hand, *never* did anything like that, but had us all made up and in costume anyway because of the possibility he *might*. I was unsuccessful in trying to get him to drop the concept, and this is what must have led to my frustration the day he wanted all of us to practice playing football with him. This would end up being for one brief five-second cut in the movie where Warren, in preparation for his return as a quarterback for the Los Angeles Rams, practices with his household staff. I'm sorry, to me, you don't even rehearse that. You have a lot of people who couldn't possibly catch a football—middle-aged English butlers, etc. When you shoot it, you tell them to go out for a pass and if you just film that—no rehearsal—it would look like what it looked like *with* rehearsal—even better. I promise you, I wouldn't do this today, but that day as the household staff, men and women, ran out for passes, I walked away and sat in a distant gazebo. I could faintly hear people calling, "Where's Charles?" "Where's Charles Grodin?" "Would someone get Charles Grodin?" I just sat there and stared at the trees. After about forty-five minutes I got bored hiding out and drifted over to the practice field. Warren was busy passing the ball to a heavy-set actress playing a woman servant when he saw me and said, "Chuck, go out for a pass." I went over to him and said, "Y'know, we might have a problem here. I'm not supposed to be a good athlete as your secretary, but in life I'm an excellent athlete. It could look strange. What would you like me to do?" He stared at me, not sure what I was up to. It's actually because of Warren I eventually dropped a very high percentage of my put-on humor. He's a very sharp guy, and when he told me he couldn't "read" me in life and alluded to how that could be discomfiting, I decided to straighten out the curve a little. Anyway, this day, after hearing what an excellent athlete I was (a little true), he said again, "go out for a pass." I shrugged and jogged out. He threw me one, and I reached up and pulled it in with one hand. I probably couldn't have done that again in a hundred tries. Warren stared at me. I jogged over to a bench and said, "I don't think it's in the scene's interest I practice too much." Anyway, looking back over the whole *Heaven Can Wait* filming experience at the estate in Palo Alto, I think I'll visit San Quentin.

Shawn just knocked and said, "Ten away." Yeah. Right.

It's now fifteen minutes since "Ten away." There's no question reporting for work at bedtime doesn't bring out the best in me. I will still never consciously, nor hopefully unconsciously, behave disrespectfully toward anyone because, along with every other reason—most of the people working have been here longer than I have. Earlier I watched my Knicks play the Orlando Magic on TNT. The Knicks won in overtime, so I definitely have that thought to fall back on tonight.

I ask Clay to put *Patriot Games* in the VCR. You never know when an unexpected hour or more wait will hit. The movie looks good.

It's an hour later, a little after 2 A.M., and we're on the bus. Ron Underwood comes over and allows, "It's a good feeling" that we're winding down. It's his first concession that we've even been through something. It's actually better not to even talk about a long journey—best just to take the next step and eventually if you're lucky the next one will one day be the last one.

It's 2:30 A.M. The bus is about to pull out. There's a camera truck in front of us towing the bus and about five motorcycle police accompanying the whole deal.

Ron continues to act as though we're at a kid's party. The cheerful look seems to say, "Hi, howya doin'? Want a balloon?" The lights go out in the bus regularly, so it's late, cold, dark— definitely a time for some humor, but we're all too tired.

It's 3 A.M. I'm back in the trailer with *Patriot Games* while they light the next shot.

Patriot Games has got me to 4:45 A.M. without looking at my watch. I still haven't done anything but be in the distant background on one shot where if the shot's in the movie I seriously doubt I will be visible. I just read the last sentence to the assistant director, Shawn, who said, "I doubt it, too." We have one more shot where I am even less likely to be seen, and then I can go home, which will probably be around 5:45 A.M. It's not fun, but it's part of being in the movies. Again I'm really grateful there have been so few times like this.

We end the night with Academy Award nominee David Paymer literally driving our old bus down a San Francisco street and back several times. The bus is vibrating wildly and as a result so is David's entire body.

We have a day off, and Clay and I head for San Quentin. It's a beautiful drive, but once there, I decide to stay in the car and just check it out from the visitors' parking lot. Like Alcatraz, it has great views, but the windows look like they were painted green—probably not, but they looked that way. Clay learned there was a museum we could go to on the grounds to see prison stuff, but I chose to pass on that. I mean, what would I look at?—a pipe that was used to bonk a guard—what? Basically I had to wonder what all the people who lived in the nearby houses thought when they woke up in the morning and looked out the window. Do you just get used to the idea that the building across the way has a working electric chair?—not to mention just thinking about the clientele in the place.

The next day before coming to work tonight, I watch *Born on the Fourth of July*. I was really moved by it and thought first it was too bad something like that wasn't done when the Vietnam War was still going on. Then I wished I had made something of that sentiment. Amazingly, I forgot I had. In 1969, I made the anti-war Simon and Garfunkel television special that was actually shown on CBS at nine o'clock Sunday night, always an entertainment slot. I wrote about this extensively in my first book, so suffice it to say that where Oliver Stone properly won an Academy Award in 1990, in 1970, for our show AT&T removed its name as sponsor, the Nixon White House requested a tape of the show, and the *Washington Post* wrote an editorial marveling that it got on the air. *TV Guide* objected that it aired in an entertainment time slot, prompting the biggest outpouring of mail against their position the magazine ever received—talk about a split country. I've been doing lighthearted things for so long I actually forgot once I made something like that.

We have a full night tonight and tomorrow night, then back to L.A. for a couple of days. It's a beautiful night, and I've brought the movie *JFK* in case we get into some heavy waiting. We watched it for about a half an hour before we were called. What a piece of filmmaking!

Robert is driving and Tom, Kyra, Alfre and I are jammed into this tiny car again. Robert backs it to the bottom of a hill where two policemen assigned to assist us are stationed. One of the officers starts talking to Robert in kind of a sharp way—not sharp to someone breaking a law—sharp to an actor about to play a big scene. Tom says, "We're in the movie," in case the officer wondered what we were doing, but clearly he knew we were the actors. He's just giving us attitude that climaxes with him saying to Robert in a really edgy tone, "Would you step out of the car?" It was upsetting, and the guy was truly out of line. Robert felt abused, but tried to stay cool about it. I didn't. After the shot I went to two of our producers and told them to back the guy off. They sent their police liaison—someone from the San Francisco Police Department—down to the bottom of the hill to talk to the guy.

When we backed down the hill again, the liaison guy was standing there in a leather jacket next to one cop and our rough cop was standing back a little. I checked him out. I'm sure he would like to have turned our car over, but he was holding it together pretty good. I guess police officers don't speak to the public unless they're at least chastising, if not busting them, so maybe they sometimes don't have the chops to talk to someone in a different context—especially not to an actor about to go in front of the camera. The actors were friendly. The cop was not.

We're filming next to what I understand is a big drug park. Our lights have clearly limited park activity.

I find it necessary to back off the still photographer. We have an absolute understanding he doesn't shoot when I'm filming. I guess because I don't say anything in the scene he thinks it's O.K. to shoot, because he did, and standing close to me, too. An excellent young actress, Elisabeth Shue, is mostly on camera, but my head is right next to her, and when I look over at Robert, there's the still-guy popping away a few feet behind him. It's an amazing distraction for me and plenty of other actors. From now on I'm going to put it in my contract they can shoot whenever they want, but they're off the set when we film. That way I can finally stop thinking about it. As I've said, I'll do it—we all will, especially for them, once we've filmed it. I'm truly tired of thinking about it. I think these people should be doing this selectively for particularly interesting still possibilities—not every day for everything for months.

I spend a couple more hours waiting and watching *JFK*. Again the filmmaking is breathtaking, and I thoroughly enjoy the picture, but the certainty with which each set of circumstances in the story suggests another conspiracy almost starts to be satirical to me. I would satirize it something like this. "I cut my toe, you had lunch and Fred took his car to the garage, all at 1 P.M. Don't you see what that means?"

Both Kyra and Tom were in *Born on the Fourth of July*. I'm deeply moved by Kyra's work and tell her so. Tom is only in it for about eight seconds, and I tell him it's so short, it's like Oliver Stone was only fulfilling some contractual obligation that would call for a penalty if Tom didn't get his eight. What's great about Tom Sizemore is he loves to laugh and have fun along with being plenty talented. I find myself really rooting for him to have a nice career. Next he plays a leading role in a picture called *Natural Born Killer* for Oliver.

I get to go home at 4:30 A.M. instead of 5:30 only because I ask them to think ahead whether they'll need us. I still manage to get only four hours' sleep before I'm awake again waiting for tonight, which is our last night in San Francisco. I will lie in bed all day, before I'm called for 6:15 P.M. rehearsal. A doctor who treats the company up here told a friend of my wife's who told me that "Everyone up here got sick except Charles Grodin." I doubt that anyone addresses the preventive issue as aggressively as I do, either.

I run into an actor playing a small part in the picture with whom I worked at the beginning of my career. I don't recall seeing him much, if at all, over the years. I would assume it's been a difficult road. There is some uneasiness as we greet each other. He remembers working with me as well. Neither of us recalls exactly where. I never even considered the possibility that I'd be struggling past a certain point. For me the struggle really stopped when I was thirty-three. If my career had continued to be uncertain much longer—I might have gotten out and gone into something else. I can't imagine a lifetime of waiting for the phone to ring.

In Michael Caine's book, he talks about working with Laurence Olivier in *Sleuth*. Olivier says to Michael Caine, "When we began, I thought I had a very skilled assistant. I now see I have a partner." It reminded me of an encounter I had with the great English actor Eric Portman, who was a star when I was driving a cab in New York in the late fifties. I recognized him when he got into my cab and said, "Mr. Portman, you may not believe me, but I feel you are one of the five greatest actors in the world." Without missing a beat, he responded with great confidence, "I believe you!" He was appearing on Broadway with Geraldine Page, who was then and for decades after until her death considered one of our finest actresses, if not *the* finest. I told Mr. Portman of my admiration for Miss Page, and he patronizingly commented, "Well . . . she's a student." Even though I was new to the profession, I bristled on her behalf. I responded, "Well, of course, we're all students." There was less chat in the cab after that, but he did invite me to see the play and, I'm sorry, Geraldine Page was in a whole other league—the highest one.

I arrive at work excited that this is the last night—that I get to go home to my family tomorrow. I tell Ron on the set something to that effect, and he smiles one of his bigger smiles and says, "Don't be so sure!" I'm startled. What is he saying?—I have to stay here and work some more? I do some digging. It wouldn't be right to go to Ron directly and ask him, "What's up?" because he's up to his ears addressing the night's shooting issues. I learn that the studio is thinking of releasing the picture at Christmas rather than rushing it out in August, which would allow only four months for postproduction work, which may not be enough. I don't honestly know why it needs to take that much time for editing and scoring and mixing of a lot of effects tracks, but it clearly does. I learn the studio has a lot of faith in the picture, which is expensive, and wants to spend more to make it even better, which might also mean more stuff I'd do—but not tomorrow, and that's the main thing. I'm actually pleased to hear it. Unless they think highly of it, studios don't spend more money on something.

Eventually I take Ron off to the side and ask him what he meant with his cryptic remark, really to verify what I've heard. I learn I got it all wrong. In confidence, he tells me the issue is nothing I've just heard but is whether the film we shot last night is in appropriate focus. It may be one person in one shot, and that may be O.K., if we cut around it. Ron and some of the others will check it out in a couple of hours at around midnight, when it arrives on a flight from L.A. There is a possibility we may have to stay over and reshoot tomorrow night and go home a day later. Most of us are already packed—cast and crew— around a hundred people, I would guess. I know in the overall scheme of things—what does one more day matter, but when you're all packed and anxious to see your family, as so many of us are, well . . . you know.

It now seems word of what could happen has spread all around the company. We'll know if the film is all right or not shortly.

I am watching *Unforgiven*. I've heard people love it or hate it. I'm in between. There seems to be much good work, but I don't fully "get" it. Maybe I'm preoccupied over whether we can leave or not. It reminds me of the time I teased Warren Beatty that my appreciation of his film *Reds* was affected because I wasn't seated in the roped-off section at a big screening of the picture. It was a joke, as I really liked the movie enormously.

Our film is O.K.! We go home tomorrow as planned! A cheer went up from the company when the announcement was made!

I wait around long enough to see all of *Unforgiven* and half of *A Few Good Men*. By 4 A.M., when I'm released, we're all so tired and out of it we could do a good job on a sequel of *Night of the Living Dead*. As we head to the car, Clay calls out, "Have a good trip" to no one. When I asked him to turn off the music in the car, he says, "Music?" and when I say, "Let's leave for the airport at eleven forty-five tomorrow," he thinks a quarter to twelve might be better. I mean, we're *tired*! But it's over here, and two more days next week in L.A. and it's over—period. Everyone will be happy, as it's been a long one and hopefully a really good one.

After almost a week off, I'm back at Universal Studios in Los Angeles for the last day of this nineteen-week movie. It turns out I'm only needed for this one day, not two. I arrive with mixed feelings—happy a long schedule has come to its end, and surprisingly sentimental as we souls have been a group with the common bond of being souls. Even though it's a movie—a soul is still a soul.

I have some flying shots today and then some still shots for poster art and then my dreaded interview with what they call the electronic press kit. This is where everyone talks about their character and the movie, which I find not only boring but counterproductive. That leaves me only with an option of kidding around, and extended kidding around is a job. I'm comforted in knowing they will use only the parts they find entertaining.

There will be a party for the cast and crew tomorrow night that I'll attend, and that's it for *Heart and Souls*. The picture will be in theaters in a little over four months, and by the time you read this we'll all know if the effort was worth it. Hope really springs eternal when all this work and money have been expended. In any case, the picture certainly makes a positive statement about life, and I'm proud to have been a part of it.

Every time I come on the set, I look for my chair. As I've said, I believe in sitting whenever possible, even if I don't feel like it, as it pays off later in the day. Today when I came on for my flying, Kyra was already up there and after looking around, I asked for my chair. It was flying high above the floor as a joke. I called to Horst, the prop man, "You finally made the book!" The joke was I always wanted the chair moved as close to where I was going to be working. We all had a good laugh.

I've flown. I'm finished! There were five different angles with me plenty high up there, and when I finished, our sound man, Richard Goodman, played "The Thrill Is Gone." Very nice. Ron Underwood came over, and we had a genuinely warm good-bye. What a great pleasure he has made these four months.

I'd like to close this chapter with excerpts from the interview that I filmed for the electronic press kit right after the completion of my work in the picture.

ME

(to interviewer)

I would like to take this opportunity to say publicly that just because you play an invisible soul in the picture, as I do, that doesn't mean, as the studio feels, that you don't need dressing room accommodations. The studio took the position that because I was invisible, I didn't need to break for lunch, and I think that was inappropriate. It's been a lot more difficult, because I had to stand outside the sound stages and change clothes, just kind of lean against a pole most of the time, and hope that some of the production people would, you know . . . if they didn't finish a sandwich or something. I just think that the studio behaved in a very bizarre way regarding all of us souls in this picture. There was never a chair, there was never a meal break, there was never a dressing room, there was never even a glass of water, even when working on some of the hot, hot days outside.

INTERVIEWER

Sounds like it was quite a challenge. I mean—

ME

It *was* a challenge. It just called upon . . . resources that I haven't been used to calling upon. And you know, as Nietzsche said, "If it doesn't kill you, it makes you stronger," so possibly that's true . . . but in the future if I ever play this kind of a role again I'm going to make sure that the contract has certain stipulations. The studio should not be able to get away with that.

INTERVIEWER

Okay, good. Was there any special preparation that you undertook to play the role of someone who is there but not really there?

ME

No, because that's what I basically am in life anyway. I haven't really been there for years, I think since grammar school.

INTERVIEWER

Okay, good. Charles, is there ... Can you maybe define a little bit for us, you know, what the souls can do and cannot do. I mean you observe reality as it goes on around you, but you can't interact with it.

ME

I never really understood what the souls could do or not do. I didn't know whether they could touch each other ... I knew we couldn't eat ... on or off camera as I mentioned. Frankly, in the picture you will notice that I am often trying to sit down, 'cause only in the movie itself, on the set can I sit, because there was no place to sit off the set. They had chairs for everybody connected to the studio, and everybody working on the crew. They felt these were hard-working people, but I just don't understand their logic, so in the picture itself I would always be sitting. I didn't even ask, frankly. They started a scene; I sat down, 'cause I was exhausted. So the hardest part of this role was really off-screen, because the conditions were so deplorable; but on-screen, you know, living rooms, bedrooms, it was nice, you sit, you relax.

INTERVIEWER

Okay. Maybe a few words about what it's like working with Ron Underwood.

A pause.

ME

Ron Underwood . . . He was the director, right?

INTERVIEWER

Yes, the director.

ME

Yeah, he was there. He's very happy, he smiles a lot. I think he's got something else going on that keeps him pretty happy most of the time, because nobody working fourteen-, fifteen-hour days on a movie could be that happy. So I think Ron probably has some personal investments that were going very well during the picture, 'cause he always had a big grin from ear to ear. I can only imagine that's what it would have had to do with.

INTERVIEWER

Okay. Charles, what will the viewers take away after sitting in a theater and watching this movie? Will they carry anything with them out to the bright daylight?

ME

I just think with any movie you have to remember to take what you came in with.

308

You know, you don't want to leave your jacket or your purse or anything. Not only in the movies, but really anywhere, when you get out of a cab, whatever, make sure you've taken all your valuables, because the movie theatres or the cab companies or the airlines, they're not really responsible for your belongings, and I think when you come away from *Heart and Souls* that the same would be true. Just make sure that you've got your jacket with you.

INTERVIEWER

Okay. They have you strapped into this contraption flying around on wires. Tell me a little bit about that.

ME

We were harnessed to fly on these wires. In fact, as you know, I'm sitting in a harness now, and I'm kind of in devastating pain, but I'm paid a great deal of money, so I don't mean any of this complaintively, I just mean it as a statement of fact regarding the facilities, or lack of facilities, and the . . . excruciating pain of the harness. These are just facts of life and you just live with it. That's the way it is. It's a painful experience, it's an experience of considerable deprivation, but you know, so is life.

INTERVIEWER

If you were given the little details, you know, getting chairs, food, etc., etc., would you play the role of the soul again?

ME

You know, for the right amount of money I'd really do anything, to be honest with you. I mean they're talking to me about a movie, playing the nice side of Hitler, and the money is incredible, because nobody wants to play this, so we're talking about it. Just a question of definition of gross points is what we're really into now.

INTERVIEWER

Okay. All right, good. That's pretty much— Well, would you say that this is a special effects movie? I mean, you're talking about souls and invisible people and, you know, there's flying . . .

ME

I don't really know. I haven't seen any of the movie. I don't go to the dailies. The people who go to dailies have really mastered sleeping standing up, because if you work for sixteen hours and then you go to dailies for three hours, I mean if you think about it, there really is no time to go home. So, there are a number of people on this picture who just can sleep in place, standing, like horses, and . . . it's tough. You've got some very odd expressions on the people on this picture as though they've been somewhere, and they're not sure quite where that is, but I don't think they're making plans to go back.

INTERVIEWER

Anything else that you'd like to add?

ME

I'd like to salute you for your continued
good work. You know, I haven't seen you
since you interviewed Martin Short with an
IV tube, and he fell out of the chair in a
coughing fit. Did you conduct those interviews or you were just there? Because I
don't remember your face. But then I don't
remember people's faces . . . or names. It's
just the kind of person I am.

INTERVIEWER

Well, that's okay. I mean . . . there's a lot of
crews that come through here.

ME

I know who I am and that's about as far as I
can go.

END OF INTERVIEW

The first person I showed the video of the above to said, "Gee,
did the studio really not give you a dressing room or meal
break?"

EPILOGUE

It's a few months later now. *Heart and Souls* has completed its postproduction work and been received enthusiastically by test audiences.

One day about a month ago, I went in to work with the director Ron Underwood on some looping. Looping, for those of you who may not know, is a process where we redo some lines that are not as intelligible as they might be, due to background noise when filming.

I had a small awareness that Ron, always the picture of cheerfulness, was a bit subdued. Toward the end of our session he turned to me and said, "Something terrible has happened." I stared at him as he went on to tell me that one of our producers, Dirk Petersman, was dying.

Dirk was the producer who had the day-to-day responsibilities for making sure that everything gets taken care of. It is a position filled with stress, and it's easy to understand why the person in that position is often the one to "blow."

Epilogue

Dirk Petersman never blew. In fact, Dirk had such a constant grace about him it was surprising to know he *was* the producer. I once overheard him on the phone with the lab that processed our film. We were having some problems that temporarily suggested we would have to reshoot. It turned out to be lab negligence. Dirk spoke most respectfully to the person at the lab and yet communicated the problem we were having with them. "I'm sure you can understand how our cinematographer feels when we look at the film in that state and he hasn't been told the problem is in the lab." He went on in his gentlemanly fashion for a few minutes, as my admiration for him grew.

Of course, life is a series of unending problems, and the only thing that can ever change is our attitude in dealing with them. Because of his grace under pressure, Dirk was a role model.

Sometime, about halfway through the filming, Dirk began to limp. At first it seemed funny, as I've always said anyone making movies eventually begins to limp, one way or another. It wasn't funny when the limp persisted, and Dirk in response to my inquiry casually said, "The doctors don't know what's causing it." It turned out to be lymphoma and Dirk died June 13, 1993. He had plans to take a trip with his wife, Sabra. He had plans to start another project.

Dirk Petersman probably never would have made The Most Powerful list, but he might have made The Most Happy Successful list. The excitement of *Heart and Souls* has been hollowed for us. This is Dirk's first on-screen producer credit. He was forty-eight.

Life does have a way of getting in there.

Index

Index

Index

Index